Why Students Underachieve

What Educators and Parents Can Do about It

Regalena Melrose

Rowman & Littlefield Education
Lanham, Maryland • Toronto • Oxford
2006

Published in the United States of America
by Rowman & Littlefield Education
A Division of Rowman & Littlefield Publishers, Inc.
A wholly owned subsidary of The Rowman & Littlefield Publishing Group, Inc.
4501 Forbes Boulevard, Suite 200, Lanham, Maryland 20706
www.rowmaneducation.com

PO Box 317
Oxford
OX2 9RU, UK

British Library Cataloguing in Publication Information Available

Library of Congress Cataloging-in-Publication Data

Melrose, Regalena, 1970–
    Why students underachieve : what educators and parents can do about it / Regalena Melrose.
        p. cm.
    Includes bibliographical references (p.).
    ISBN-13: 978-1-57886-439-3 (hardcover : alk. paper)
    ISBN-10: 1-57886-439-9 (hardcover : alk. paper)
    ISBN-13: 978-1-57886-440-9 (pbk. : alk. paper)
    ISBN-10: 1-57886-440-2 (pbk. : alk. paper)
    1. Mentally ill children–Education.   2. Problem children–Education.
3. Learning, Psychology of.   I. Title.
LC4165.M45   2006
371.94–dc22   2006005693

Manufactured in the United States of America.

To Todd and James
for teaching me, by example,
everything I need to know:
Love never fails.

Contents

Preface

Educators are faced with new challenges in the twenty-first century as students are exposed to growing numbers of images and stories related to violence, turmoil, and trauma. School shootings and school terrorist attacks have claimed the lives of numerous children around the globe, shaking the very core of our students' sense of safety and security in this post–9/11 world.

Since 9/11, the advent of war in Iraq, and the recent devastation of Hurricane Katrina, students of all ages are viewing terrorist images, hearing gruesome stories, and experiencing terrifying events that contribute to an overall sense that these are dangerous times and, ultimately, no one is safe. When such a global environmental context combines with students' own personal histories and living conditions, especially when these are problematic, their abilities to learn and behave in the classroom as expected can be impacted in devastating ways.

Students experience direct and indirect exposure to violence and trauma in their schools, homes, and neighborhoods, sometimes on a daily basis. Such exposure has the potential to change who students are and how well they are able to meet the demands of their world. Research conducted over the past decade has explicitly revealed how trauma changes the brain and, ultimately, affects learning and behavior. To be fully effective as educators, we need to learn about these new findings in order to know how best to intervene with some of our most troubled students.

In the years I have worked as an educator, I have witnessed the change in how much more we now need to know about helping students overcome crises or traumatic events, whether experienced directly or vicariously. After taking detailed developmental histories of children of all ages, it became apparent to me that a growing number of students' academic and behavioral challenges began with a crisis or with one or more traumatic events. Without considering the source of the problem when developing interventions, I have seen firsthand that, regardless of excellent intentions, we have needlessly exacerbated problematic conditions for our students.

Our most troubled students can sometimes be the most baffling to us. However, regardless of how ill informed or unprepared we may feel at times to help them, we need not despair. There are many simple yet powerful ways to help support traumatized students at school so that the damage of terrifying events is minimized and learning is maximized. Educators play an important role in helping resolve the impact of trauma. If we mistakenly take ourselves out of the equation, we run the risk of becoming part of the problem rather than the solution.

After years of working in schools, I have learned that *every* classroom includes a number of students who have experienced trauma and who display some residual impact of the event or events. I have also seen the power of educators to make a difference to those students. Each and every educator that comes into contact with traumatized students has a chance to contribute to their healing and recovery or contribute to their suffering and despair. Once educators learn about these students and how to help them through the contents of this book, I believe they will feel more than equipped to do their part in helping one child at a time until the success of every student is possible.

In part I, we will learn about common barriers to learning. We will learn about traumatized students—who they are and how they are commonly misunderstood. We will learn how to assess them better so we can more accurately understand their unique needs.

In part II, we will learn that trauma is not just a large catastrophic event such as 9/11, Columbine, or Hurricane Katrina. Trauma is much more common than we ever knew before. It is a greater part of our students' everyday lives than we ever imagined. We will learn what trauma is, how common it is, and how seemingly benign events that we may never have considered traumatic before can leave long-lasting scars that require our compassion and intervention.

Part II includes a review of recent research findings on trauma's impact on the brain and nervous system and how that relates to the learning and behavior problems of our students. Once we understand these relationships more clearly, we will be able to develop interventions that work not just now but in the long term.

In part III, we will learn about our unique role as educators in helping students who have been traumatized. Concrete tools will be reviewed that can be readily used in classrooms and school offices to promote greater success across academic and behavioral domains.

In part IV, prevention of traumatization is emphasized. Previous chapters reviewed activities to be used by educators with students who struggle in school because they have already been traumatized. However, educators must also be equipped with knowledge and tools for how to *prevent* traumatization in the event of a crisis at school or in the community when it impacts students. A critique of current crisis intervention practices will be presented, as well as an alternative approach, all based on the most recent research in the field.

The book's "final words" will revisit the barriers to learning presented in chapter 1, emphasizing the need to reconsider how we intervene with traumatized students within both general and special education. Most importantly, these final words will ask the scientific community to continue what it has started in its study of trauma and the brain. Now that we know how trauma impacts brain development and subsequent educational functioning, and we have created interventions specific to these findings, we must accumulate outcome studies to determine whether or not these approaches are as efficacious, valuable, and worthy, as suggested by numerous case studies and anecdotal examples.

Acknowledgments

I have numerous people to thank for their contributions to both my personal and professional lives, contributions that have made this book possible.

I first want to thank the students I have been honored to serve. Their trust in me and faith in the therapeutic process have taught me precisely what I need to know about letting go and letting God, about the body truly being a naturally healing mechanism, and about the power of what it means to be witnessed.

I need to thank Peter Levine, though I struggle with words to convey the depth of my gratitude for a life lived with such insight, wisdom, and dedication. Peter, your work has changed my life in ways I am still discovering. You have been a gift to me and are a gift to this planet. Thank you for the tireless effort you continue to make locally and globally to heal this world. We are all better for it.

Thank you, Maggie Kline, for introducing Peter and his work to me, for the time we spent as friends and "sisters," for your teaching and mentoring, and for continuing to inspire me with the important work you do.

I want to thank the Somatic Experiencing community, especially Stephen Sova and Steven Hoskinson, for the difference they have made to my life and work.

I am indebted to Long Beach Unified School District and all the wonderful people I have worked with there who have supported me, cheered me on, and helped me attain my goals and dreams.

Thank you, Judy McBride. How could I ever thank you enough for believing in me the way you did from the very beginning, for taking me into your impressive fold, for teaching me all that you did, and for picking me up when I needed just that? You are a marvelous inspiration to every one of us.

Kathryn Goria, thank you for being such a wonderful listener, and for giving me your support. Your life experiences have taught me well. I thank you for sharing them so generously.

Alberto Restori, thank you for your friendship, your intellect, and your conversation. Your thoughts and ideas have been so valuable to my work. Your encouragement has meant the world to me.

A very special thanks goes to my original crew from McGill University in Montreal, Canada, where it all started and where the standard was set.

To Todd, Judy, and Charlie, the value in my life of your love and support cannot be measured. It means everything to me. Thank you for your generosity, thoughtfulness, and care, and for being so proud of me.

To my mother, father, brother, and sisters, I want you to know that I remember what we had that was right and good. There were happy times. I will always cherish the moments when our heads were clear and our hearts were pure and we were able to extend ourselves in true love. Thank you for those times. I will take them with me every day of my life.

Finally, and most importantly, I thank God for everything, good and bad, especially for helping me realize my own value and capacity to live a life worth living.

1

MISUNDERSTOOD

1

Barriers to Learning

BARRIERS TO LEARNING
WITHIN GENERAL EDUCATION

The word *barrier* is defined in Webster's dictionary in different ways, primarily as a material object or set of objects that separate, demarcate, or serve as a barricade. For the purposes of this book, a second definition is most relevant, and that is as something immaterial that impedes or separates. Keeping this latter understanding of *barrier* in mind, we will come to understand why too many students do not benefit from their educational experiences, despite the best efforts of educators. Examples of well-understood barriers to learning include, but are not limited to, chronic illness, second-language issues, socioeconomic factors, and environmental conditions such as limited access to school and academically related materials.

Let us briefly consider each of these identified barriers. Chronic illness afflicts many of our students each year and keeps them from attending consistently or, when at school, from being able to benefit from instruction. Examples of chronic illnesses in our students include diabetes, asthma, kidney disease, and leukemia among others. Second-language issues and their impact on learning have stirred great debate and controversy in education over the years. Educational scholars continue to study the effects of learning more than one language in the home or having limited exposure to English before and after entering school where English is the predominant language used. A barrier to learning may exist for our second-language learners depending on whether or not other confounding variables are involved. Students who live in poor socioeconomic conditions face overwhelming challenges, such as simply getting to school on a regular basis. Some do not have the opportunity to receive exposure to a rich learning environment before and after they enter school, making the process of academic learning a difficult one. As we know, poor attendance, thus limited exposure to school, impedes students' abilities to achieve academically. These and other of the numerous barriers to learning that exist for students will be discussed in this chapter.

First, it is important to state that many good things are happening in schools today to address the various challenges students face. The majority of educators, including school psychologists and other student support personnel, are well trained to handle a variety of important and recurring issues. Each year teachers do an excellent job of identifying students who are "at risk" for underachievement due to some of the factors mentioned, and many others. Educators meet regularly in teams to discuss these children and how best to intervene with them in the classroom and on the school campus as a whole. Teachers identify students who struggle physically, academically, behaviorally, emotionally, and environmentally.

Students' needs vary tremendously. Some need clean clothes, food, glasses, reading support, math assistance, behavior management, occupational therapy, medical attention, and so on. Schools are quick to respond. Each member of the team does his or her part. The nurse may do a medical screening and refer to a doctor for follow-up for the student with physical ailments. The school psychologist may work with the teacher on developing a behavior plan for the student who cannot sit still or who engages in excessive attention-seeking behaviors. The counselor may begin a friendship group for the students struggling with making and keeping friends. Administrators follow up with discipline issues to ensure that our students grow to become respectful and responsible citizens.

Despite these multiple efforts, there is always a group of students at each school each year that remains resistant to intervention over time. The school-based problem-solving team may meet on several occasions to modify interventions and apply new approaches with the most challenging students. While most learners will excel with some kind of intervention, others will continue to struggle no matter what is done to help.

There comes a time when the problem-solving team, including the parent or guardian, needs to consider whether or not to assess a student for special education services. All members of the team know the importance of ruling out language, environment, and other factors that may explain the ongoing difficulty of the student, including cultural issues and lack of exposure to school and academic material (e.g., attendance). Psychoeducational assessments are only done after such factors are found not to be the primary reason for the lack of educational success. This is not an easy process and educators need to be applauded for meeting continually to carefully address these issues and rule them out one by one before considering an assessment for special education. Of course, it is not that interventions are unnecessary for students struggling due to second-language issues, poor attendance, illness, or environmental factors. They require interventions within general education as all struggling students do. However, it is only when there is resistance to such general education interventions over time *and* each of the confounding issues has been ruled out as a primary contributor to the lack of educational success that a referral for an assessment for special education is ethical and appropriate.

Once a psychoeducational evaluation is complete, there often comes a greater understanding of what the interfering factors were in the case of a student who was resistant to intervention over time. Finally, there may be an explanation for why the student continued to have such difficulty despite varied and ongoing assistance. Through the evaluation process, school psychologists identify whether or not students "fit" into one or more designating special education categories. They do so according to the federally mandated Individuals with Disabilities Education Act (IDEA), as well as each of their respective state's "composite of laws" manual for special education.

Students qualify as individuals with exceptional needs when the results of the assessment process demonstrate that the degree of the impairment requires special education. The individualized educational program (IEP) team, which consists of the school team involved with a struggling student as well as the student's parents, decides whether or not the assessment results have demonstrated that the degree of the student's impairment requires special education. The team takes into account all relevant material that is available regarding the student and uses no single score or product of scores as the sole criterion for the decision. Once students are identified as requiring designation in one of the categories, they are often served through IEPs designed to meet their unique learning needs.

According to IDEA, a "child with a disability" is defined "in general" as a child who needs special education and related services for either mental retardation, a hearing impairment including deafness, a speech or language impairment, a visual impairment including blindness, (serious) emotional disturbance (hereafter referred to as emotional disturbance), an orthopedic impairment, autism, traumatic brain injury, other health impairment, a specific learning disability, deaf-blindness, or multiple disabilities. Additionally, IDEA generally defines the term "child with a disability" as a child (aged three through nine) who needs special education and related services due to the experience of developmental delays in one or more of the following areas:

physical, cognitive, communication, social, emotional, or adaptive development.

A brief overview of each of the six categories that pertain specifically to the purposes of this book will be presented.

BARRIERS TO LEARNING
WITHIN SPECIAL EDUCATION

For each of the categories reviewed, students are identified as requiring formal designation in special education *only* when their educational performance has been adversely affected by their disability. "Educational performance" entails far more than academic performance. Students' educational performance includes their ability to meet the age-appropriate demands of being on a school campus. This involves social, emotional, and behavioral demands in addition to academic expectations. These are considered carefully when assessing a student's educational performance. For each of the categories reviewed, students are designated as requiring special education services only when their educational performance in any of these areas—social, emotional, behavioral, or academic—is adversely affected by their disability.

The following six categories are most relevant to the purposes of this book and will be reconsidered in the final chapter, chapter 12. They include *autism, developmental delays (aged three to nine years), specific learning disability, emotional disturbance, traumatic brain injury,* and *other health impairment* (see appendix A for the additional designating categories defined by IDEA.

Autism

A number of school districts more comprehensively label this category *autistic-like behaviors* because the category is broader than the name *autism* implies. Autism is part of a larger umbrella category of disorders called, in the *Diagnostic and Statistical Manual for Psychologists* (DSM-IV-TR), pervasive developmental disorders (PDD). This larger umbrella category includes autistic disorder, Rett's disorder, childhood disintegrative disorder, Asperger's disorder, and PDD-not otherwise specified (NOS), hence the use of the more encompassing label *autistic-like behaviors*. This discussion will focus on the more commonly observed conditions of autistic disorder, Asperger's disorder, and PDD-NOS.

Autism, Asperger's, and PDD-NOS have in common extreme challenges in the areas of social interaction and/or communication with, in the case of autism and Asperger's, repetitive and/or stereotyped behaviors and interests. Students with autism oftentimes have a co-occurring condition of mental retardation, but there are at least 25 percent who are considered "high functioning" because their general cognitive ability is anywhere from average to very superior. One hundred percent of students with Asperger's, on the other hand, have at least average cognition and no significant language delay as part of their developmental history. A language delay is specific to cases of students with autism.

Autism	*Asperger's*	*PDD-NOS*
Social interaction (SI) deficits	SI deficits	SI deficits
Language development (LD) delays	No LD delays	Possible LD delays
75% Mental Retardation (MR)	No MR	No MR
25% Average (A) or above IQ	A or above IQ	A or above IQ
Repetitive/Stereotyped (R/S) Behaviors	R/S Beh.	No R/S Beh.

It is important to note that the deficits of students with PDD, such as the social interaction or communication problems of students with PDD-NOS, must be severe. The deficits must significantly and negatively impact the student's functioning in at least one major area of life, usually school. Often, developmental delays are found in the histories of these students, but not always. Sometimes early development, in infancy or beyond, was precocious because it was excelled rather than delayed. Toileting skills, for instance, or other self-help/adaptive skills, may have developed either slowly or at an accelerated rate. This is the art of psychoeducational assessment. Well-trained school psychologists acquire the knowledge and experience necessary to recognize the importance of a precocious rate of development regardless of direction. School psychologists are required to know what the relevant information is, and how to sift through all the data and come to the best conceptualization of an individual. When this occurs thoughtfully, parents and educators often breathe a sigh of relief, knowing that they finally have a more clear and thorough understanding of their child.

Developmental Delays

This designating category is reserved for students aged three to nine who have significant delays in one or more areas. The areas typically assessed include gross and fine motor development, self-help or adaptive behavior, cognition and preacademic functioning, social or social-emotional skills, and communication. If the youngster is determined to have at least a 50 percent delay in one category or 25 percent delay in two or more categories, he or she is recognized as developmentally delayed and in need of intervention as provided through the services of special education.

Developmentally delayed students are sometimes too young for educators to identify more definitively, as either autistic or mentally retarded, for example. The category is helpful as a "watch and see" provision, with intense intervention, of course. The hope is that particular deficits will be outgrown or that the youngster will make the gains necessary to normalize through the services provided. Every three years, and before the student turns ten years of age, a thorough reevaluation is necessary to determine whether or not special education services are still necessary. If the student is about to turn ten years of age and special education services are still necessary, then a more definitive designation is required.

Oftentimes, developmental delays are diagnosed when children have not yet begun their formal education, at the age of three or four. They are referred to preschool assessment teams by centers already working with the children and their families. Alternatively, parents may refer their own child as they begin to recognize that their child is not developing at the same rate as his or her siblings. Typically, cases referred to preschool assessment teams fit into one of the more definitive designating categories, such as *autism, speech or language impairment,* or *mental retardation,* sometimes as the result of a congenital anomaly or medical condition (e.g., cerebral palsy). The category of *developmental delays* is used only when the criteria for these conditions are not clearly evident yet a child demonstrates an inability to function age-appropriately in at least one domain.

Careful collection of the histories of pre- and perinatal development, as well as birth experiences, and keen observations of family functioning, can point to the difficulties related to delays in development and help us to understand a child's inability to regulate age-appropriate functioning in various domains. Chaos within an individual or family during or after pregnancy can produce the kind of neural disorganization that significantly impacts the developing fetus, infant, or toddler. This topic will be discussed in more detail in the chapters ahead.

Specific Learning Disability (SLD)

Currently, there is much controversy, research, and discussion in the area of SLD regarding whether or not to continue using the discrepancy model to designate students as "learning disabled." The model is linked with what many educational professionals are calling the "wait-to-fail" model of identification and service delivery. This is because the discrepancy between cognition and ability required by the current definition of a learning disability is often not evidenced clearly until the second or third grade. Even then, when a discrepancy exists for a student, it may not be "significant" or great enough for the student to be eligible for special education services. Common practice today indicates that a student's academic achievement is only *significantly* below his or her general cognitive ability when it is one-and-a-half to two standard deviations below. Only then is the student considered learning disabled and in need of special education services. What that currently means in a practical sense in the schools is that third-grade students, for example, may be performing academically at a first- or second-grade level, and not display a significant enough gap in statistical terms to qualify for formal help through special education.

This also means that students with lower-than-average cognitive abilities who often have low achievement commensurate with their cognitive capacity, go without services because they do not demonstrate the discrepancy needed to be considered learning disabled. These students do not exhibit mental retardation, but they do not have average cognition either. They demonstrate borderline cognitive capacities (IQ 70–79) and achievement to match, and in many cases, are not accommodated with the curriculum adjustments they need in order to have a successful educational experience.

The "severe discrepancy between intellectual ability and achievement" that is the defining element of SLD is usually demonstrated by a student in one or more academic areas, such as math, reading, or writing. As part of their psychoeducational evaluation, school psychologists often identify a processing problem that is proposed to help us understand why it is that the student is not achieving up to his or her ability. Visual processing problems, visual-motor integration challenges, auditory processing deficits, and other difficulties in the areas of attention and memory are examples of processing problems that may contribute in some way to the disability. Controversy exists around this particular issue as well, however. Many researchers in the field, after examining all the available data, have concluded that processing problems have little if anything to do with learning disabilities and the discrepancy between ability and achievement.

More recent and comprehensive research has pointed to a different way of understanding the gap. Some researchers have identified specific "marker variables," such as phonological processing and short-term memory, that predict and are related to the acquisition of academic skills (e.g., reading). How this current research will impact the practice of school psychology— how students will be identified and served—remains to be seen.

What is certain is that professionals governing the field of special education are currently *un*certain about the best way to identify students with SLD.

There are numerous students not achieving to their potential given their cognitive abilities. Research is not conclusively finding that processing problems, as traditionally understood, are at the root of the underachievement. The question of whether or not to keep the current model in place at all is at the foreground of thought. The California Department of Education (CDE) has acknowledged that the current SLD eligibility criteria is technically unsound and imposes an arbitrary and instructionally incoherent consideration of the student's educational needs (Reed 2000). The National Association of School Psychologists (NASP) has been asked to address the identification process and eligibility criteria. NASP recommended that eligibility be interdependent upon instructional supports and other interventions provided through general education. As a result, the requirement of achievement below expectations would not be established through a discrepancy formula but rather through the collaborative clinical judgment of a multidisciplinary team based on a comprehensive array of data.

This proposed alternative method of identifying students with SLD would require the collection of data throughout the course of implementing interventions within general education. When a student who appears to have a learning disability fails to make progress despite the implementation, adaptation, and monitoring of multiple interventions—or when the interventions that prove to be successful are so specialized or intense that they cannot reasonably be provided within general education—a referral to special education would be initiated. With such controversy and reconsideration at the forefront of the field today, perhaps what we are learning is that the traditional ways of understanding students and their challenges are unsatisfactory. Traditional assessment and identification do not seem to adequately account for or explain the reasons why such a broad number of students are unable to regulate their own learning.

Considering an additional group of students with learning disabilities—those with "nonverbal learning disabilities" (NLD)—seems to be another effort on the part of educational professionals to understand and more effectively intervene with students who have achievement as well as behavioral problems. Descriptions of these students sound much like the descriptions of students with pervasive developmental disorders—PDD-NOS, for instance—because of their social skills deficits. However, students with NLD, as opposed to students with PDD-NOS, have strong language or verbal skills, and often use these to compensate for their problems in different domains. For this particular reason, it is important to carefully distinguish PDD students with Asperger's disorder from NLD students. Both groups of students have high-functioning language skills and deficits in social interaction. The distinguishing characteristic in the case of students with Asperger's disorder is restricted, repetitive, and stereotyped patterns of behavior, interests, or activities not found in students with NLD. The primary deficits of students with NLD are in three areas: (1) motor (lack of coordination, poor balance, and/or difficulty with fine motor tasks, such as writing), (2) visual-spatial-organizational (lack of ability to form and retain visual pictures, faulty spatial perceptions, and or difficulties with spatial relations), and (3) social (lack of ability to comprehend nonverbal communication, difficulties adjusting to transitions and novel situations, and/or significant deficits in social judgment and social interaction).

Emotional Disturbance (ED)

According to IDEA, the term *ED* refers to a condition that involves one or more of the following characteristics over a long period of time and to a marked degree:

1. An inability to learn that cannot be explained by intellectual, sensory, or health factors.
3. An inability to build or maintain satisfactory interpersonal relationships with peers and teachers.
4. Inappropriate types of behavior or feelings under normal circumstances.
5. A general pervasive mood of unhappiness or depression.
6. A tendency to develop physical symptoms or fears associated with personal or school problems.

The terms "over a long period of time" and "to a marked degree" have received attention and debate. As a general rule, many school psychologists consider six months to one year a "long period of time" for children. Careful consideration must be paid, however, to students who are experiencing loss from separation, divorce, or death. These children may grieve for an indeterminable amount of time and appear as depressed or anxious when in fact they are passing through a normal stage of functioning considering the circumstances. A conscientious effort on the part of educational professionals is made to reserve this category for students who, for a minimum of six months, have displayed significant or severe behavioral or emotional problems that have negatively impacted their educational performance. Such a severe emotional problem may be suicidal depression or anxiety or both (they often co-occur). Such a behavioral problem may involve self-mutilating or other self-destructive behaviors. These are *severely* disturbed students who require intense services not just in their schools but also within their families and communities.

As with other designating categories (e.g., SLD), an important criterion for the use of the ED designation is documented resistance on the part of the student to attempted interventions. The behaviors must persist regardless of all the help the student receives to decrease the behaviors. This is, again, where the school psychologist is required to mount and sift through all relevant information to determine whether or not general education options have truly been exhausted. What is sometimes determined to be an intervention is highly questionable. Visits to the principal's office, suspensions, and detentions are examples of what some call interventions. When a student is being considered emotionally disturbed, is it not best practice to require that significant assistance be directed at the student's social-emotional functioning? That kind of help can only be provided by a mental health specialist, not a principal or assistant principal whose focus on discipline may be necessary but is not sufficient.

Another consideration is the too common view educators have that students who are problematic behaviorally are, in fact, behaviorally or emotionally *disturbed*. Students who make regular trips to the principal's office for defiance, challenging authority, or truancy, for example, may not necessarily be students with an "emotional disturbance." A distinction exists but educators do not always find it clear, leading to an overidentification of ED students in many school districts today.

The overlap that exists between emotional disturbances and many other conditions may also account for the problem of overidentification. For example, students with social interaction deficits—students with PDD-NOS, for example—often exhibit "an inability to build or maintain satisfactory interpersonal relationships with peers and teachers." Are these children best understood, identified, and served as students with an emotional disturbance? Or do we better serve the student by understanding the deficit as part of a condition that is fundamentally different from an emotional disturbance? What is best practice? How, conscientiously, do we do no harm? School districts continue to struggle with these questions and with the question of who ED students genuinely are. State and federal laws continue to modify the specifics of the criteria to assist educators in their struggle.

Traumatic Brain Injury (TBI)

According to the practice of a growing number of school districts across the country, a student may be designated as having TBI when an official document from a physician indicates the condition in medical terms. However, the education, training, and experience of school nurses and psychologists make this unnecessary. Through a thorough psychoeducational assessment, a multidisciplinary team that includes the school nurse and psychologist may determine that there existed a premorbid level of functioning for a student that was interrupted by an incident. As the result of an accident involving a head injury, for example, the student may now have significantly lower levels of ability than he or she had prior to the event.

The brain can be profoundly altered by any physical blow, whether related to an accident or injury, causing small lesions at specific sites (Elliott 1992). Even a seemingly or at least relatively benign event, such as rough shaking, can cause multiple microscopic lesions throughout the brain (Karr-Morse and Wiley 1997). This evidence points to the fact that TBI can be the result of incidents that do and do *not* involve a direct blow or injury to the head, making the detection of such changes to the brain nearly impossible for doctors to detect. Most medical doctors in emergency rooms, for example, do not typically conduct tests that reveal such subtle yet profound damage. Many parents are sent home from emergency rooms with their injured children and the message that their children are "fine." Educators, however, are in a unique position to notice more readily how students have been impacted by an event. They have the opportunity over time to observe how students' academic and behavioral functioning may change. They have more access to relevant data than medical doctors, as well as opportunity to collect such data, to determine whether or not there has been a significant change in ability due to accident or injury.

TBI involves physical damage to the brain and can be caused by early injuries that are often cumulative from multiple incidents of abuse. These early injuries are hard to detect because they leave no external marks. The damage from such injuries often does not appear until later as the affected neurological system matures (Karr-Morse and Wiley 1997). Significant impairments in self-regulatory behaviors required for learning and adapting to the social environment are implicated. For instance, individuals who have sustained injuries to their frontal lobes show impairment in their control of emotional expression and an absence of awareness of the impact of their behavior on other people (Golden, Jackson, Peterson-Rohne, and Gontkovsky 1996). Temporal lobe injuries, by contrast, are associated with "episodic dyscontrol," in which violent behavior erupts seemingly out of nowhere, is unpatterned, and occurs without provocation or premeditation (Golden et al. 1996). These findings have large implications for educators who care about knowing their students and thoroughly understanding what is causing their inability to benefit from their educational program. We have to be willing to learn about the findings of these recent research efforts, and to incorporate them in both our evaluations and designations. This is the only way we will conceptualize our students accurately and thus intervene with them effectively.

Other Health Impairment (OHI)

This category is reserved for students with chronic or acute health problems that cause limited strength and vitality or alertness that negatively impact educational performance. Such medical conditions commonly include asthma, diabetes, cancer, leukemia, epilepsy, infectious diseases, hematological disorders, kidney disease, and heart conditions among others. Revisions to IDEA in recent years have included attention-deficit/hyperactivity disorder (ADHD) (with or without hyperactivity) in this category. Many professionals from varying fields regard ADHD as a medical condition or chronic health problem because of its neurological base. The heightened activity and distractibility that is often the result of the condition causes, in many cases, limited alertness or attentiveness to the educational environment. Some students neurologically impacted by ADHD require the use of medication to help them manage their impulsivity and inattentiveness in order to meet the demands of the educational environment.

According to Karr-Morse and Wiley, in their comprehensive book *Ghosts from the Nursery: Tracing the Roots of Violence*, the label ADHD actually covers disabilities in several discrete brain functions that most of us take for granted in both learning and social situations (Karr-Morse and Wiley 1997). The five basic capacities involved in the attention disorders (ADHD with or without hyperactivity) include the capacity for planning, selecting, resisting distraction, attending continuously, and self-monitoring:

Planning: Students with ADHD often act without thinking. They generally lack an ability to be reflective, thus problem solving suffers.

Selecting: Students with ADHD often struggle with tasks that require them to determine what is salient and what is not, what the relevant part of the information is, and what details should be most attended to.

Resisting: The ability to resist distractions is often impaired in students with ADHD. Filtering out extraneous stimulation can be next to impossible at times, as can inhibiting movement and vocalization or verbalization.

Attending continuously: Sometimes students with ADHD can attend for long periods of time, when the subject matter is something they are very interested in. However, in most educational situations, concentration is unpredictable at best. Related to this ability, Karr-Morse and Wiley mention that many students with ADHD have sleep and arousal irregularities that cause fatigue. They can be wakeful at night and tired during the day. Yawning and stretching in the classroom are common signs of their fatigue.

Self-monitoring: Self-awareness is an ongoing challenge for students with ADHD. They struggle with monitoring how they are doing on a task or how others experience them when in a social interaction.

Each of these abilities requires relatively intact brain functioning, not that social factors cannot help ameliorate biological vulnerabilities. However, based on a review of much of the research done in this area, Karr-Morse and Wiley write, "What we know is that, while it may be exacerbated by them, ADHD is not caused by social factors. . . . True ADHD has a neurological basis" (1997, 115, 116). It is a brain-based condition attributed to heritable genetics 50 percent of the time and to insults to the neurological system occurring primarily prenatally and at birth 50 percent of the time (1997).

The OHI category is not the only category considered for students with ADHD. Many children with the disorder qualify for special education services as students with coexisting learning disabilities, for example, when their achievement is significantly below their level of cognition. Between 19 and 26 percent of ADHD students have at least one learning disability in math, reading, or spelling (Karr-Morse and Wiley 1997). However, when their achievement remains within the expected range despite problematic behaviors that negatively impact their educational functioning in other areas, the OHI category is considered. As mentioned earlier, educational functioning includes far more than academic performance. Social interactions with peers and adults are a necessary part of the school day and can be problematic for these children, causing adverse educational performance.

Mounting and striking empirical evidence may require professionals in the field of educational law to broaden their understanding and definition of medical conditions within the category of OHI. Through diligent research practices, neurologists and other medical and mental health professionals are beginning to more fully understand the long-term effects of significant medical histories, such as compromised gestational periods, birth complications, surgeries, prolonged stays in hospitals—when isolated, especially—and other medical situations that compromise children's nervous system and self-regulatory functioning. An abundance of research assessing the effects of stressful pregnancies and birth experiences on the developing fetus, infant, and toddler is impacting our understanding of the roots of learning and behavioral challenges. A consideration of this will be highlighted later in the book.

ONE SIGNIFICANT BARRIER MAY UNDERLIE THE REST

The designating categories of special education have been carefully conceptualized by educators and are conscientiously considered in the cases of students who appear to have a barrier or barriers to learning. Most cases referred to school psychologists are straightforward and well understood. The majority of students referred and evaluated clearly meet criteria for one of the designating categories and are appropriately served as a result of the designation specified. Time and time again, we have seen that when the student, designation, and assigned services match, the services received by the students lead to their progress. However, there is a growing number of students in every school district each year for whom we cannot seem to find an accurate match. These students continue to baffle educational professionals, despite their best efforts to understand and intervene. These are often the students who arrive at school, no matter how young, with a significant history already in the making. Some have been asked to leave their daycares or preschools. Some have been given disciplinary transfers from one school to another. Others come to school with long, often conflicting psychological and/or medical reports from outside agencies and hospitals with various diagnoses and recommendations, some tried, some abandoned, or are students quickly acquiring such reports. Numerous traditional forms of intervention were tried with little success. School psychologists review, observe, and consider what the situation may be with these students but cannot seem to put their finger on the specific challenges and needs of the students—on what the actual barrier to their successful education is. Designing and implementing effective interventions becomes futile because the problem is not clearly understood.

When the problem is not clearly understood, we miss not only the opportunity to intervene within general education in an effective way but also the opportunity to use the designating categories of special education in a more accurate and comprehensive way. Some designating categories are broader and more encompassing than their current use implies, other health impairment and traumatic brain injury, specifically. They are underused as a result. A number of the more baffling students assessed would be better understood as having health impairments or brain injuries because of their significant medical histories or traumatic experiences. Educators have not yet considered these designations for many of the students who need them, most likely due to limited knowledge of current brain and nervous system research. The findings of the past decade—"the decade of the brain"—are critical to the work we do. Such findings point to the importance of considering pre- and perinatal development, trauma, and stress, in both the student and the student's caregivers when we assess for potential barriers to learning.

Rather than simply identifying the problem and developing solutions for the problem as defined, we need to understand the source of the problem. That is what we do when we consider pre- and perinatal development, trauma, and stress. Understanding the source of learning and behavioral challenges is more important to best practice than ever before. In light of compelling research on the developing brain and its effect on the nervous system and self-regulatory capacities, we now know that without understanding the source of the problem, we do not understand its solution. Reconsideration of both the criteria for the designating categories, as well as the use of the categories, is implicated.

Identifying barriers to learning is one of the most important things we do as educators. Within general education we have identified poor attendance, cultural and environmental conditions, second-language issues, chronic illness, and economic disadvantages among others. Within special education we have assessed for developmental delays, physical disabilities, learning disabilities, emotional problems, and health impairments among others. There remains a group of students, however, whose inability to access their education with success is still not understood. There remains, in this twenty-first century, a misunderstood child.

We first heard about the "misunderstood child" in the 1980s when a book by the same name was originally published (Silver 1984). The author helped us put a name to those students who were struggling with learning disabilities that, at the time, we did not know enough about. We rose to the challenges then of those students and learned to intervene with them in more effective ways. We learned at that time, just as we continue to learn today, that when we misunderstand children, we leave them behind.

This is a new era. Twenty years after the publication of *Misunderstood Child: Understanding and Coping with Your Child's Learning Disabilities,* we have new challenges to face in education. Post–9/11, in light of numerous school shootings, terrorist attacks, and natural disasters, and with media and Internet access at an all-time high, our students experience exposure to local and global violence in frightening proportions. We would not only be naïve but also dangerously ignorant to think that this exposure is not having a significant impact on our students. In fact, we witness that impact in our classrooms and on our playgrounds every day. We hear more now than ever before about bullies, crises, and school violence. The growing focus of education on prevention and intervention in these areas is because we realize these problems are on the rise.

As we face this new era, having committed to "no child left behind," a reconsideration of our priorities and commitments in education is called for. We need to ask important questions. Have we identified, in either general or special education, all the possible barriers to learning and behaving in school with success? Are the designating categories as they are currently being used comprehensive enough to account for the barriers our students face? Why is there a growing number of students who do not fit into the categories as they are currently being used? Who are these students who do not fit? What are the barriers to their education? What do we need to start doing to assess them more accurately, identify them more comprehensively, and serve them more effectively?

In an attempt to answer these questions, the chapters ahead will review current research findings on the developing brain and nervous system, research that is completely relevant to education yet largely ignored. The findings of this research demonstrate that there is a direct and significant effect of experience on the brain and ultimately on learning and behavior. While the findings point to a single barrier that may underlie the struggles of both general and special education students, we must also acknowledge that our own limited awareness of these findings and their implications is also a barrier to the success of our students. We can only know how to help them when we know how their experiences have impacted their development. As the relationship between experience, the developing brain, and subsequent learning and behavior is made evident, it will become clear why no one needs this information more than educators.

2

Traumatized and Misunderstood

Who is the misunderstood student? Who are the students who continue to baffle educators despite their best efforts and expertise training? As a school psychologist, these are the students I am asked most often to consult about, not just with teachers and administrators but also with school psychologists and mental health professionals. While most educators know what to do with more typical cases involving learning and behavioral challenges, there is a growing number of students each year who are not helped by our more traditional approaches. My colleagues often state that they feel there is "something else" going on with a particular student, something they feel they are missing. They realize that until they figure out what that missing piece of the puzzle is, their efforts at creating and implementing interventions will have limited success.

At each of the schools I serve, I keep a mailbox where I receive written referrals from teachers and administrators alike. On one occasion, I was left a copy of a correspondence between the school's nurse and principal. The nurse had downloaded a page from the Web and wrote on it asking the principal if she knew anyone who fit the profile described. The description provided on the Web was of students who had committed acts of violence on their school campus. The nurse wondered if the description applied to anyone we needed to be aware of at our school. She wanted to be proactive, as all educators do, and intervene as early as possible when signs of at-risk behaviors were evident. With early intervention, we hope we will prevent school shootings and other violent acts that occur daily on campuses everywhere.

In response to the nurse, the principal wrote down one name on the page. Because it was left in my box, it became my job to follow up in whatever way I could, enlisting the help of whomever was needed, in order to prevent a violent act on our campus. The same day I received the correspondence in my mailbox, I met Joel for the first time.

JOEL

When I met Joel, he had already been on a behavioral contract with his teachers and administrators. I asked him about the contract and he told me that it had worked well for him the year before. In fact, he asked me if he could be on another contract. He said that he "behaved better" when he had the opportunity to earn rewards and meet with "that nice man" every week to talk. The intervention services Joel had been receiving were interrupted by the summer vacation and did not resume when the new school year had started.

Joel started acting out again. His teacher described him as a "good kid" who did not present as a behavior problem on a daily basis. There were a few occasions, however, on a sporadic basis that Joel "flipped." It would come "out of the blue." No one could identify a precipitating event or trigger, the "thing" said or done that would send Joel into a tailspin. Without warning, he would go into a rage and verbally, sometimes physically, assault the person in front of him, the principal included. One day, despite having Joel back on his behavioral contract experiencing many good days, he hit the principal four times and was "referred for immediate action" to be transferred out of the school.

When I met with Joel, a nine-year-old fourth-grade student, it was clear to me that he had a big heart full of great pain. He was often remorseful after an upsetting event during which he would lose his temper and yell at or hit someone. Two incidents we reviewed together over the few weeks I had the opportunity to work with him involved a minor trigger, such as losing his turn at a game on the playground. He reported that such an incident would upset him so much he would become "furious!"—a nine on a scale of one to ten—and then he would "handle himself badly." On each occasion that I met with Joel, he said he wanted to handle himself better but that "it" happened so quickly he did not know what he could have done differently at the time.

When students state that they do not know how they could have acted in a nonviolent or nonaggressive way when provoked, educators do not want to hear or accept that. We want to hear that students like Joel know how to walk away, seek the help of an adult, ignore the trigger, or count to ten. How many times, in situations just like Joel's, have we taught students to consider these options, choose one, and act on their choice responsibly? The problem is that most students are not Joel and these generic tactics that sometimes work with some students, often do not work with students like Joel. He really did not know what to do—because "it" did happen too quickly for him to operate in such a cognitive, rational, and reflective way.

What is the "it" that happens so quickly that rationale and reason and strategies and well-taught tools do not work? It is the same "it" that happens to all of us when we become so completely overwhelmed that we cannot think straight or understand our actions or words after we have completed them. This overwhelming instant is not a cognitive process. It is not experienced in our mind alone and cannot be intervened with effectively at that level of processing. The "overwhelm" experienced is physiological. It is in our body. It is sensory overload.

During overwhelm, our body becomes governed by the oldest part of our brain, the reptilian brain or brain stem, that when activated is very powerful. It overrides the cognitive rational part of us that says, "Walk away" or "Count to ten." The brain stem simply cannot listen, not at the particular time it feels threatened. It does not have that choice. The nervous system and brain functioning of this process will be reviewed in the chapters ahead (see chapters 4 and 5) so that we can come to understand why it is that under certain circumstances our brains and bodies are so inflexible.

If you have not had the experience of overwhelm I am describing, you are a fortunate anomaly who, as an educator today, needs to learn about, and have compassion for, those who have such experiences. It can be terrifying, confusing, and the cause for much shame and grief in a person's life—especially when no one talks about what that experience is. Our students, too many of them, know what sensory overload is like because they feel it, over and over, without ever understanding what is happening to them.

SHANTE

An exasperated mother sat with me at school one day and pleaded for help. Her eight-year-old daughter, Shante, had already been "kicked out" of a number of schools, including her YMCA playschool at the age of two. The mother reported that since her daughter was two years of age, she had displayed behavioral problems such as tantrums that continued into the present day at least two to three times per week. She, and the educators involved, remained confused by Shante. The mother described her as "fine one minute, the next I don't know what's going on. Minor things set her off in a big way." The teacher reported that Shante was out of her seat "constantly," "glued" to one of her neighbors. She described her as defiant, stubborn, and as someone who liked to boss people around, ready to engage in a "power struggle" at any given time. If someone upset her in the slightest way, the teacher said that Shante acted as though "the world had come to an end."

Shante's mother also recalled a time when her daughter was three or four, she went "on a rage" and "attacked" another little girl. The mother said she would never forget seeing her daughter that way, "full of rage and sweating" profusely. She remarked how much sweat covered her young girl's body and face, fully engaged in this attack. Shante's grandmother grabbed her and held her tightly, up against great resistance. Shante kicked and screamed trying to break loose for what seemed an endless amount of time, but her grandmother held on tight with love and concern until the mother recalled a deep breath came over Shante and she was calm. The mother recalled to me that in that moment of calm, Shante looked at her grandmother and quietly said, "I love you, nanna."

The principal was clear when she met with me about this student that she did *not* think Shante was emotionally disturbed (ED), despite her history of difficulties. Having two ED classrooms on her campus, the principal felt strongly that this was not a student who "fit" that profile. The student's academic history, as well as her current grades and test scores, did not indicate the possibility of a learning disability either. We were not going to be successful in understanding or intervening with Shante as long as we continued to try to fit her into a "box" utilizing the special education designating categories as we currently do. Shante, just like many other students today, required us to dig deeper and consider a new way of doing things (see chapter 8 for more on Shante).

DANIEL

Daniel, aged twelve, was a gifted student in middle school. He was in an accelerated academic program because of his superior cognitive and academic abilities. He was bright and accomplished as a student. He came to my attention because of an out-of-control tantrum behavior that he exhibited in his classroom to the point, on one occasion, of throwing a chair in the direction of another student. This was a boy who displayed rigidity and inflexibility, despite his cognitive astuteness. His behavior regressed to that of a two-year-old when he felt threatened or afraid. The fear he experienced often presented itself as anger, not uncommonly, and thus Daniel became known as having a problem with rage.

While most teachers and administrators in Daniel's case felt the tantrums "came out of nowhere" without a precipitating event, as in the case of Joel, there were triggering events. As with Joel and Shante, the triggers were so minor to most people that no one could believe they could activate such extreme regression. For example, Daniel threw a tantrum when he came back to school after being ill for a few days and found that someone was sitting in the seat he normally occupied. The teacher had moved the room around while Daniel was gone and everyone was assigned a new seat. Daniel could not be reasoned with or consoled by a rational explanation. His nervous system was physiologically inflexible enough that this change was too much for him to tolerate. Instead of feeling relief by the cognitive explanation, Daniel was already "on automatic." His instinctive reptilian brain was activated and he was out of control. Despite everyone's best efforts, he could not be soothed or consoled. His behavior could not be redirected. Daniel's instinctive response to defend himself against a perceived threat kicked in and he could not be stopped. This unstoppable physiological process is precisely what we need to know more about in order to understand the increasing number of students who leave us so confused.

During interviews with his teachers, Daniel was described as appearing to be on "sensory overload" at times, impatient, easily overwhelmed, and prone to "freaking out over small things." In reviewing these descriptions, notice that they are largely sensory based. They actually describe experiences of the nervous system, an inability to tolerate uncomfortable feelings and sensations. Educators may have a sense of the student's difficulty and may describe it well. However, many of us do not yet know what our impressions and descriptions really mean. This is because the world of sensations is relatively unknown to us, yet this is the level at which our most troubled students fall apart. Without understanding and intervening at the level of sensation, we misunderstand the problems and needs of our students.

We all know that trying to talk with someone when they are extremely upset is ineffective. This is because when we *talk* we engage the cognitive brain. The cognitive brain is *not* the brain most activated at the time of sensory overload or overwhelm. That brain is reptilian. When it is activated, students cannot be reasoned with and cannot, with their cognitive processes, stop themselves from acting out. Under conditions of threat or rage, when the brain is flooded with stress hormones, the "fight or flight" human is not under the governance of the analytical cortex, the seat of rationality and wisdom

(Karr-Morse and Wiley 1997). It is under the governance of the brain stem or reptilian brain. Thus, cognitive-based therapies are an exercise in futility. To be effective, interventions need to be directed at the reptilian or brain stem level (Levine 1997). Normal, rational thoughts are totally unavailable until fear or fury subsides (Karr-Morse and Wiley 1997).

Dr. John Stewart, of Hastings Clinical Associates in Maine, developed a program to understand and intervene with acting-out, aggressive students in the public school setting (Stewart 1998): *first, to understand*; second, to intervene. As educators, we need first to comprehend that these particular students, those who go largely misunderstood in schools today, are operating under high degrees of anxiety, according to Dr. Stewart, even if this anxiety is not readily visible to the eye. He describes anxiety as a psychophysiological response to a sense of threat—a response that involves the student's hormones, especially adrenaline. A highly anxious state can inhibit learning and promote the primitive response pattern of fight or flight.

Some educators wonder why these students feel so threatened so often. Why do they so often appear to be paranoid or easily startled, hypervigilant to anything going on in the classroom or on the playground? It is a good question. What we have learned through years of valuable research is that there is a baseline of anxiety that each of us has when our nervous system is idle. This baseline is set by a number of variables, including genetics and early experiences in utero, during the birth process, and after birth. Anxiety also has a rate of escalation, when the system begins to accelerate in response to an external stimulus. The rate at which our nervous system escalates is also affected by both our genetic predisposition and the environmental conditions in which we live.

The regular students of our schools, the students who learn steadily, negotiate and navigate their way through problems, manage their lives without an inordinate amount of difficulty, have normal levels of anxiety—baselines and rates of escalation that are within the normal range. The highly labile, hypervigilant students that educators often do not know how to help are those students whose baselines of anxiety, as well as rates of escalation, have been compromised. Conditions that compromise the developing brain and nervous system include biochemical factors, unpredictable environments, and low competency, according to Dr. Stewart, thereby creating a higher fight or flight threshold. These students are physiologically overwhelmed much easier and more quickly than other students. Because the escalation happens so quickly, and at the level of sensation, students may demonstrate explosive behavior about which they have little or no insight.

Dr. Stewart offers another explanation for why these students do not have insight concerning the origin of their acting-out behavior. He describes the acting-out behavior as a defense mechanism or unconscious effort on the part of the student to avoid conscious awareness of the feelings associated with the event. Perhaps the student is experiencing a reminder of how "no one in my life stays" or "I'm not lovable" or "I can't depend on anyone." Keeping these thoughts, and the feelings and sensations they provoke, out of consciousness is accomplished by behaving—*mis*behaving usually. When we become frustrated as educators because the students we question will not give us a reason why they did what they did, it may serve us well to remember Dr. Stewart's words—the purpose of the acting-out was to *not know why*. The behavior becomes another level of psychological containment, according to Dr. Stewart—a way to *avoid* thoughts and feelings, as well as sensations.

Students who experience physiological overwhelm or sensory overload, do not necessarily act out by raging, becoming violent, or throwing a tantrum like a two-year-old child, as in the cases of Joel, Shante, and Daniel. Some students simply cannot stop crying, or feeling ill without medical reason, or performing odd ritual behaviors to somehow organize and calm the inner sensations of the body, often experienced as anxiety.

ANN AND MARIA

Two young girls, aged eight, from the same class began seeing the nurse regularly at the beginning of their year in third grade (the girls did not know each other and did not know that the other was reporting illness to the nurse). Their visits were not necessarily remarkable, considering that both Ann and Maria were quiet, sensitive girls adjusting to a new classroom, a new teacher and a new, more difficult curriculum. Yet each day, as the year progressed, the students' symptoms did not get better, they got worse. There was no medical reason for the illnesses, yet they persisted. Between the two of them, they reported dizziness on some days, headaches on other days, and sick stomachs. Alarmingly, one of the girls began to stick her fingers down her throat until she vomited. Her feelings and sensations were so intolerable to her she was willing to go to that extreme length to experience relief.

Ann and Maria were girls with "psychosomatic" complaints, physical complaints of illness that had no medical explanation. The girls did not run a fever or, according to the nurse, display any other indicator that they had a genuine illness. Yet they continued to come to the nurse's office asking for comfort and relief. They were experiencing something in their body—the somatic piece of psychosomatic—that they had no words for, that they did not understand. Something in their classroom was overwhelming them physiologically and, like many other children, they did not have the cognitive capacity to comprehend it or put it into words (more on Ann and Maria later in the chapter).

One young boy I worked with briefly before he experienced relief and resumed his normal level of functioning came from a solid, loving family. His parents were concerned for him because, at ten years of age, he cried excessively at school.

JESUS

For weeks, Jesus was unable to function in class without breaking down into tears and asking to go to the counselor's office. He ate his lunch with the school counselor every day, too emotionally upset to go out to the playground and play with his peers. His parents, teacher, and school administrators spoke with him, tried to help and support him, but Jesus could not verbalize what he was experiencing or why. All he could do was cry as he held his head in his hands with exhaustion.

While working with Jesus' school team and parents, I learned, as I did with each and every one of the students described thus far, that there had been a significant traumatic experience in the student's history. Jesus had been molested at his previous school. When he was ten years old, a number of his same-age peers held him down and took turns violating him.

Joel, the boy who had been transferred out of our school for hitting the principal, fell off the balcony of his second-story home between the ages of two and three, his mother recalled.

Eight-year-old Shante fell from her bunk bead at the age of two and broke her elbow. When her mother, in a panic, unknowingly forced her daughter's arm into a jacket to bring her to the hospital, Shante screamed in anguish and lost consciousness. Her mother noticed in that moment that her two-year-old daughter's elbow was the size of a large lemon.

Daniel experienced a stressful birth or what is known as fetal distress. Both his heart rate and that of his mother lowered rapidly as they struggled to complete the birth process. Doctors believed they would need to perform a C-section quickly if conditions did not improve. Daniel was born with the umbilical cord wrapped around his neck. He developed normally it appeared, according to his parents' report, until he had another traumatic experience when, between the ages of two and three, he was taken to the doctor to have a buildup of wax removed from his ear. His parents recalled that after that event, Daniel displayed extreme tantrum behaviors any time he had to return to a doctor. He remained, at twelve years of age, highly sensitive to anyone coming around the side of his head where the doctor, years earlier, had restrained him and dug for the earwax. In elementary school, Daniel experienced two significant incidents of bullying as well. His parents said he never forgot those experiences and that they had somehow changed him. It was after the bullying incidents that Daniel began exhibiting tantrum behaviors more frequently at school, over seemingly insignificant events. As the incidents mounted, the behaviors became increasingly threatening to the people around him.

Ann, the young girl who began putting her fingers down her throat to throw up so she could get out of class and find solace in the nurse's office, had recently heard about a drive-by shooting at the swimming pool she swam in that summer. She heard stories of the senseless event, as well as the robbery of a family friend, and the stories repeated in her mind before she went to sleep at night. Ann reported that she was having nightmares and sleeping poorly. She was coming to school tired and anxious.

Maria's father, when interviewed, told me about a frightening fall Maria had when she was approximately two years of age. The fall was so severe, he and his wife rushed her to the emergency room to be sure she was going to be all right. The hospital staff, as in Joel's case, x-rayed Maria and sent her home with her parents stating she was "fine." Maria's parents knew she was not fine, and were aware that she began to develop differently from her siblings after that event. Similarly, Joel's mother recalled how different Joel was from his brother Sam, asking, "Why can't he just be more like Sam?"

Both Ann and Maria, such sensitive girls, were in a classroom with a teacher who was a harsh disciplinarian. With the best intentions perhaps, the teacher raised her voice often, waved her finger in front of her students' face when upset, and used sarcasm, as well as threatening words and stances, to get her students to behave. Both girls, on separate occasions spoke with me privately about how scared they were to be in their classroom. Their nervous system could not regulate the sensations and emotions provoked by their teacher's harsh style of teaching. Their earlier traumatic experiences had left their mark, leaving the girls more vulnerable to anything frightening or threatening. Together we worked on ways they would be able to tolerate the experience of being in their classroom. They needed to be able to withstand their sensations of anxiety—the jumpiness they felt inside, the impulses they felt to get up and get out of the classroom to find relief. We worked to find a way for them to experience relief without needing to leave the class on a regular basis (more on "resourcing" and "tools for tolerance" in chapters 6 and 7).

The cases presented in this chapter serve only as examples of the many students who are misunderstood despite the best efforts of educators. In the case of Daniel, many different kinds of professionals, including psychologists, psychiatrists, and therapists, in addition to school personnel, were involved in trying to sort out the problem and how best to intervene. When I met with Daniel's parents, they came prepared with records and reports from years previous that detailed several different diagnoses and varying medications that had been prescribed and tried. Daniel was described in the various reports as exhibiting ADHD, oppositional defiant disorder, major depressive disorder, bipolar disorder, and/or intermittent explosive disorder. Medications rotated as often as the diagnoses with little to no success. In fact, not uncommonly, some of the medications made the symptoms worse. It is often the case that until a precise diagnosis is agreed upon, medicating such a student can be like throwing gasoline on a fire. Traditional psychotherapy was not effective in Daniel's case either. Yet the family did not give up. Daniel continued to participate in a social skills development group with other students his age.

When I met with Daniel's parents, I asked many detailed questions about Daniel's developmental history, including gestation, the birth process, and his history of accidents, falls, surgeries, and hospitalizations. What became clear was that Daniel's parents, not unlike many professionals, had not considered the importance of these early experiences. Many educational, medical, and mental health practitioners, to the disservice of our students, fundamentally disagree on the importance of identifying and intervening with the source of the problem. Eleven-year-old Manuel is a case in point.

MANUEL

Manuel was being treated for ADHD by one of the psychiatrists at the clinic I interned at, and he was not getting better. In fact, he was quickly getting worse. The medication he was given appeared to be exacerbating his symptoms. A long period of different medication trials began as Manuel's behaviors continued to deteriorate. Stimulant medications and antidepressants were tried and abandoned as they each failed to bring about the behavior change that everyone hoped for. Meanwhile, I worked with Manuel and his family to try to understand why it was that so many different medications often effective with children with ADHD were not working for Manuel. After collecting a detailed developmental history, it became clear that Manuel was not ADHD at all. It was not hyperactivity he was displaying, but hypervigilance. The source of his inattentiveness was not the neurological condition of ADHD but the experiential condition of anxiety—the result of having witnessed his uncle shot and killed in front of him in front of a liquor store at age eight. Manuel's symptoms of nightmares and intrusive thoughts about the event were consistent with a diagnosis of posttraumatic stress disorder (PTSD). The source of Manuel's symptoms was trauma—multiple traumas, in fact—and his treatment needed to account for that.

In an effort to change Manuel's diagnosis and treatment, I met with my supervisor and two psychiatrists to discuss the case. Very quickly the psychiatrists insisted that they treated symptoms and symptoms only. Manuel presented as someone who was "hyperactive," they said, and therefore needed to be treated for that cluster of symptoms specifically. Because they did not consider the source of Manuel's behaviors, the symptoms were misunderstood. He continued to receive medication for the wrong illness and before long became psychotic. It is now well known that PTSD, when left untreated, can lead to psychosis over time. Progression of the disorder is avoidable when we are diagnostically accurate and tailor our treatment to manage the specific symptoms involved. In Manuel's case, what needed to be intervened with was ignored.

My conversation with the psychiatrists occurred before we knew as much as we do now about trauma in children. We have begun to realize, through the help of recent research, that there is an important difference between hyperactivity and hypervigilance. We are starting to recognize that these similar yet different symptoms can look the same in children, and that without a thorough assessment we can make grave mistakes in our diagnoses and treatments. We now know that children who have been traumatized are not helped but harmed by stimulant medication. Children with a volatile nervous system who experience emotional swings from elevated states of happiness to extreme irritability and aggression, as evidenced by Manuel, are not helped but harmed by antidepressant medications. The psychiatrists did not know Manuel's story; they did not know what he had experienced and therefore who he was. They had the knowledge and training and experience they had, and they were sticking to their diagnosis. This is how we fail children.

Many different kinds of professionals, not just the psychiatrists mentioned but also educators, operate largely in the here and now. This is a valuable place to be operating from. Children with problems are experiencing difficulty in the here and now and need to be intervened with in the here and now. However, without an appreciation for where the behaviors stem from, there can be no understanding of what kinds of interventions will lead to relief. Too often we want to be able to take students aside, talk with them in a way that elicits their description not only of the problem but also the solution, and then begin to see improvement because we took time to counsel them. Our cognitive mind is hoping to intervene effectively with students at a cognitive level because that is our comfortable mode of operation. Our society focuses on cognition, we are trained cognitively, and we value the cognitive mind. We insist that our mind is more powerful than our instinctual responses and that we have what it takes to control overwhelming experiences if we concentrate enough, think enough, or talk enough. This is one powerful reason why our troubled students continue to have problems even though we feel we have intervened.

MARTIN

The principal asked me to meet with ten-year-old Martin's very concerned mother who was "willing to do anything" to help her son. When I met with her, she stated that the main reason she needed help for Martin was his "lack of concentration in class." She went on to say that "he's so bad." He "tips his desk, throws his paper during silent reading, cannot study on his own, and always has to have someone with him." The mother said that she wanted him tested for being "extra active," stating that at home, Martin is "fidgety, can't sit still, argues over homework, and ends up in tears."

Does this student sound ADHD to you? Clearly, based on the descriptions of current symptoms, Martin has a neurological condition readily helped by psychostimulant medication, right? Wrong. Consider Martin's history. Martin has a kidney disease for which, since the age of five, multiple hospitalizations and surgeries were necessary. Many of the times Martin needed to be in the hospital for extended stays, his mother could not be with him. She is a single parent and needed to be at work. As a young boy, one can only imagine how frightened Martin was, left with strangers at a hospital to be probed, prodded, needled, restrained in some cases, and operated on. Martin's mother stated that since the time of his last hospitalization—and "that one was really bad," she said—Martin began flinching anytime someone who was physically close to him moved. She was extremely concerned at the time of our meeting because his once good grades had dropped.

Are students like Martin understood when we ignore history—the source of the difficulty—and simply treat current symptoms? Medicating his "extra active" behaviors with the typical medications used for such symptoms would have been throwing gasoline on a fire.

TRAUMATIC STRESS, ITS SYMPTOMS,
AND WHAT TO DO ABOUT THEM

Not all students who experience trauma become traumatized. Some students are more resilient than others. Some students have more resources than others. Many factors combine to determine whether or not there will be a residual impact of a traumatic event on a student (see chapters 4 and 5 for more). Additionally, not all students who have been traumatized exhibit all the symptoms required by the DSM-IV-TR for a formal diagnosis of posttraumatic stress disorder (PTSD). Focusing simply on students with PTSD is a mistake and is not the intention of this book. Though there are no statistics, one can guess that there are a significant number of students who experience posttraumatic stress who fall between the cracks, who are not recovered from their trauma yet do not have the degree of debilitation involved in PTSD (Rothschild 1996). It is vital to the safety of our schools and the health of our students that we intervene with anyone with any degree of posttraumatic stress, students whom I simply call "traumatized."

One striking sign of the traumatized student is rage. Not all students who are traumatized exhibit rage and not all students who display rage have been traumatized. In my experience, however, I have often found a traumatic history in the students referred to me for anger management, students who have a tendency toward fits of extreme frustration, anger, and aggression. The amount of rage in our students today is particularly alarming to educators. It is seemingly unexplained, and yet, when one considers the world our students live in, it really should not be so alarming. According to the *Northern California Psychiatric Physician*, for example, both exposure to violence and violent behavior among our youth continue to escalate. California statistics recently released by the Children's Defense Fund indicate that three children die from child abuse each day, nine are murdered, and thirteen are killed by firearms. Violence in the United States is the major contributing factor to posttraumatic stress, depression, and behavior problems in our youth (Menvielle 1998). Twenty-five to 50 percent of all children exposed to violence in the United States are at risk for PTSD, a number that is comparable to U.S. combat veterans (Menvielle 1998).

It has become increasingly evident through research studies on the effects of violence that posttraumatic stress negatively impacts the physiology of traumatized individuals (van der Kolk, McFarlane, and Weisaeth 1996), as do birth complications and early infant and childhood experiences (Karr-Morse and Wiley 1997). Physiological and neurological development is sequential. The organizing and sensitive brain of a fetus, infant, or young child is more malleable to experience than a mature brain. Experience provides the organizing framework for a fetus, infant, or child (Perry, Pollard, Blakley, Baker, and Vigilante 1995).

Early experiences in utero, infancy, or childhood, including anything the organism perceives as threatening to its survival, can result in malorganization and compromised function in the affected brain systems. Examples include toxins, such as drugs or alcohol, as well as overexcitation or extreme stress of any kind. Understanding the organization, function, and development of the human brain and brain-mediated responses to threat provides the keys to understanding the misunderstood child. It is the brain that processes and internalizes both traumatic and therapeutic experiences. It is the brain that mediates all emotional, cognitive, behavioral, social, and physiological functioning (Perry et al. 1995) (see chapter 5 for more).

With consideration for physiology and brain development research, I work with traumatized students at the level of sensation. Sensation is the language of the reptilian brain or brain stem, the part of us that is so involved in our response to perceived threat and danger. *Talking* about thoughts and feelings, on the other hand, engages the part of the brain *least* involved in the experience of trauma, the neocortex. This can make things worse for the traumatized student, not better. Rather, our goal must be to access and soothe the brain stem. We can do this by encouraging students to notice and describe their sensations within the context of either a resource to strengthen them or a traumatic event to help resolve it (see chapters 6 through 9 for more). That is how I intervened with Jesus.

JESUS REVISITED

I met with Jesus two times several weeks after he had been molested. We did not need to go into the story of what happened to him. In fact, it was better not to because of how telling the story can retraumatize. Instead, I helped him establish a safe place in his mind and at the school where he could get grounded and connected to someone and something that helped stabilize his nervous system. I helped Jesus experience his body as a safe place again. We accessed his sensations. I asked him to notice what he was experiencing and sensing in his body and then invited him to focus there to see how things might change. Within a few short moments of focusing on the sensations in his body, Jesus felt his body change from "jumpy and scary" to more "relaxed and smooth." His parasympathetic nervous system kicked in, as it always does, and brought the sympathetic nervous system down to a more relaxed state. He went from feeling anxious to feeling relaxed and became aware of this in his body. We engaged the brain stem through sensation and found relief that was palpable.

Jesus took the body memory of that experience with him, remembering at an instinctual level—and perhaps at a cognitive level—that "what goes up must come down." He knew experientially that his nervous system might get activated but it is also designed to relax itself again. Just as our anxiety has a rate of escalation, it also has a rate of de-escalation. I had two sessions with Jesus working in this way, as well as a session with his family to teach them about the processes at work and how to create calm in their own nervous systems in order to help Jesus feel calm. Jesus began playing on the playground, making new friends, not because of anything technical or complicated I did, but because the body is a natural healing mechanism that does what it needs to do when we let it (see chapter 11 for greater detail).

How else are traumatized students misunderstood? Many display behaviors that cause educators to consider special education placement, because "something" is wrong, educators know that much, but what precisely is a mystery. Are these students autistic? Emotionally disturbed? Health impaired? It is not that they do not have some of the characteristics of students who have a developmental disorder, emotional disturbance, or some other special education consideration. The problem is, first, that these designations do not capture the whole picture, and second, without the whole picture, we intervene in ways that may actually do more harm than good. When the source of the problem is not considered, we are uninformed about best practice when it comes to designation and intervention.

Intervention is different from treatment. It is not the responsibility of educators to provide treatment per se. That is the job of medical and mental health professionals. However, in many cases, educators are often the only professionals that families can afford to access, or feel comfortable accessing. School psychologists are trained to evaluate and make recommendations. They are, according to Bert Racowitz, PhD, psychologist specialist for the Dallas Independent School District, "boundary-crossers," professionals who are in a unique position to work to fill in the gaps in children's services and work with families and communities to improve mental health services (Clay 1998). School psychologists are therefore in a unique and responsible position. When they evaluate students and their needs thoroughly, taking into consideration their developmental histories and individual experiences, planning interventions and placements based on that information, students and families benefit tremendously.

The problem arises when school psychologists and other educators operate with an incomplete or insufficient knowledge base. This is when we tend to refer for evaluation and placement in special education, when we are faced with students we do not understand. Having them placed in classes or schools apart from regular students, however, means we expose them on a daily basis to other students with the same kind of volatility. Such exposure has the grave and likely potential to contribute to a vicious cycle of nervous system overwhelm that for some students never ends. We do not make these placements lightly, in all cases, or with mal intent, but we can do better.

Self-contained special education classes, ED classes in particular, can be high-strung, tense, and relatively unsafe places for traumatized students simply by virtue of the fact that so many problematic children are in the same place at the same time. While there are some students who are helped by these placements when the teacher manages an excellent program, too many times, the reality of the situation is far from ideal. Many educators make such placements because it is the only choice we have. The ED designation in particular often becomes the "catch-all" solution to our failure to understand (see chapters 8 and 12 for more).

To date, our conceptualizations of our most troubled students are incomplete. Our understanding of trauma and its impact on development is incomplete. Our knowledge of how to prevent trauma and intervene when a student has experienced a traumatic event is incomplete. We have felt the frustration when we simply do not know what to do anymore. The number of these challenging students is increasing while the number of much-needed resources is decreasing. We can no longer be, as those psychiatrists were when I was an intern, comfortable in our current knowledge and training, especially when it is often no longer current. Knowing that our students and families rely upon us as they do necessitates that we take action to fill in the gaps of our knowledge and learn about new possibilities to create more choices. Educators are doing terrific things and many students get better, but that has not equated to "no child left behind" and we know it.

3

Filling in the Gaps

As educators, we need to be asking the right questions. School psychologists, in particular, perform numerous psychoeducational evaluations each year and are often the only person with the responsibility of telling a student's story. In my review of hundreds of reports produced by school psychologists, I have found that the majority of the stories of troubled students are incomplete. What is often missing is history. School psychologists typically do not neglect to give background information, but that information usually focuses on whom the student lives with, what schools the student has attended, what the student's attendance in school has been, and what language the family speaks in the home. These are currently considered the important variables when evaluating a student for learning disabilities and other special education considerations.

Popular belief as reflected by these reports is that any information related to the experiences the student had before entering school, especially before the age of two or three, is irrelevant. Any preverbal, and thus "precognitive," experiences are not important, do not have a lasting effect, or have little meaning. The infant, and certainly the fetus, is considered "exempt from thought and the capacity to record enduring experiences" (Karr-Morse and Wiley 1997, 4). This is the common belief and yet, according to Karr-Morse and Wiley's research, "nothing could be further from the truth. This overlooked chapter of early growth sees the building of the capacities for focused thinking and for empathy—or the lack of these" (1997, 4). Accordingly, our understanding of the inability of a student to focus, learn, and behave in expected ways depends upon a careful consideration of these earliest months of life.

Early developmental information is very important to the understanding of students and yet is not commonly part of the stories educators tell. Too often we leave out of the reports we write the details of the conditions of the conception or gestation of our students, when such information can be exactly what we need in order to understand and intervene with success. For instance, several studies have documented links between being prenatally unwanted and increased rates of both youth suicide and juvenile criminality (Karr-Morse and Wiley 1997). For decades we have known that what affects the mother emotionally also affects the fetus. Drs. Sontag and Wallace as long ago as 1934 found that when their pregnant patient was pursued by a psychotic husband, the fetus was physiologically alarmed right along with the mother, as measured by heart rate and respiratory activity (Chamberlain 1995). Understanding this stress response system and its impact on brain development has large implications for working with individuals with attention problems and/or impulsivity. According to Perry (1997), when experiences of overstimulation of the alarm system occur early enough in development, a state of hyperarousal or numbing may become a permanent trait in the student, setting the stage for a host of learning and behavioral problems.

The oversight of this early developmental information is not unique to the field of education. It is common for many professionals. In *Ghosts from the Nursery: Tracing the Roots of Violence,* Karr-Morse and Wiley wrote that the stories of our most troubled individuals are told over and over again by "events, psychiatric reports, interviews . . . [delving] into adolescence, grade school and childhood" (1997, 4). The beginning of the stories, however, goes untold. "One chapter is nearly always missing—the first chapter, encompassing gestation, birth, and infancy. And because it goes unseen and unacknowledged, it repeats itself over and over at a rate now growing in geometric proportions" (4).

Making the collection of detailed developmental history information our responsibility as school psychologists is vital to the assessment process. In many school districts, the nurse or social worker is solely responsible for collecting this information and providing a summary of it in their own reports, often separate from the psychologist's report. Other districts do a good job of having the nurse and/or social worker and school psychologist work together to provide a joint report. A more complete story is told in these cases. Yet having the information does not mean it is understood. The impact of the student's early experiences is rarely fully comprehended or appreciated by professionals of any kind, not just educators. School personnel often do an excellent job of gathering information because of greater access than other practitioners to family members who attend or visit the school. However, like most other professionals, they are uncertain of what the information they have gathered really means.

Without knowing the implications of early developmental information, we are less likely to make the effort to gather it. There still exists today a common belief that fetal development and birth experiences cannot be that important unless, perhaps, drugs or alcohol were indicated. This belief prevents us from understanding our most troubled students and what we can do to have a lasting effect on their educational development.

In 1998, Steve Bagby Sr., a representative from the American Guidance Service, spoke with school psychologists around the country to remind them of the importance of history taking (Bagby 1998). His argument was that history taking is more relevant than standardized testing when assessing to formulate diagnostic impressions. He indicated that formal training in history taking is conventionally only provided in the fields of medicine and social work and argued for why this needed to change in the field of school psychology.

According to Bagby, important information needed for the formulation of diagnoses and treatment not provided by standardized testing includes *age of onset, course, etiology, treatment design,* and *risk* as well as *resilience factors,* all information that is best gathered through detailed history taking. *Age of onset* of the problem is important, for instance, when one is considering the possibility of ADHD because of the set criterion that onset of symptoms must occur before the age of seven. In terms of the *course* of the disorder, in order for a student to genuinely be learning disabled, for example, the student's particular learning problems must be consistent over time. A learning disability, by definition, is not something that is outgrown. When considering *etiology,* should a student have a history of a thyroid condition, for example, their symptoms may be the result of that medical condition and not some other consideration. *Treatment design* information is crucial to understanding problems that may be the result of a relapsed condition, when medication is stopped in the case of depression, for example. Finally, *risk* and *resilience factors* are paramount to understanding and planning for a student's success. If we do not know the factors that either place the student at greater risk of difficulty or make success more likely, then we cannot develop interventions that will be effective. This information is not derived through standardized testing. It comes from prioritizing the intention to really know a student by asking the right questions related to history.

Treatment plans are best devised by asking solution-focused questions that are also based on history. For instance, asking about past attempts to find a solution or implement an intervention, finding out about what was tried before with some success or no success, informs treatment planning in an invaluable way. Knowing about the exceptions to the problem—when and where and with whom the problem has not occurred, for example, or has not been observed—is revealed only through conscientious history taking, not through the use of standardized tests. Learning about the students' resources—how they have been able to manage themselves despite their problem and how they accessed what was helpful to them—helps us understand the student in a comprehensive way and informs our treatment planning extensively.

From the most recent research findings, valuable information that we need to be sure to gather includes the conditions of the conception, the pregnancy, and the birth of the student in question. Karr-Morse and Wiley, based on their review of hundreds of research studies, documented in their book that the infants whose birth was compromised by physical difficulties coming into the world, such as struggling with a breech birth or having been threatened with suffocation from a cord wrapped around the neck, were highly vulnerable and in need of reassurance and comfort. "When a traumatized baby is instead rejected by his mother, the stage is set for rage and often for violent criminality in adulthood" (1997, 90). We need to know about this particular combination of factors. When there was pre- or perinatal stress of any kind, asking what the early care of the infant and toddler was like thereafter is a very important part of any assessment.

Dr. Patricia Brennan at the University of Southern California (USC) studied more than four thousand males and found that children who suffered birth complications together with maternal rejection in their first year of life were far more likely than others to become violent offenders as adults (Brennan and Mednick 1997). Poor social circumstances, including poverty, combined with birth complications did *not* produce violent outcomes. Instead, it was the particular combination of birth complications and *maternal rejection* that led to the maladaptive outcomes. Also out of USC, researchers concluded that the highest rates of violent crime occurred when individuals experienced both a high number of delivery complications and a mentally ill parent (Kandel and Mednick 1993).

This early developmental information is vital to our understanding of the students we serve yet can be challenging to gather. Many excellent tools are available to educators and other professionals to aid in the process. One such comprehensive tool is the Structured Developmental History (SDH) form from the Behavior Assessment System for Children (BASC) (Reynolds and Kamphaus 1992). This form is an extensive, twelve-page history and background survey that provides a thorough review of social, psychological, developmental, educational, and medical information about a student. The BASC-SDH provides key information for determining whether disorders are acute or chronic, for documenting developmental progressions, for identifying age of onset, and for differentiating among clinical disorders. Jerome Sattler, in his comprehensive text *Assessment of Children*, also provides sample interview forms that are thorough and helpful in gathering relevant historical information (Sattler 1992).

Many examples illustrate the imperative nature of gathering historical information in order to develop the most precise diagnostic impressions possible and therefore most appropriate treatment plans. Students with behaviors on the spectrum of a pervasive developmental disorder, for instance, may be autistic if language was delayed in their early development, or Asperger's if there was no language delay early on. The diagnosis informs treatment. What is helpful to the student with autism may exacerbate the difficulties of the student with Asperger's. Our diagnostic impressions must be precise. An eight-year-old overactive, inattentive student may be ADHD if these behaviors were observed consistently throughout early development, before the age of seven specifically, or may have an anxiety disorder (e.g., acute stress disorder or PTSD) if the behaviors appeared for the first time related to a traumatic event. Without asking the right questions, professionals cannot be sure of exactly what the challenges and needs of a particular student are. Having the BASC-SDH or any other thorough history-taking tool in front of you, as an evaluator, is an excellent way of approaching any case in a structured, detailed way. It serves as a reminder to ask all the important questions that are sometimes forgotten or assumed to be unimportant.

Sometimes, it is only when we get an answer that we suddenly realize why the question needed to be asked in the first place. In the case of Daniel (see chapter 2), when I met with his parents and completed the SDH form, they did not remember the details of the pregnancy and birth until the questions became more and more specific. Professional expertise combined with the effective use of the tool led to a complete picture of the student's experience. It was important to patiently ask more and more detailed questions, to probe and listen, and to provide space for the answers to come.

In *Assessment of Children*, Sattler stated that much of the art of interviewing lies in the ability to listen creatively and empathically and to probe skillfully beneath the surface of the communication (Sattler 1992). He reviewed a number of distinct advantages to the interview as an assessment procedure. The detailed and structured interview allows one to motivate the interviewee to provide accurate and complete information while obtaining the chronology and history of events. Through interviewing techniques, such as reflecting content and using summary statements, the importance of historical information becomes clearer to everyone involved. For instance, when I interviewed Daniel's parents, they first responded that there was nothing remarkable to report about Daniel's delivery at birth. As I asked detailed questions about the event and reflected their answers back to them by summarizing their statements, Daniel's parents began to realize how stressful the delivery had been. They remembered that their son's heart rate was rapidly declining, as was the mother's, and that the medical staff cautioned they might quickly need to perform a C-section. Each parent remembered through the interview process that the experience had been "very stressful" to each of them. The C-section was not necessary in the end, but when Daniel was born, the umbilical cord was wrapped around his neck and he had difficulty breathing. He was placed in an incubator immediately after birth and kept there for two days until mother and child were released from the hospital.

Other information gathered that became important to the understanding of Daniel came from an expansion of the BASC-SDH interview. In addition to asking the questions outlined in the protocol, I took a detailed trauma history from the parents. Had their child ever experienced any serious accidents, falls, injuries, illnesses, hospitalizations, or medical procedures? It did not take either parent long to recall the seemingly benign visit to the doctor's office during which Daniel needed a buildup of wax removed from his ear. This would not seem significant to the average person, except that Daniel many years later still had extreme reactions when anyone came close to that side of his head or when he needed to visit a doctor, especially in the years immediately after the event. Furthermore, the developmental history taking helped us to understand the significance of the bullying incidents that greatly affected Daniel's functioning at school. Together, these pieces of information told Daniel's story and helped us to appreciate where his rage came from and how we could help.

The first time I noticed that we began helping Daniel was at the meeting where we discussed the results of his evaluation. As the team reviewed the details of his story, Daniel listened with remarkable focus and ease. His body language and facial expressions clearly stated a sense of relaxation and relief that we finally understood him and what events had had such a lasting impact on his nervous system. He could then trust that we would operate within the context of our understanding of him and head in the right direction in terms of intervention.

Daniel's nonverbal communication was as clear a communication as any that the right questions had been asked and that they had helped to derive an understanding of Daniel that had not existed before. Sattler highlighted listening as crucial to the interview process and stated that a good listener is attentive not only to what is said but also to how it is said. The interviewee's tone, expressions, gestures, as well as physiological cues (e.g., pupil dilation, tremors, blushing) are important parts of the assessment process. Posture, fluidity versus rigidity of body movement, and physical tension may be evidenced through a strained facial expression or forced laugh. None of this information should go unnoticed.

In addition to asking the right questions in order to more comprehensively understand a student, we need to be attentive to numerous and varying indicators. Sattler wrote that we need to be attentive to the feelings invoked in us by the interviewee in order to determine how to regulate the pace of the interview and to gain appreciation of how the interviewee affects others. Good listening, he wrote, requires that we be attentive not only to the interviewee, but also to ourselves. Noticing the student's relationship to us furnishes an important clue as to his or her perception of adults (Wenar 1990). It is natural for students to be reserved initially, since in reality the interviewer is typically a stranger. However, as they discover that the interviewer is interested, friendly, and benign, they should become relaxed, cooperative, and communicative, although still reluctant to talk about sensitive topics (Wenar 1990). If this does not happen over time with the student, this can become relevant diagnostic information. Perhaps the student never warms up, or becomes provocative, or attempts to engage the interviewer in a power struggle. These are all important pieces of information that cannot be derived from standardized tests but can only come from an interview process that includes keen observation. The student's body and body language, according to Wenar, provide important clues to physiological intactness as well as to personality variables. All inform diagnostic impressions and treatment.

It is important to note, as pointed out by both Wenar and Sattler, that the interview with its focus on history taking can have disadvantages, such as when interviewees provide inaccurate information or have biases that make them susceptible to subtle, unintended cues from the interviewer. Wenar makes the excellent point that while some research studies assessing the reliability of interviews disqualify parents or students as sources of accurate information concerning aspects of development, the studies do not render their histories useless. It is still important for the interviewer to know the parents' and students' perceptions of the facts.

While there are limitations to knowing perceptions only, we can compare the information gathered by different interviewers at different times to verify what can be considered more reliable and valid. If the nurse collected data a year previous and that information matches the information shared with the psychologist at the time of the current evaluation, it is probably safe to rely on the information as accurate and true. If information gathered by different people at different times does not match, then effort must be made to verify what is true and what is not, by checking medical records or comparing the information to that gathered by other professionals involved in the case (e.g., therapists, social workers, doctors).

At the end of the interview process with Daniel's parents, they remarked that out of all the professionals they had been to, and there were many, not one had taken the time to ask the detailed questions that needed to be asked in order for them to more fully understand their child. Like their son, they too appeared more relaxed and relieved that someone took the time to consider the whole story of who Daniel was—what all of his challenges and needs were. As educators, we are in a privileged position to work with families in the context of their children's world—at school—to gather the most comprehensive information possible. Caring about the source or sources of the problem is our obligation to these families. Depending on the circumstances, they come to rely on school personnel the most. Parents are at their children's schools more often than at doctor's offices, medical or mental health clinics, and therefore, they often ask their children's educators for help first. We are the ones who can go beyond the medical doctor's focused interest in symptoms and how to treat those with medication.

As a clinical psychologist, I worked within the medical and mental health fields. Some of the medical doctors I knew, as I mentioned in chapter 2, were very direct with me when they stated that their concern was for the symptoms of the problem and not the source. Many times since my work with Manuel (see chapter 2) I have been concerned about children being diagnosed with ADHD when their histories had been so traumatic. Their symptoms could have been more comprehensively understood as anxiety as a result of their experiences. Hypervigilance, an exaggerated startle response, and high levels of anxiety in general can easily be observed as hyperactivity, especially because ADHD is such a popular diagnosis and seemingly easily treated with medication. Again, this speaks to our misunderstanding of children. We do not yet appreciate that children are as affected by disturbing external events as adults are—that they pick up on the stress and tension involved in their parents' lives and that they have their own extreme levels of stress to tolerate and rise above. Neither do we appreciate that events need not happen to children directly in order to be terrifying or traumatic. Children simply need to *hear* about frightening or threatening events to suffer from their vicarious effects.

It is up to us as educators to fill in the gaps of our knowledge and training and have our students be the deserving recipients of our greater understanding of them. Global events, as well as personal experiences, impact the development of our students across domains in direct and specific ways and we need to know how. What is traumatic for our students? How are traumatic events affecting our students' functioning in all areas, social, academic, and behavioral? The answers to these questions require our effort and time. We need to take the time to learn what the right questions are; we need to make the effort to ask those questions; and we need to know what the answers mean once we have them.

Although this chapter largely focused on the role of school psychologists as assessors, other school personnel working with students—teachers, counselors, and principals—need to be aware of all the issues reviewed. As educators, each of us needs to be asking historical questions and putting the answers into a meaningful context. The success of our students depends on it.

II

TRAUMA AND THE BRAIN

4

Trauma

The healing of trauma depends upon the recognition of its symptoms.

—Peter Levine, PhD

TRAUMA IN CHILDREN

Children are not any less impacted by trauma than adults. No matter how young, even preverbal children experience trauma and remember terror in the very cells of their body. Infants and toddlers may be too young to verbalize and cognitively process traumatic experiences but they are not too young to be changed by them.

We are now learning through scientific research that trauma changes brain chemistry and, as we already know, brain chemistry changes behavior. Based on their extensive review of recent data, Karr-Morse and Wiley stated that, "for children *of any age, long-term damage* can occur from a single searing trauma or prolonged exposure to chronic stress or fear" (1997, 156). Trauma that occurs during infancy and early toddlerhood—because this is the most explosive phase of brain development—can cause injury that reverberates beyond anything we imagined possible (Karr-Morse and Wiley 1997).

Many parents and professionals believe that children, especially preverbal children, cannot be as affected by trauma as adults. We have subscribed to this notion because preverbal children cannot talk about their experiences. They have no words. They cannot verbally convey their horror. What they can do, however, is act it out, and that is precisely what more and more educators are witnessing in schools today.

Researchers have documented our observations. In one study, eighteen out of twenty young children who had experienced trauma between birth and two-and-a-half years of age replicated their trauma in their play (Karr-Morse and Wiley 1997). Studies done by Joseph LeDoux revealed that early precognitive emotions continue to play out in later life even though the person may have no conscious memory of the event (LeDoux 1993, 1996). Dr. Leigh Baker, author of *Protecting Your Children*, concluded that infants have preverbal memories that are stored in their body that may resurface at any point in later development, causing unexplainable and uncomfortable physical sensations (Baker 2002).

The symptoms children display after being traumatized are not any different or any less intense than those observed in adults. In fact, for decades, since Dr. David Levy's important study on the aftereffects of trauma, we have known that children who experienced surgeries and invasive medical procedures thereafter displayed traumatic symptoms comparable to those manifested by soldiers returning from war (Levy 1945). The symptoms were not only comparable but also as intense and debilitating.

TRAUMA DEFINED

Trauma for children is any event—real or *perceived*—that is terrifying or threatening *to them*. It does not matter whether or not others are terrified or threatened by the same event. What matters is how it is experienced by the individual. Dr. Peter Levine, after twenty-five years of experience studying trauma, wrote in his book *Waking the Tiger: Healing Trauma*, that a traumatic reaction is valid regardless of how the event that induced it appears to anyone else. For some, for reasons that will be discussed, the same particular event may not be traumatic while, for others, it may cause affliction that even those who suffer cannot understand.

In schools, the term used for a traumatic event is "crisis." For the purposes of this book, the terms "crisis" and "trauma" will be used interchangeably. Crises are typically unexpected events that can be life threatening and that may or may not involve a degree of violence. "Crisis intervention" is the term used to describe the immediate response of schools to a crisis involving students either at the school or in the community in order to prevent traumatization of students. Crisis intervention will be reviewed in chapters 10 and 11.

Knowing how to prevent traumatization is important to schools, making the recent efforts by educators to develop better crisis intervention approaches a relevant focus. The growing number of students who arrive to school already traumatized from events in their communities, neighborhoods, and homes, however, cannot be ignored. We need to address what educators can do to understand these students better and intervene with them effectively. The following chapters (4–9) will help us do just that.

Examples of traumatic events that occur every day in the lives of our students include

- domestic violence
- emotional, physical, and sexual abuse
- physical neglect and abandonment
- fetal distress (high levels of stress during gestation and delivery)
- birth complications
- rape, molest, and incest
- surgery and other invasive medical or dental procedures
- general anesthesia
- car accidents
- falls, injuries, or other accidents
- community violence (e.g., witnessing, hearing about, or experiencing a violent act)
- being threatened, attacked, or bitten by an animal
- sudden death or loss of a loved one (including divorce)
- natural disasters (e.g., earthquakes, fires, tornadoes, floods)
- chronic disease or serious illness (e.g., leukemia)
- prolonged immobilization from casting and splinting
- high fevers, accidental poisoning, exposure to extremes in temperature
- being lost (e.g., at the mall, in a strange neighborhood)
- near drowning, near suffocation
- bullying
- acts or words of racism and prejudice in one directed at another

As we can see from this list, if we are working with school children, we are working with trauma. The experiences listed are varied. Some are obviously traumatic and others are not so apparent. Depending on the particular kinds of neighborhoods our students live in, some are more exposed to certain acts of violence than others. There is no question, however, that regardless of socioeconomic status, trauma is a part of almost every student's life.

STUDENTS WHO BECOME TRAUMATIZED VERSUS THOSE WHO DO NOT

Not everyone who experiences a traumatic event becomes traumatized. Some do very well in the face of danger and carry on without any noticeable sign of what they went through. Others, *even if at first they seem all right*, later develop signs and symptoms that something is not the same. Traumatic effects are not always noticeable immediately following the incident(s) that caused them. An early fall that causes shock or injury may produce no obvious problems at first. It may not be until years later, until another frightening event occurs (such as a medical procedure or when a stressful period commences, such as entering school) that the effects of a previous incident begin to show. According to Dr. Levine, "symptoms can remain dormant, accumulating over years or even decades. Then, during a stressful period, or as a result of another incident, they can show up without warning" (1997, 45).

As weeks, months, and years pass, students who seemed "just fine" immediately after a crisis event may begin to struggle with their sleeping patterns, eating patterns, level of concentration, and/or ability to focus and be in the here and now. Some may become more agitated, more easily upset, and more difficult to soothe. They may report a sore tummy, headaches, or pain in their limbs. Others may report nightmares, difficulty remembering, and "jitteriness" inside that will not go away. Students who experience trauma may develop a sense that something bad is going to happen and they need to be ready for it.

Students who become traumatized after a terrifying event differ from students who do not. Two factors in particular distinguish these two groups of students: *different trauma histories* and *differences in availability of resources*.

Students with *different trauma histories* vary in their level of vulnerability to future traumas. A student who had a difficult gestation and/or birth experience may have arrived on the scene of life with an already vulnerable nervous system. Antonio Damasio (2003) wrote in his book *Looking for Spinoza: Joy, Sorrow, and the Feeling Brain* that all organisms come to being with the capacity to regulate life and thereby permit survival. It is our birthright as mammals to come into this world with the biological groundwork necessary to develop into creatures capable of handling the threats to our survival that are a natural part of our existence. However, due to varying conditions during gestation and birth, not everyone comes to being with the same amount of fluidity with this self-regulating capacity. Research on the brain is now helping us understand more clearly that this very capacity, so critical to the management of all of life's challenges, can be compromised by high levels of stress during pregnancy, the birth process, and the weeks and months following birth.

Some of our students come into the world with a deregulated nervous system. The internal homeostasis that is vital to our well-being is not balanced in them. (I use the term "homeostasis" as Damasio did, a "convenient shorthand for the ensemble of regulations and the resulting state of regulated life" [2003, 30].) This does not have to be a life sentence, however. Despite having an unregulated nervous system, *differences in availability of resources* can change the course of how future traumatic incidents impact functioning.

A student with a nervous system that was compromised by trauma in the past can in the future experience repair. Repair can be the biological result of living in a stable nurturing home with at least one caregiver who responds to the student's needs with attunement in a generally consistent manner. The body's innate and natural healing capacity will restore balance when it experiences these and other resources. On the other hand, when vulnerable children are parented in chaotic or unstable homes, or are left with caregivers who, for reasons such as postpartum depression or chronic mental illness are not attuned to the needs of their children, this repair will likely not happen. Homeostasis, balance, and well-being may continue to elude these children.

Many infants experience no fetal distress and come into the world just as Damasio envisioned, with the "entire collection of homeostatic processes govern[ing] life moment by moment in every cell of [their] body" (2003, 35). They may experience accidents, falls, or injuries, often a normal part of development, and manage them well with the help of loving caregivers. There may occur one or more of these incidents however, that proves to be beyond what some students or their caregivers are prepared for. A student's frightening fall at an early age that causes shock or injury may trigger strong emotions for the student's caregiver, who is then less able to respond to the incident in the moment with healthy attunement and care. A simple medical procedure a year or two following such a fall that requires physical restraint to the student, or one that is somewhat invasive, may seriously frighten the student further. Together, the events can have reverberating effects on the student's nervous system for years to come.

MEREDITH

At seven years of age, one student referred to me for counseling required three separate surgeries for a condition the mother identified as "myringotomy." The mother reported that her daughter, Meredith, "thrashed and screamed" as she was put under general anesthesia each time the surgery was conducted. Days after the first surgery, the student repeatedly asked her mother, "Why did you let them do that to me? How could you let them do that to me?"

Just as army MASH medics once said when speaking of injured soldiers who required general anesthesia for their surgeries, "As they go in, so they come out." Meredith went under anesthesia thrashing and screaming and came out with problematic behaviors that over time mounted and intensified. She was eleven years of age by the time she was referred for counseling, at which time her mother reported behaviors such as "compulsive talking, attention-seeking behavior, nightmares, sleepwalking, and excessive eating." The mother repeatedly described her daughter as "overwhelming." Not only was Meredith experiencing her world, postsurgeries, as overwhelming, her mother's nervous system was also on sensory overload from having to cope with the aftermath of her daughter's traumas.

Terrifying experiences can be, and often are, traumatic for both parent and child, regardless of who the event happens to directly. Life and all its challenges can seem insurmountable thereafter. The culmination of frightening events over time can make the nervous system of some students less readily capable of regulating both future traumatic events as well as life's daily challenges. Traumatized students may develop low levels of frustration tolerance and tantrum behaviors in response to seemingly small and insignificant everyday challenges. They may begin to display angry behaviors, lashing out at siblings or other playmates with little or no provocation. They may begin to cry excessively and not be able to calm down with soothing techniques that were once helpful to them.

BEN

A family came into the school for help with their five-year-old boy, Ben. Mother, father, and baby sibling were present for our meeting. The family thought Ben was ADHD. With the behaviors he displayed in the classroom, according to the teacher's report, they believed he needed to be treated for hyperactivity and inattention. Was medication the only next step? they wondered. We talked at length and, as I took a detailed developmental history, it became clear to each of us what their son was going through. They recalled the invasive medical procedure he experienced as an almost three-year-old, when he was kept in the dark in his hospital room and woken up throughout the day and night for multiple injections. During our meeting, the parents relived their horror of having experienced numerous "jolts" in the middle of the night as medical staff came into the dark room, flicked on the bright light, woke their child as they searched for another vein, and injected him once again. The tears streamed down their faces as they talked about how different their son was after that experience. They recalled that it was after that event that their son began crying more easily. He became more fearful of things and his sleep was restless ridden with nightmares and feelings of danger.

How easily Ben's symptoms were misunderstood. How readily we see symptoms of ADHD—restlessness, "squirreliness," agitation, hyperarousal, "ants in his pants"—without knowing anything about the history of the student, the student's story, and his or her experiences. These symptoms of trauma are readily misunderstood as symptoms of ADHD because educators and parents alike have been given so much information about ADHD. As educators, we have learned a great deal over the years about the signs and symptoms of ADHD and about the medications that can be helpful for the condition. On the other hand, we have not been told about trauma. We do not yet know the signs of this particular challenge and how to help. We are not equipped to accurately recognize our students' suffering even when it is right in front of us.

The two factors that distinguish students who become traumatized from those who do not, *different trauma histories* and *different availability of resources*, are related. Students who do not have a significant trauma history often have more resources available to them. For instance, students without unresolved trauma in their history already have a valuable *internal* resource: Their nervous system is biologically better equipped to navigate through frightening events when their early development has been without debilitating incident. Students do better after a crisis when they have *external* resources available to them as well, such as a stable family to go home to, close friends they can rely upon to help them cope, and recognition for their talents and abilities that serve as outlets.

Developmental age and stage can make a difference in the amount of resources students have available to them. Younger students often have fewer resources to protect them. The younger the students are the more dependent they are on the help and protection of others. They are smaller, weaker, and less experienced than older children and therefore more at the mercy of the event.

While age makes a difference in how traumatic a particular event can be to a child, contrary to common belief, level of intelligence does not. Researchers have found that intelligence serves as a resiliency factor that helps individuals (who are intelligent) do well when faced with trauma over time. Abused children, for example, who because of their intelligence do well in school, have successes to offset their experiences of abuse. As far back as the seventeenth century, according to Damasio (2003), the Dutch philosopher Spinoza in his book, *Ethics*, stated that an affect cannot be restrained or neutralized except by a contrary affect that is stronger than the affect to be restrained. Research on resiliency has found that intelligence can bring about such "contrary affects" to the experience of abuse that "restrain or neutralize" the impact of the abuse over time.

It is true that intelligence can serve as an invaluable buffer against the negative effects of *developmental* trauma, which has to do with disruptions in getting needs met throughout the life span, especially from the fetal period through adolescence. However, as we will learn about in the next chapter, intelligence has less to do with how well we fare in the face of *shock* trauma. Shock trauma, as opposed to developmental trauma, is a one-time specific event that begins in the body with an instinctual response to a perceived life-or-death situation, causing alterations in the central and autonomic nervous systems. It involves not so much the rational, cognitive brain as the reptilian brain or brain stem and its millisecond response repertoire of fight, flight, or freeze. (This is not to suggest that shock trauma is not involved in developmental trauma. As one can imagine, abusive events and other traumas in childhood that are more chronic can also involve shock to the nervous system and thus have not only developmental implications but also a physiological impact comparable to a one-time specific event.)

Well-known educators in the field of crisis intervention today believe that students who are less intelligent are not as traumatized by terrifying events as are more intelligent students because they do not have the cognitive capacity to understand what has happened. The faulty line of reasoning that supports this belief is that if students cannot cognitively understand what has happened to them, they cannot be harmed by what has occurred. Only through knowledge of current research findings in the field of trauma will we eliminate these and other false beliefs that have the potential to harm our students.

Trauma is not a cognitive event, although it involves the mind. It is not something that happens to the intellect. Traumatization does not occur to smart people as opposed to people with mental retardation. People do not need to be able to analyze whether or not an event is particularly terrifying in order to feel its traumatic effect. We do not need to make rational judgments about what is fearful in order to feel fear. Trauma is an event of the *body* and mind. We know this as a result of the concerted effort of numerous researchers over the past decade. Because of these researchers, we now know more than ever before how trauma impacts the functioning of all students, intelligent or not.

PRIMAL RESPONSES OF FIGHT OR FLIGHT

Sudden, unexpected, life-threatening events mobilize powerful primal energies of fight or flight. These energies involve the brain, the endocrine system, and the autonomic nervous system. The body undergoes profound physiological changes in order to meet threat—muscles contract, bracing occurs, breath quickens, eyes narrow, chemicals flood the body—all in preparation for survival. These responses are instinctive and automatic and cannot be derailed by the cognitive, rational brain.

The enormity of these energies, of the responses we muster when we face threat, cannot be overstated. Dr. Michael Leeds (2003), a researcher in the area of anger, hostility, and aggression, detailed the fight-or-flight response by outlining the physiological changes we go through in milliseconds in order to defend our survival:

- release of catecholamines
- increased blood glucose and fatty acids
- skeletal muscle tension
- increased heart rate, breathing rate, blood pressure, and perspiration
- vasoconstriction in extremities
- increased clotting factors
- changes in eye tracking behavior
- increased sensory modality tracking: voice, volume, and pitch

In *Discover Magazine* in March 2003, Jocelyn Selim contributed to an article on fear written by Stephen Johnson. Selim described the anatomy of fear in a way that may help us to appreciate how quickly the body readies all biological systems for survival.

> Within seconds of perceiving threat, the primitive amygdala [see chapter 5] sounds a general alarm. The adrenal system promptly floods the body with adrenaline and stress hormones. Nonessential physiological processes switch off. Digestion stops, skin chills, and blood is diverted into muscles in preparation for a burst of emergency action. Breathing quickens, the heart races, and blood pressure skyrockets, infusing the body with oxygen while the liver releases glucose for quick fuel. The entire body is suddenly in a state of high alert, ready for fight or flight. (Johnson 2003, 36)

Damasio (2003) referred to these physiological changes as "low branch" reactions. They "are and should be stereotyped," he stated. "One does not want to interfere with nature's wisdom when it comes to . . . running away from danger" (2003, 52). The brain is prepared by evolution to respond with specific repertoires of action, automatically. According to Damasio, there is first a change "in the state of the body proper" and then "in the state of the brain structures that map the body and support thinking" (53). The "thinking" does not come first. Students who have the cognitive capacity to think quicker or with higher order function are not more afraid or fearful faster than less intelligent students. Regardless of intelligence, all students, all human beings for that matter, share the same biology and biological drive for survival. The ultimate result of our instinctual responses to danger "is the placement of the organism in circumstances conducive to survival" (53).

When these primal energies are mobilized for fight or flight and the threat is successfully overcome by either fighting or fleeing, there often comes more than just a tremendous amount of relief, but actually a greater sense of mastery and power. In the wild, ethologists observed rabbits that successfully fled from coyotes and termed their exuberant movements after the escape as "pronking." Humans too, after successfully protecting themselves or running away from danger, feel a sense of exuberance that they overcame such a challenge. They may feel a sense of completion and integration that is not simply psychological but physiological. The human body, when it completes what it set out to do, uses up all the chemicals released for fight or flight. Thus, the chemicals and energies discharged from the body leave no residual excess. Even though people are exposed to terribly traumatic events, when they are able to fight or flee and thereby use up all of the body's mobilized primal energies, they are not later plagued by traumatic symptoms.

It is when there exists no possibility of successfully fighting or fleeing that trauma rears its ugly head. All the energies become mobilized for movement, but movement is not an option. Biologically, the body makes the only other choice available at such a time. The instinctive choice to freeze is made when that is the best way to ensure survival. As is often the case with our students, they become immobilized by trauma not only when the body instinctively goes into freeze, but also when, out of shear physical limitations, they simply cannot override what is happening to them. Children are often rendered helpless. Their attempts to fight or flee are thwarted by the physical impossibility of the task. It is in this helplessness response, this immobility or freeze, where the seeds of traumatization are planted. Without being able to move, expend, and thereby discharge all of the chemicals and energies mobilized to meet the threat, our students are left with these powerful energies and chemicals trapped inside their body.

The best-documented example of what I am describing comes from *Too Scared to Cry: How Trauma Affects Children and Ultimately Us All* (Terr 1990). In 1976 in Chowchilla, California, twenty-six children were kidnapped from their school bus. Months and years following the event, almost every single child displayed posttraumatic stress responses (PTSRs) that interfered with their daily functioning. They suffered the residuals of trauma. The one exception was Bob Barclay, who was fourteen years old at the time of the event. He was able to respond during the crisis by enlisting the help of another boy and digging his way out of the enclosed space he and the others were left in. While Bob was able to move and remain active, functionally using up all of the chemicals and energies that were mobilized by the event, most of the other children were frozen with fear. Their primal energies—strong enough, as we have seen and heard, for a mother to lift a car off her own child—remained stuck in their body, unused, only to surface later as posttraumatic symptoms.

This is not how this event was first understood. In the beginning, two hospital physicians and one psychiatrist examined the children immediately as well as within days after the event and determined that, for the most part, the children were fine. They ran tests and found no physical reason to believe that the children had suffered any trauma. (This happens every day!) Eight months later, however, Dr. Lenore Terr began one of the first scientific follow-up studies on children and trauma and found that almost every child had been traumatized by the event. The children reported sleep disturbances, including nightmares, and had become more prone to violent outbursts and reactions.

It cannot be stressed enough that initial checkups by physicians following the event did not reveal evidence of trauma. These were children ages five to fifteen who were kidnapped and buried alive in a "hole," as they called it, an underground vault, and were left there for thirty hours. Yet physicians and a psychiatrist felt the children were fine.

THE AUTONOMIC NERVOUS SYSTEM

What we now know about trauma, thanks to studies such as Dr. Terr's and the brain research of the past decade, is that traumatic symptoms are largely the result of primitive responses, and are thus, according to Dr. Peter Levine, difficult to recognize. It is the autonomic nervous system that becomes deregulated by trauma. It sometimes takes time to see the demonstration of this in everyday signs and symptoms. For instance, children are often in shock following a traumatic event and can remain in shock for months, even years. These are the children who many falsely assume are doing well because they are not acting out and getting into trouble like other children who experienced the same event. These children who look like they are doing so well are, in many cases, actually living outside their own body, dissociated, numb, or in a daze. They look as though they are looking through you. They cannot concentrate or remember what someone has just said to them. They look spacey and disoriented. They may sleep too much or too little. They may eat too much or too little. These symptoms reflect as much of a deregulation of the nervous system as any.

When the autonomic nervous system becomes deregulated by trauma, any or all of the basic human drive functions can begin to operate irregularly, effectively out of balance. Body temperature may become irregular, such as in the case of shock when the body becomes cold. Children who are traumatized may then chronically experience a cooler body temperature than before the event. They may begin experiencing sleep disturbances and/or eating disturbances—gaining or losing weight, having difficulty falling asleep or staying asleep. These are functions mediated by the autonomic nervous system, the same system that is highly aroused when preparing for survival.

There are two branches of the autonomic nervous system: sympathetic and parasympathetic. Sympathetic nervous system responses are those that have to do with the body revving up for action, such as blood pressure accelerating, heart rate accelerating, face flushing, sweating, and muscles constricting. Parasympathetic nervous system responses are those that de-escalate or relax the responses of the sympathetic branch. Healthy, untraumatized students have a balance between these two branches. They are able to navigate through life's challenges with the ease of an ebb and flow. They may become upset by daily events but are able to self-soothe or receive the help of another without becoming stuck on high, or stuck on low. The traumatized student's nervous system, on the other hand, is out of balance. It does not ebb and flow with ease. It is either too revved up too much of the time, easily upset and difficult to soothe, or is too shut down lacking in vitality and participation in life. We will understand these differences better when we study trauma and the brain in the next chapter.

CALVIN

Calvin is nine years old. He currently goes to school in an alternative educational setting. The setting consists of one room divided by partitions to make two classrooms, and is a storefront in a strip mall. Calvin has been required to attend this alternative program because he has been unable to control his impulses to act out inappropriately on a regular school campus. At his regular school, Calvin repeatedly gave notes to female students asking them if they wanted to have sex with him. Despite being smart and capable academically, Calvin refused to do class work and obey teacher requests. He often refused to speak at all. One day, he put a fellow student in a trash can, stating that a voice in his head told him to do it. Now that Calvin is on a small dose of antipsychotic medicine he appears to be doing better in some areas of his life. However, under any kind of stress, Calvin's problematic behaviors escalate, making the alternative setting an ongoing need.

On the surface, it may seem that Calvin has lived out his genetic propensity to develop a psychotic disorder and will always require medication management with antipsychotic drugs. However, Calvin has no family history of schizophrenia or bipolar disorder or any other illness that would explain the development of psychotic symptoms, especially at such a young age. What he does have is an extensive history of trauma.

The inordinate amount of stress that is experienced in a traumatic event, when left unresolved and untreated, can lead to psychotic symptoms, as it did in the case of Manuel in chapter 2. Mental health providers are only now slowly coming to appreciate the necessity of recognizing the difference between similar-looking symptoms to be certain posttraumatic stress responses are being treated as such and not as symptoms of another disorder. We need to be much less concerned with whether or not students who have been traumatized meet criteria for PTSD, and more concerned with intervening with students who have any degree of a posttraumatic stress response.

The term posttraumatic stress *response* (PTSR) was coined by Dr. Peter Levine in an effort to recognize that the so-called symptoms of trauma are simply the natural way our bodies respond to trauma. According to Levine, they do not constitute a disorder. The problem lies not in the symptoms but in the lack of opportunity to use up the energy mobilized during the threat. The symptoms simply signal where in the body the energies need to be discharged from. Furthermore, as stated in chapter 2, there are many different degrees of responses after a traumatic event. All degrees need to be recognized as worthy of consideration of treatment and intervention. PTSD is reserved for persons who exhibit a certain number of symptoms to a particularly debilitating degree. The terms PTSR (as suggested by Dr. Levine) and "traumatized" (for the purposes of this book), however, help us consider all individuals who are having difficulty following a trauma, regardless of meeting criteria for a disorder.

At one of my schools, I served as the coordinator of the School Based Mental Health Program (SBMH). I received one referral after another of students whose school functioning was being dramatically disrupted by depression, anxiety, inattention, hyperactivity, or some other DSM-IV-TR cluster of symptoms. There was not a single referral I can recall that did not involve either one traumatic event or series of traumatic events, even though such incidents were rarely mentioned initially. The symptoms that the students were referred for had traumatic antecedents in every single case, yet trauma was rarely indicated on the initial paperwork. Similarly, in a study conducted by Dr. Bessel van der Kolk of Harvard University and Boston Medical Center, the many symptoms of trauma that the patients at a large mental institution exhibited were overlooked because no one recognized their significance (van der Kolk 2002). We are only now beginning to appreciate the significance of trauma.

Michael, aged eight, was referred for the SBMH program for ADHD symptoms. Michael had an extensive history of surgeries and medical procedures due to a lifelong kidney condition. Marisa, at five years of age, was referred because of "behavior problems" in her kindergarten classroom. Her ear was severed and sewn back on after a dog attacked her as a three-year-old. David, aged nine, as a two-year-old, fell from a second-story balcony and had a large scar on his upper forehead to show for it. Oliver, as a six-year-old, displayed memory problems, reading problems, and behavior problems after being hit by a car when he was riding his tricycle in an alley. Many of these children received clean bills of health from the physicians that served them at the time of their accident and thereafter. It was in the schools, however, where we saw the physiological residuals of the trauma they experienced.

THE *EXPERIENCE* OF TRAUMA

There are a number of educators who, when they see difficult or confusing behaviors in students, are tempted to simplify the situation by blaming parents, especially when students are angry, aggressive, or violent. We believe sometimes that these behaviors are the result of bad parenting. Parents, on the other hand, have blamed educators for not doing more, understanding better, or coming up with quicker solutions. The truth is that trauma is not the fault of either the caregiver or the teacher, at least in many cases. Of course, there are cases of parents who were ill equipped for pregnancy, birth, and raising children, and there are teachers who teach with a threatening disposition in order to keep their students in line. Once we more fully understand the *experience* of trauma in our students, however, we will find that blaming each other misses the point.

Dr. Peter Levine (1997) conveyed the reality of a traumatized person in his book *Waking the Tiger: Healing Trauma*:

> Words cannot accurately convey the anguish that a traumatized person experiences. It has an intensity that defies description. Many [who experience trauma] feel they live in a personal hell that no other human could possibly share. . . . [They] struggle

with: *I fear getting out of my bed in the morning. I fear walking out of my house. I have great fears of death—NOT that I will die someday, but that I am going to die within the next few minutes. I fear anger—my own and everyone else's, even when anger is not present. I fear rejection and/or abandonment. I fear success and failure. . . . I feel nervous all the time. I have shortness of breath, racing heart, disorientation, and panic. . . . When I do accomplish something, I feel no sense of satisfaction. I feel overwhelmed, confused, lost, helpless, and hopeless daily. I have uncontrollable outbursts of rage and depression.* (47)

I am reminded of so many of the students I work with when I read Levine's words. These are the experiences, the fears, and the feelings traumatized students express—not necessarily with their words. They express their anguish in their behaviors and in the things they do not say. They express their inner frazzled state in the fragmented drawings they depict, in their frenetic scribbling, with the dark colors they choose. One six-year-old boy, when asked to draw his safe place—a person, place, or activity that helped him feel safer when scared or lonely—scribbled with a dark green crayon all over the page. He showed it to me and said, "This is my dark place." When I asked him how often he is in his dark place, he answered, "All the time." He did not have words beyond that to express his anguish. He did not have the inner integration and wholeness to draw anything other than he did. "This is what I have to say," that picture spoke to me, "This is my experience."

There is an overwhelming push in this culture for our students and anyone else who has experienced trauma to simply get over it and get on with their lives. They are told to be grateful for what they have, do well in school, be a good athlete, make friends, and everything will be okay. Just forget about it, people tell them, think happy thoughts, watch a funny movie, and everything will be okay. Students are not just asked to deny their true inner experiences, their lives demand that they deny the truth. If they push those feelings down deep enough and numb those uncomfortable sensations long enough, maybe then they will be able to concentrate, follow the rules, learn to read, and get good test scores. The sensitive and caring teachers who realize when there is something wrong with a student reach out as best they can. They may have their troubled students meet with the school counselor or psychologist, for example, hoping that some counseling will help their students concentrate, follow the rules, learn to read, and get good test scores. Despite the efforts of educators, there remains in this culture as a whole little understanding and tolerance of the time it takes to repair the damage done in the wake of trauma.

HEALING TRAUMA

We cannot change what we do not understand. As Dr. Levine stated, the healing of trauma depends upon the recognition of its symptoms. We are getting a better idea of what the traumatized child looks like in the classroom. We are beginning to understand the importance of differentiating between signs and symptoms and taking detailed developmental histories to help us pinpoint whether or not we are dealing with trauma.

When it comes to understanding how to heal trauma once we have identified it, we must turn to an unexpected place—the wild. As strange as this may sound, we have a great deal to learn from animals in the wild. They face trauma daily and yet do not exhibit traumatization. This is important to humans because we share a large portion of our brain with animals. Even though we may not know it, we have the same natural and innate capacity to move through trauma as animals do. What we must do to use this innate capacity to its best potential, as efficiently as animals do, is get out of our own way. We must let our oldest, reptilian brain do what it does best without interference from our newer more rational, cognitive brain, unique to us as humans.

The key to healing traumatic symptoms in humans lies in our ability to mirror the fluid adaptation of wild animals as they shake out and pass through the freeze or immobility response and become fully mobile and functional again (Levine 1997), just as Bob Barclay did in Chowchilla.

We have all heard the saying, "playing possum." We know that in nature there is a natural and active process involving predator and prey. When a prey, such as an impala, is aware of an impending predator, such as a cheetah, it has three biological choices, just as humans do. The impala can fight the cheetah, which will most likely not secure its survival, or the impala can flee from the cheetah, which is often what happens. However, if the impala begins to flee and goes as fast as it can and cannot outrun the cheetah, the impala will "play possum." It will exercise its third biological option—freeze—in order to survive. What is important to remember is that all the energy that was mobilized for the impala to run fast and escape the cheetah is still in the "frozen" body of the impala. The impala is as revved up as ever. It simply is not moving. This will sometimes save the impala's life because of the cheetah's enjoyment of the chase, the fight, and overall challenge of catching an active prey. The freeze sometimes makes the impala less interesting to the cheetah and it will leave it alone.

That is not the end of the story. What is most important to the understanding of how to heal trauma is what happens to the impala after the cheetah has abandoned it. After the impala has determined that it is safe to come out of the freeze, it will remain in its place while gently shaking and trembling until the shaking and trembling come to a natural end. Through the shaking and trembling, the impala's nervous system discharges all the residual energy that was mobilized for fight or flight but was left unused because of the impala's inability to fight or flee. The freeze or immobility response occurred not because the energy was gone. The energy was just as great even though the body was motionless. The freeze occurred because the brain recognized that that biological choice would give the organism its best chance of survival.

The critical thing that animals in the wild do after a traumatic event that humans do not is allow the time and space for the discharge of the mobilized energy to shake itself out of the nervous system. Instead, we quickly start thinking, fearing, talking, or moving. One time, as I stood waiting at a traffic light, an older gentleman fell off his bicycle in front of me. He was clearly shaken. I encouraged him to come over to the side away from traffic and just sit and let me comfort him as he rested. "Oh no! I'm fine!" he shouted as he climbed back up on his bicycle, shaking visibly. He was unsteady on his bicycle, thrown off kilter by the fall. I let him know that it would be very helpful for him to just sit and let his body recover from the fall, that it would just take a couple of minutes, but he would not hear it. Perhaps it is the shame of the fall, the embarrassment that makes us want to act like it did not happen and carry on. The gentleman's fall was a relatively minor event. However, we often respond in this same way regardless of how major the event is. We convince ourselves that the quicker we get up on our two feet and resume duty, as if the event never happened, the better off we will be. Our newer, cognitive, more rational brains interfere with the reptilian brain's ability to shake off the event through gentle trembling and shaking that does not take longer than several minutes in most cases.

The good news is that even if the gentleman begins to develop posttraumatic stress responses from the fall, such as a fear of getting back up on a bicycle, or incessant shakiness and unsteadiness while on a bike, he can heal from the event and no longer experience such responses. The residual energy that was left in his body after the fall that he did not allow the time to shake off immediately after the event can still be discharged at a later time, only the process then becomes more involved. For instance, he would first need to learn about the body's natural ability to heal itself through the discharging of this residual energy. Then he would need to learn how to access the reptilian brain because that is where the energy stems from, and then he would need to make the time and space for the discharge to happen. These steps will be discussed further in the next chapter when we learn about the language of the reptilian brain.

SYMPTOM REVIEW

Let us review some of the "symptoms" of a posttraumatic stress response (PTSR) in our traumatized students:

- hypervigilance or hyperarousal, always on guard ready to defend or attack
- "shut down"; underarousal; sleepiness; little energy, participation, motivation, or initiative
- fears, anxieties, worries, nervousness, thoughts of doom (e.g., fear of dying/having shortened life)
- psychosomatic complaints (e.g., sore tummies, headaches, sore limbs, aches and pains)
- inattentiveness, distractibility, difficulty concentrating, confused, dazed
- daydreams, spacey, "floating through life" quality, out of body experiences
- tantrum behaviors, easily upset, difficult to soothe, excessive crying
- anger, rage, aggression, violence, threatens and/or attacks others
- self-injurious behaviors (e.g., cutting, mutilating, threatens or attempts suicide)
- difficulty learning, retaining information, retrieving information already learned
- compulsive behaviors (e.g., excessive talking, getting up and sitting down, hitting others)
- eating disturbances (e.g., eating too much or too little)
- sleep disturbances (e.g., sleeping too much or too little, nightmares, sleepwalking, night terrors)
- attention-seeking behaviors
- anxiety disorders (e.g., school phobia, obsessive-compulsive disorder, panic attacks)
- ADHD-looking behaviors (e.g., can't sit still, can't concentrate, "ants in the pants")
- reenactment of the trauma (e.g., obsessive thoughts regarding guns, death, looks for fights and/or dangerous situations, fearless, instigates punishments)
- difficult to engage, avoids or refuses to work
- perfectionist, rigid, inflexible (e.g., big upsets over small mistakes)
- enuresis, encopresis
- self-medicates (e.g., sniffs glue, smokes marijuana)
- bullies or is "the scapegoat"
- excessive clinging
- easily startled and jumpy
- irritable and agitated
- withdrawn from family and friends
- sad, listless, decreased activity
- extreme sensitivity to light and sound

- sexual acting out
- fear of going crazy

These signs and symptoms are seen at home and at school. They are observed in the classroom and on the playground. They begin to interfere over time with most daily functions and are difficult not only for the adults involved but for the students themselves. Just as we saw with the list of traumas experienced by our students, this comprehensive list of the signs and symptoms of trauma reminds us that as long as we are working with school-aged children we are, to some degree, working with the aftermath of trauma.

5

Trauma and the Brain

Bruce D. Perry, MD, PhD, is an internationally recognized authority on childhood trauma whose work has been instrumental in describing how traumatic events in childhood change the biology of the brain. At a recent conference on trauma, Dr. Perry listed the three primary purposes of the brain. They are not reading, writing, and arithmetic. They are instead survival, procreation (for survival), and caring for dependents (for survival) (Perry 2003). Understanding that the brain's primary function is not learning how to read and get good test scores is an important first consideration when thinking about the students we serve. They come to us not as a blank slate ready to take it all in, but with all of their experiences up to that point, many of them life-threatening, leaving the brain altered in specific ways that will be reviewed in this chapter.

There is no organ in the human body more important to education than the brain. There is no part of us that is more involved in the processes of learning and behavior than the brain. Yet this is the part of the body most of us know the least about. We tend to think of the brain as most involved with learning new information and remembering what we have learned in order to succeed in life, achieve goals, and set new ones. Rarely do we think of how the brain is completely hardwired to *survive first and foremost*. Only after survival is ensured does the brain concern itself with anything else. Rarely do we consider how severely altered the brain and its capacities are by experience, in ways that make learning and self-regulatory behavior a painful feat for many.

There are basic things about the brain and its impact on school functioning in all domains that we need to know in order to plan and execute interventions that work with traumatized students. If we do not learn about these facts, and we do not let them inform the development of our interventions, we will not make good on our promise to "leave no child behind." As we have now learned, the number of students we work with in schools who have experienced trauma is enormous and growing every day. Identifying and briefly discussing each important piece of information on trauma's impact on the brain as it pertains to school functioning will be the focus of this chapter.

The importance of understanding the brain in order to understand our students was well stated in an article written by Dr. Perry and his colleagues:

> Ultimately, it is the human brain that processes and internalizes traumatic (and therapeutic) experiences. It is the brain that mediates all emotional, cognitive, behavioral, social, and physiological functioning. . . . Understanding the organization, function and development of the human brain, and brain-mediated responses to threat, provides the key to understanding the traumatized child. (Perry, Pollard, Blakley, Baker, and Vigilante 1995, 273)

THE TRIUNE BRAIN

The brain as we know it is "triune." It consists of three essential parts. The newest or youngest part of the brain is the neocortex. It is largely responsible for higher executive functions, such as impulse control, planning, and language. A second and older part of the brain is known as the limbic brain, or midbrain, and is largely responsible for our emotions. Deep inside the limbic brain is the amygdala. During a fearful event, this primitive part of the brain directs the central and autonomic nervous systems to trigger an all-systems alarm (Johnson 2003) that jolts our body into high alert in the face of danger and choreographs our fear response (Utley 2001). The third and oldest part of our brain has a 280-million-year heritage that we share with every living creature on earth. It is known as the reptilian brain or brain stem. This oldest part of our brain, directed by the amygdala, is responsible for the fight-or-flight responses that contribute to our survival. While the language of the neocortex is words, and the language of the limbic brain is feelings and emotions, the language of the reptilian brain is sensations—the physical way the body feels. Connecting with our sensations, listening to them, moving through them in a conscious way, is essential to the healing of trauma and will be discussed later in the chapter.

For now, it is important to know that the neocortex is responsible for much of school functioning, including mastery of language and other higher-order executive functions. However, the neocortex is still developing when our students enter school. In fact, when we are born, we do not yet have a neocortex. We are born only with our reptilian brain or brain stem and its subcortical functions. The healthy development and organization of the neocortex within the first years of life is dependent upon the healthy organization of the limbic brain, which is dependent upon the healthy organization of the reptilian brain (Perry 2003).

The brain most involved in our responses to traumatic events is the reptilian brain with its fight-or-flight function. Therefore, we must come to appreciate that alterations in this part of the brain as a result of trauma in the first years of life have implications for higher-order learning and behavior. The limbic brain or midbrain is also involved in trauma, and alterations in this part of the brain as a result of trauma also have implications on school functioning. The neocortex, by contrast, is virtually shut down by its older, more primitive counterparts during traumatic events. This is important to remember as we attempt to understand how trauma impacts learning and behavior.

What we now know is that the brain does not stop developing at birth. While massive brain development occurs during gestation, another large amount occurs in the first four years of life. Because we are born with only the reptilian brain, the first years of life involve the growth of our limbic brain and neocortex, as well as millions of neural connections between brain systems. Whatever parts of the brain are activated at the time their neural connections are developing naturally become more charged (Perry 2003). For instance, maternal heart rate is a major organizer in the development of the brain stem, which plays a major role in self-regulation capabilities. When a pregnant mother is able to manage everyday stress levels with self-soothing and self-care, the unborn child's brain stem develops normally. However, when a pregnant mother experiences an inordinate amount of stress that is too great or prolonged to moderate, the unborn infant's brain stem and its self-regulatory capabilities will develop irregularly. Neural disorganization in the baby becomes possible. When the brain is changed in this way, regulation is difficult. External chaos leads to internal chaos or chaotic neural development, making the physiology of the pregnant mother critical to the unborn child (Perry 2003). (It is important to state that stress should not be avoided by a pregnant mother [or anyone else]. According to Dr. Perry, well-regulated stress response patterns are important to the development of self-regulation. The degree to which stress is experienced with sufficient modulation is what matters.)

STUCK ON HIGH

Trauma changes the brain. When our students are terrorized, the once linear relationship between external stress and internal experience is no longer linear (Perry 2003). For example, when we have not been traumatized, we normally wake up in a rested state and only begin to feel stressed once the external world impinges upon us with its daily demands. Our anxiety levels go up as we experience stress throughout the day. Alternatively, students who have been traumatized no longer require external stresses to feel anxiety. They wake up in an anxious state on any given day whether externally stressed or not. Essentially, their nervous system gets stuck on high. If you remember from chapter 2, Dr. James Stewart referred to this state as an elevated baseline of anxiety (Stewart 1998). Students may not appear this way on the surface, however. Some students who are struggling do not have the more easily identified pattern of acting out. They are quieter and blend more easily into the background. They try to keep from view, in fact. These two different types of students represent two different-looking trauma patterns: overarousal and underarousal.

When traumatized, some students look hyper and highly irritable—the overaroused pattern—while other students look shut down, withdrawn, or dissociated. Dissociation occurs when we disengage from life outside of us and attend to an internal world (Perry et al. 1995). Whether underaroused or overaroused, the nervous system of a traumatized student is unregulated and out of balance. It is revved high and wound tight. One trauma survivor described the dichotomy of underarousal: "You feel like a duck. You're sitting on the water all regal but you're pedaling like hell underneath." Another trauma survivor described the underaroused-looking pattern in this way: "It's like your body stops, but your insides keep moving." The underaroused pattern only *looks* like the trauma survivor is calm and less aroused than in the case of the overaroused pattern. Inside, however, the nervous system is just as revved.

Getting "stuck on high" is not unique to humans. In animal studies, prolonged high-level stimulation of the amygdala, the part of the limbic brain that becomes flooded during a traumatic event, causes a "kindling" effect. Kindling in animals is the sensitization that occurs when they are repeatedly exposed to stressful stimuli. The amygdala is most clearly related to affective states, especially fear. When it receives excessive stimulation, its neurons fire rapidly to its counterparts in the brain signaling fear and danger. When such stimulation is repeated and/or prolonged, as in the case of traumatization, the amygdala essentially fails to stop sending these signals of fear and danger, causing lasting increases in behavioral defensiveness, inhibition, and/or attack (van der Kolk 1993).

The amygdala acts like a smoke detector to ascertain whether incoming sensory information spells a threat and creates emotional memories associated with the threat (van der Kolk 2002). Through studies with rats and brain-imaging techniques in humans, we know that the amygdala lights up when emotionally aroused. The greater the arousal and activation of the amygdala, the more powerful the memory (Utley 2001). Persistence of the memories of the traumatic event, when the mind replays the event over and over again, inadvertently makes the memory stronger and the anxiety worse.

What this means for our students is that experiences of trauma, *especially when repeated or prolonged*, flood their amygdala and cause it to continue to fire as though danger is always imminent. A chronic activation of the autonomic nervous system (sympathetic and/or parasympathetic) is the result of the brain continuing to respond as if under stress, trauma, or threat, ultimately continuing to prepare the body for fight, flight, or freeze (Rothschild 1996) *even when there is no present threat*. When our students experience prolonged or repeated threatening events, the biological response of their body is to *persist* in telling the brain there is threat. As a result, the brain continues to stimulate the autonomic nervous system for defense. This is why we so often see in our students that even the slightest external triggers become experienced internally as extreme danger.

Dr. Perry describes the traumatized student as often being, at baseline, in a state of low-level fear, due to the process of sensitization just described. Again, sensitization occurs when a specific pattern of repetitive neural activation or experience (trauma) results in an altered, more sensitive system. This more sensitive system with a baseline of low-level fear can now become highly aroused or dissociated by apparently minor stressors. The student is in a persisting fear state (which is now a trait, according to Dr. Perry). The student is very easily moved from being mildly anxious to feeling threatened to feeling terrorized (Perry et al. 1995).

Parents often ask me why one of their children has so many overreactions (sometimes underreactions) to events that their siblings do not react to in the same full-blown (or detached) way. They describe their troubled child as more sensitive than their other children. Recent research on trauma and the brain is helping us more clearly understand the sensitivity of these particular students.

CALVIN REVISITED

In the case of nine-year-old Calvin (introduced in chapter 4), when taking a detailed developmental history, it became apparent why it was that he was more biologically sensitive than his siblings. It was during his gestation, not that of his siblings, that his parents' marriage began falling apart. They argued throughout the pregnancy, engaging in violent altercations with one another. By the time the birth process was underway, the mother and baby had already experienced repetitive and prolonged stress, and not surprisingly, it continued throughout the birth process. Birth complications ensued. These early experiences created a biological vulnerability in Calvin to the other problems that occurred in the home, eventually resulting in a referral to me.

Calvin's difficulties at age nine could be predicted by brain science based on his experiences throughout his gestation and first years of life. When he was three years of age, his parents had one final violent argument that ended in Calvin's father packing his bags and leaving the home entirely for two years. It was after this event that Calvin's mother remembered that her son's language development ceased. He virtually stopped talking. When he needed or wanted something he simply pointed. In that same year, Calvin was found by a neighbor in the middle of the night wandering aimlessly in the center of a high-traffic street. His neighbor returned him home and, according to his mother's report, Calvin did not speak or exhibit any kind of emotion. He was numb.

Calvin's numb exterior was not the whole story. His demeanor fluctuated from quiet, numb, and essentially shut down, to episodes of tantrum behaviors, nightmares, bed-wetting, excessive crying, clinging, and separation anxiety.

By the time Calvin entered school, he still did not use words. He did not speak to his preschool teachers at all. It was not until he was five that Calvin began using one- and two-word utterances, and although at nine he could speak in complete sentences, he rarely did. Calvin remained a quiet boy with flat affect. Not only were his language and social-emotional functioning impacted by his traumatic experiences, but also he had poor memory and attention skills. Language, memory, and attention are all higher-order skills required for successful school experiences, all mediated by the neocortex, the part of the brain that is shut down under real or perceived threat. The repeated and prolonged exposure to trauma that Calvin experienced in utero and after birth produced in his brain the same "kindling" effect found in animals—when the amygdala is "stuck on high" and continues to fire its neurons signaling danger when, in fact, danger is not necessarily present. With that part of the brain on high, the body becomes solely focused on survival and any higher-order functions of the neocortex are suspended. Calvin's nervous system remained in a hypervigilant state solely focused on survival, while his neocortex was essentially shut down making language and other higher-order functions difficult for him.

Calvin ultimately suffered what many children do when their posttraumatic responses go untreated, and when traumas continue to mount. After his mother was diagnosed twice with cancer, first of the stomach and then of the brain, Calvin became psychotic. By the age of eight, he began hearing voices that told him to do cruel things to other people. With antipsychotic medicine, these behaviors ceased and Calvin continued to exhibit his quiet, shut-down exterior, at least at school. At home, Calvin was a loving boy who did everything he could to help his mother.

The shutdown that Calvin demonstrated in his daily life at school was related to the freeze response that he entered during the times he experienced trauma. As we learned in the previous chapter, when fight or flight is not an option during a fearful event, as is often the case with children, the only other option the nervous system has is to freeze. Calvin could not stop his parents from fighting and could not stop his father from leaving. Nor could he stop the cancer from growing in his mother's body. Calvin could not fight his parents nor flee from them. What his nervous system opted to do in the face of the terrible things that happened, events that threatened his existence as he knew it, was shut down, stop, and freeze. There is a numbness that can happen at the time of such immobility. It serves to diminish the pain experienced at the time of the trauma. Calvin's freeze during the initial traumas of his life became his way of being in the world, his way of responding to any challenge that he felt was too great for him, as his teacher often observed.

THE LOW ROAD

What traumatized students lack—due to the imbalance created in their nervous system—is the critical ability to self-regulate emotions, sensations, responses, and experiences. Whereas most students may get upset over daily hassles and annoyances, they are most often able to self-soothe and adjust, or at least receive and benefit from the assistance of others. Alternatively, traumatized students become easily upset over minor events and situations and often cannot be soothed or calmed. We have recently learned why this is. People who have been traumatized develop abnormalities in the release of brain chemicals or neurotransmitters that regulate arousal and attention (van der Kolk 2002). For example, in untraumatized students, acute stress activates all the principle antistress hormones, including cortisol and catecholamines. These hormones enable active coping behaviors. In traumatized people, relatively low levels of cortisol exist while levels of norepinephrine and other neurotransmitters are chronically increased. It is this particular combination, together with traumatized students' increased arousal, that provokes indiscriminate fight-or-flight reactions. Because cortisol shuts off other biological reactions turned on by stress and is decreased in traumatized people, they are unable to modulate their biological responses to stress (van der Kolk 2002).

What this means for our students is that when traumatized and without the help needed to set their systems back to normal, they become biologically disposed to overreact and jump to their defense by attacking, accusing, or threatening. They behave irrationally in response to events that are objectively neutral. Even more frustrating for educators is that these students cannot be reasoned with nor can they explain their own behavior. Remember, when frightened or aroused, the frontal areas of the brain (the neocortex) that help us analyze and understand experiences are *de*activated. Furthermore, high levels of arousal interfere with the region of the brain responsible for helping us put our experiences into words—the Broca's area. This is why our traumatized students "suffer speechless terror" (van der Kolk 2002). It is not the sophisticated brain regions in the neocortex that are involved in our response to trauma. These are the areas that are shut down during threat. Sensations of fear and anxiety come from the more primitive or subcortical areas of the brain—the limbic/midbrain and the brain stem or reptilian brain—and these are what are activated during real or perceived threat.

In 1996, a neuro-imaging study using PET scans found in traumatized people both decreased activation in Broca's area and increased activation of the limbic system in the right hemisphere of the brain (van der Kolk 2002). As many educators know, the right hemisphere of the brain is less involved in language processing and analytical thinking than the left hemisphere, and is more involved with bodily, emotional, and interpersonal processes. Another study looked specifically at the brains of abused children, and found similar results (Teicher 2000). The brains of the abused children were altered by their experiences. Researchers found both elevated activity in the right hemisphere and decreased activity in the language center (Broca's). These specific alterations in the brain in combination with the "stuck on high" activity of the amygdala, cause traumatized students to react to even neutral events as though they are being retraumatized in the current moment. Not only do they lose control in the face of minor stress and/or neutral events but they are also robbed of their abilities to analyze and talk about what is happening to them.

Some researchers call this the "lower mode of processing" or the "low road." In this state of mind, as we have seen, the usual higher, integrative functions that enable learning and healthy social relating are temporarily suspended. Dr. Dan Siegel has proposed that unresolved trauma or grief, as we see in so many of our students, involves the low road such that it (a) becomes triggered more easily, (b) is entered more rapidly, (c) when entered, remains longer, (d) involves more harmful behaviors, (e) is more difficult to recover from, and (f) when recovery occurs, repair of the disconnections [in relationships caused by trauma and loss] is less likely to occur (2003, 15).

PATTERNS OF RESPONSE TO THREAT

As discussed earlier, there are two major response sets to threat. Overarousal leads to fight-or-flight behaviors, and underarousal or dissociation leads to defeatist or giving up behaviors (Perry et al. 1995).

Picture the student who is up and out of his seat constantly, getting involved in other people's business, putting his hands and feet where they are not wanted. Consider the student who looks for fights, using his body and face to intimidate, threaten, and provoke. Think of the student who looks at people suspiciously and often complains that people are looking at him funny, trying to start a fight with him. These are the students who are overaroused, who get noticed, and who are more obviously having difficulty often related to trauma. Biochemically, these students have elevated levels of norepinephrine, dopamine, GABA, and serotonin in their nervous systems, as well as decreased levels of cortisol needed to stimulate coping behaviors. Specific regions of their brain are more activated, such as the right hemisphere involved in the processing of body language, facial expressions, and emotional functioning, as well as the brain stem or reptilian brain involved in fight-or-flight responses.

Alternatively, think of the student who has given up. The one who does not try anymore, who sits at his desk claiming he is bored, or he does not care, or it does not matter, or there just is not anything he likes. Picture the student who is withdrawn from friends, teachers, or other adults, who looks like he is trying to disappear. This is the student who is underaroused or dissociated. He may stare blankly, daydream, look through you, not hear what you are saying, or forget what you just told him. Biochemically, these students have elevated levels of opioid peptides, serotonin, and dopamine in their nervous system, causing a numbing effect. The parts of their brain that are more activated actually correspond to the overaroused student. Their right hemisphere is also more activated than their left hemisphere. Their fight-or-flight mechanism is also on overload. Their sympathetic nervous system is also on high, so high that the parasympathetic counterpart to the sympathetic system has to work overtime to override it.

The two systems—both sympathetic and parasympathetic—are highly elevated and working overtime in response to threat, whether real or perceived. In the case of the dissociated, shut down, or numb student, the parasympathetic branch of the autonomic nervous system is winning over the sympathetic, however slightly. That is how they appear to be shut down. If the sympathetic branch of the autonomic nervous system is the gas of the car, the parasympathetic branch is the brake. In the case of the dissociated pattern, the gas and the brake are both going strong, with the brake winning over the gas. But that can change on the turn of a dime, as many educators have witnessed. Out of the blue, the quiet student who is usually spacing out or blending into the background may inexplicably "blow his top" and demonstrate reactions and behaviors that look very much like the overaroused student.

Educators have observed that although some traumatized students may demonstrate only one or the other response pattern most of the time, others may display both of them at different times throughout the same day. Some students alternate between shutting down completely when something challenges them, and jumping out of their seat to look for a fight for no apparent reason. They may alternate between staring blankly for several minutes at a time, daydreaming, and then accusing their neighbors of looking at them funny and threatening them violently.

These swings from one pattern to another can be common in traumatized students. In fact, when experiencing a trauma, young children commonly use a combination of responses that are designed to enable their survival. They may initially respond with an overaroused pattern in order to signal to caretakers that they are in need of defense. If the threat continues, and caretakers do not come to the aid of their children, they move into the underaroused or dissociative continuum, initially becoming immobile (freezing) and compliant, later completely dissociating (Perry et al. 1995). One can understand how the combined responses *at the time of the trauma* can lead to a combined pattern of responding to future threats, real or perceived. In fact, brain research supports that this is the case. The brain changes in a use-dependent fashion and organizes during development in response to experience. The specific ways in which the body responds during trauma is related to the pattern of response present in future threatening situations (Perry et al. 1995). This is what we read about in the case of Calvin.

NOT NECESSARILY DEFIANCE

Calvin's tendency to freeze and shut down when challenged is not unique. The freeze response is often the automatic response of traumatized students when they feel anxious, afraid, or threatened. Dr. Perry cautions that too often these responses are readily interpreted by adults as defiance. In fact, many students who have been traumatized end up diagnosed with, among other things, oppositional defiance disorder (ODD). Their sensitized neural system reacts to the inordinate amounts of stress they experience by shutting down more and more as threat or anxiety persists. These are the students who do not readily comply with requests, who seem to get stuck in a place that no amount of reasoning or choice or bribery can get them out of. While it looks like they are calm ducks on the surface of the water, simply refusing to comply, their nervous systems are actually "pedaling like hell" underneath.

When Calvin was asked to comply with teacher and parent demands, it was not that he *would* not comply in the moment. He actually *could* not respond in the moment. His nervous system was too tightly wound, so rigid and inflexible, and without the ebb and flow and fluidity necessary to readily respond to life. When asked to comply on the spot, Calvin went into overwhelm. Not all the time, but many times. It was as if one more demand was one more input into a nervous system that could not take in another thing. Imagine being a five-pound sack of potatoes with ten pounds of potatoes already jammed into it. The thought of having to take in one more potato is beyond the tolerance capacity of many traumatized students, especially in the moment of the request.

With students like Calvin, it can be helpful to provide them with a written copy of the daily agenda at the beginning of the day so they can see what they will be required to do hour by hour. The more structured and predictable things are for them, the less they need to respond on a moment's notice. Also providing them with a longer response time helps them to create time and space between the demand and their performance, creating an opportunity for their nervous system to settle and for them to get used to the idea of the behavior expected of them. Positively reinforcing them as soon as they begin to comply is also important. These interventions begin first with our understanding of the student (see chapters 6–9 for more intervention ideas).

TRAUMA AND THE DEVELOPING BRAIN

As previously discussed, when our students come into this world, all they have is their most primitive, subcortical brain—the brain stem (Stern 1985). Pictures of a three-month-old brain, for example, reveal in the infant a brain stem and only fractions of the visual and auditory cortices. The brain continues to develop long after birth. Because we are born with a relatively small number of neural connections in the brain, the infant has a massive increase in complexity of neural connectivity shaped by both genetic information and by experience. Experience leads to neural firing, which activates genes that lead to the production of proteins that enable the formation of new synaptic connections (Kandel 1998; LeDoux 2002).

Furthermore, at birth, the sympathetic branch of the autonomic nervous system is all that is available to the regulation of the infant. Thus, the infant is ready for responses of excitation and arousal, but without the parasympathetic branch, still undeveloped, the infant has no way of calming or decreasing sympathetic responses. The two branches of the parasympathetic nervous system include the dorsal vagal and the ventral vagal. It is the ventral vagal branch specifically that gets larger as children develop. This is the branch that modulates arousal and helps us feel calm again. This is extremely important. Newly born infants, until that ventral vagal branch of the parasympathetic nervous system is fully developed, are completely dependent on their caregivers for regulation of their experiences, sensations, and emotions. This has large implications when we consider the body's response to trauma.

When extreme stress or trauma is experienced in the earliest years of life, during gestation or the first years after birth, the unborn or newly born child has no way of modulating their sympathetic nervous system's responses. Their heart rate, blood pressure, motor constriction, and endocrine and neurotransmitter levels all escalate during trauma or stress and then have no way *on their own* of returning back to baseline. The nervous system stays on high exhausting all efforts and resources. The infant is a subcortical creature who lacks the means for modulation of behavior that will only come with later development (van der Kolk 2002).

As young children grow, their ability to regulate their own physiology in a balanced manner develops a more autonomous capacity. However, until this happens, infants and young children are dependent upon the responsiveness of their caretakers. Perry (2003) and Schore (1994) among others argue that, in conjunction with genetic endowment, the nature of the interactions between infant and caregiver literally organize the infant's brain. The more a particular pattern is used, the more it fires that same pattern of neural activation. Perry and Schore believe that experience within the context of the caregiver-infant dyad provides the organizing framework for the infant's brain.

THE PARENTING FACTOR

The importance of at least "good-enough" parenting cannot be overstated when we consider the infant's dependence on caregivers to modulate their arousal. When pregnant or new mothers actively modulate their own stress levels, they directly and indirectly modulate the stress levels of their babies. When this does not happen often enough, the baby's nervous system remains revved by the stress it experiences as a result of the anxiety the mother experiences. Stress hormones, released throughout the body during times of stress, remain in a baby's tiny body, impacting the rapidly developing brain until he or she is sufficiently soothed. If soothing does not happen, or does not happen enough, babies are left in a state of high arousal until so exhausted they collapse into a complete shutdown. Such an unregulated and imbalanced state takes a serious toll on the developing brain and nervous system.

It is the primary caregiver-infant relationship that regulates the infant's psychobiological states, thereby allowing the child to tolerate more intense and longer lasting levels of heightened, yet modulated, arousal (Schore 1998). When the caregiver actively helps the infant move from negative states of discomfort, hunger, and frustration, for example, to more positive ones, the infant's emotions are successfully regulated and balanced. When infants are not helped by their caregivers to move out of negative states, they are left without any means of balancing out their own system, setting them up biologically for little tolerance of stress in the future.

When the caregiver is unable or refuses to cocreate an attachment bond with the infant that allows for the dyadic regulation of emotion, the result is a state of shame in the infant (Stroufe 1996). Shame is a painful infant distress state that is the result of the misattunement of infant and caregiver. Misattunement occurs when the infant comes to expect a positive response from the mother, such as a loving gaze, and receives instead a look of disgust or despair, for example. When this happens unexpectedly for infants, they are propelled further into the negative state they were already experiencing, one that they cannot yet autoregulate or modulate on their own.

Shame itself does not cause the lack of self-regulation we later see in many of our students. Shame can be successfully regulated through a process of "disruption and repair." If caregivers are able to monitor and regulate their own affects and reengage with their infant regularly, then shame does not necessarily lead to problems for the child later. It is when caregivers do not monitor and regulate their own affects, and when they are unable or unwilling to repair, that an enduring disposition to shame is possible (Schore 1998).

When shame becomes an enduring disposition for a child, as a result of multiple experiences over time of misattunement and poor attachment between infant and caregiver, the child is set up for physiological and psychological "shutdowns" that become easily triggered. Shame triggers a rapid de-energizing state that involves depletion in energy, withdrawal, recoiling, and attempts to disappear (Schore 1998). As opposed to processes that promote and prolong contact and facilitate "merging with sources of satisfaction" in order to generate euphoric emotions and pleasurable activity, shame induces "ending contact and halting arousal" (Knapp 1967; Schore 1998). Shame is involved not just in challenged early parent-child relationships, which can in and of themselves be traumatic, but also in the independent experience of trauma.

Poor attachment and multiple experiences of misattunement between caregiver and child can be traumatic experiences for infants who are left in an aroused and negative state to fend for themselves without the resources to do so effectively on their own. Traumatic events themselves, separate from parenting issues, have the same effect. Underdeveloped infants or toddlers who experience trauma also experience aroused and negative states that they are unable to modulate themselves. The results on the developing brain and nervous system, and thus the children's ability to later self-regulate learning and behavior, are devastating. What happens over time with poor parenting, for example, is that the core relational shame transaction becomes internalized in implicit, procedural memory as a visually stored image so that by the end of late infancy, the elicitation of shame does not require the presence of an external person (Schore 1998). Rather, shame can be activated by an internal image making it much more difficult for the child to experience a wide range of positive and negative affects without going into "shutdown."

ATTACHMENT

There are extremes in parenting that can be traumatic for our students and can have specific effects on later school functioning. First, let us consider the various attachment patterns, the possibilities created by parents as they respond to their infants. A secure attachment is the result of contingent communication between parent and infant; it is when a parent is able to share and amplify positive emotions as well as share and soothe negative ones (Siegel 2003). Insecure attachments are the result of inconsistent responding of parent to child and there are two forms of these: organized and disorganized. Insecure, organized attachments are less extreme than the insecure, disorganized pattern, which can be either avoidant or ambivalent. The avoidant attachment pattern between parent and child is often the result of an emotionally impoverished relationship while the ambivalent pattern is often the result of inconsistent availability of caretakers for sensitive, contingent communication with the infant.

For the purposes of this book, we will focus on the more extreme pattern of the insecure attachment, called disorganized. It is predictive of later difficulty with social relationships and balanced emotional regulation (Siegel 2003). This pattern is the result of a parent-child relationship in which the parent is the source of terror and alarm in the infant. The parent creates a state of alarm in the child by various means, including threat of, and actual, violence, leaving the child in a "biological paradox." The child's brain is motivated to move toward the caregiver for soothing, yet that same person is the very source of the child's alarm. Researchers Maine and Hesse have called this paradox "fright without solution" (Maine and Hesse 1990).

These early experiences within the parent-child dyad lead to the shame response reviewed earlier, during which the child shuts down, recoils, and attempts to disappear. This becomes their only biological solution for survival in such a paradoxical situation. Such dissociation or shutdown results in the fragmentation of normally associated cognitive processes, such as emotion and memory (Siegel 2003). The child's brain becomes sensitized, creating a biological vulnerability to developing serious self-regulation imbalances should any future trauma occur.

What Dr. Siegel and his research colleagues have found is that children with this disorganized pattern of attachment have parents who have their own unresolved trauma or loss. The transmission of trauma appears to be multigenerational. Unresolved trauma and grief in a parent may produce the frightened, frightening, and in other ways alarming and disorienting parental behaviors that lead to disorganization in the child (Siegel 2003). When parents have a compassionate understanding of themselves, they are able to provide the emotionally sensitive, contingent communication that children need in order to thrive (Siegel 2003). The question is not the presence of disruptions in the bonding or attachment between caregiver and infant, but the balance between disruption and repair. The more likely that mismatches between caregiver and infant are repaired, the more likely that the infant will be securely attached. Repair is much more likely when caregivers have a compassionate understanding of themselves and their own traumatic experiences. Considering the implications of trauma on later development throughout generations, we can see why it is so important that as a culture we find ways to understand trauma and effectively intervene in order to resolve it in all generations.

When parents resolve their own trauma and loss, they can be more responsive to their children. Better attunement of the parent to the child enables the child's brain to achieve bodily balance and later mental coherence (Siegel 2003). Parent-child interactions shape the genetically programmed maturation of the brain to alter the ways in which emotion regulation and response to stress develop. In this way, secure attachment relationships promote well-being by supporting the integrative capacities of the child's developing brain (Siegel 2003).

TRAUMA'S IMPACT ON MEMORY AND LEARNING

Research in the field of psychology, in the area of learning specifically, has for decades taught us about the need for an optimum level of arousal in order for learning to take place. In undergraduate psychology courses, for instance, students are given the teaching example of preparing for, and taking, an exam. Spaced studying versus "cramming" is recommended because of the overwhelming amount of arousal in cramming situations. When arousal is too high, concentration can be impossible. While starting to study too soon is associated with little arousal and is, therefore, not the best scenario for learning either, there is an optimum period before an exam when arousal levels are at their most functional. This is when learning readily takes place.

As with preparing for an exam, when it comes to taking an exam, memory for what was learned is more available when arousal is optimal. When well prepared for a test, there is still a good amount of arousal stimulating the best performance because it is a testing situation. However, even if some studying and learning took place before an exam, if arousal is too high during the exam, what was learned is forgotten.

Arousal has the potential to stimulate learning, memory, and performance when it is optimal, and has the potential to inhibit learning, memory, and performance when it is in excess of what can be comfortably modulated by the student's nervous system. Dr. Pat Ogden has called this optimal arousal zone the "window of tolerance" (Ogden 2003). When functioning within this window, our students are able to process, integrate, and remember information. It is within this window of tolerance that both learning and successful educational performance are possible.

We have learned in this chapter that students who have experienced trauma, especially when prolonged or repeated with few resources to help them recover, remain in a state of alarm. As long ago as 1889, the psychoanalyst Pierre Janet, described the combination of intense arousal and paralysis of action in response to threat—a combination too often experienced by our traumatized students—as what interferes with proper information processing and appropriate adaptation (Janet 1889, 1909). The high level stimulation of the amygdala of traumatized students, and the kindling effect this produces, keeps their nervous system stuck on high. This is critical to our understanding of these students and why they have such a difficult time learning and performing in the classroom. The amygdala screens incoming data and decides what to focus on. In fact, all limbic systems (the amygdala is a limbic system) appraise incoming data in this way. The amygdala changes the attentional focus of the brain's perceptual system away from what is least important to survival and toward what is most important to survival. When traumatized, the amygdala implicitly encodes experiences so that a fear state in *un*fearful situations becomes standard. What we see, therefore, when their trauma remains unresolved, is that our students are left in a world of terror. Their amygdala is activated more quickly, more deeply, and more intensely. They then screen information in the classroom in a biased manner that ignores much of the curriculum and focuses mostly on what they need in order to survive readily perceived threats. This kindling effect causes a disconnection between vital brain areas, including a disconnection from the orbitofrontal cortex and its nine critical functions (Siegel 2003), causing the "low road" functioning discussed earlier.

The orbitofrontal cortex is part of the neocortex or youngest part of the brain. Its nine critical functions include bodily regulation, emotional regulation, response flexibility, empathy, self-awareness, fear extinction, being in touch with intuition, communication attunement with others, and morality (Siegel 2003). We know that these processes are mediated by the orbitofrontal region largely from brain research that involved the study of people with tumors and/or lesions in that area. For instance, studies have found that tumors in the orbitofrontal cortex have caused amoral attitudes and behaviors (Siegel 2003). Antonio Damasio (2003) cited several studies in his book *Looking for Spinoza: Joy, Sorrow, and the Feeling Brain* that involved damage to this area, causing disturbances in social behavior and a lack of empathy. Healthy development, including secure attachment and not necessarily the absence of trauma but the resolution of trauma, are necessary for the orbitofrontal cortex to successfully mediate these important functions.

There is not a single aspect of learning that does not require at least some of the functions mediated by the orbitofrontal cortex. Self-regulation, for instance, is critical to learning and successful educational performance. Bodily regulation keeps the nervous system in a balanced state within the window of tolerance or zone of optimum arousal that we know is important for learning to take place. Emotional regulation works in the same way, keeping the nervous system in balance and within an optimal state for taking in information, integrating that information, and remembering it later. When stuck in a highly aroused state, the nervous system, rather than being balanced and regulated, is out of balance and unregulated, making learning extremely difficult. Other orbitofrontal functions, aside from bodily and emotional regulation, are also necessary for learning and appropriate behavior. They include response flexibility, self-awareness, communication attunement with others, and certainly fear extinction. We know that being left in a state of fear, for example, as in the cases of traumatized students, is to be left in a constant state of defense rather than in an open, fluid, and adaptive state more conducive to learning.

The chronic high state of arousal that traumatized students live in interferes with learning also because it interferes with the functioning of the hippocampus, that part of the brain that is responsible for memory. For instance, one study found that victims of physical and/or sexual abuse had lower memory volume in their left-brain hippocampal areas than did nonabused victims

(Bremmer, Krystal, Charnez, and Southwick 1996). Another study (Yang and Clum 2000) found that the stress involved in "early negative life events" or trauma, induced the release of glucocorticoids, such as cortisol, that damaged the left hippocampal area of the brain and thereby increased memory deficit. We also know that REM sleep is disturbed in those with unresolved trauma (Siegel 2003). REM sleep is a critical agent in the consolidation of memory, especially long-term memory into permanent memory. It is nearly impossible for students to consolidate memories—for instance, working memory into short-term memory and short-term memory into long-term memory—when they cannot concentrate. Students are less capable of concentrating when they are in a constant state of alarm. Both short-term (Starknum, Gebarski, Berent, and Schterngart 1992) and verbal or explicit memory (Bremmer et al. 1996) suffer when people are in a highly aroused state.

When our students are left in a highly aroused state, they are more anxious, and when more anxious, they pay closer attention to nonverbal than verbal cues (Perry et al. 1995). Remember, we learned that when traumatized, the left hemisphere, the part of our brain involved in language processing, is less activated than the right hemisphere, the part of the brain involved in nonverbal cues such as tone of voice, body posture, and facial expressions. According to Dr. Allan Schore, the right brain is involved in the vital functions that support survival and enable the organism to cope actively and passively with stress (Schore 2001a, 2001b). It is the right brain where the dominant reactions to stress occur. This means that traumatized students are less capable of processing verbal cues and language-based tasks than nonverbal cues and tasks that do not involve language processing. In fact, traumatized students become fixated on nonverbal cues that may aid in their survival to the neglect of the curriculum and other classroom demands. This is because, as we now know, the brain is programmed for survival first. When the amygdala remains highly activated due to unresolved trauma, the brain notices only those cues that will enable survival to the exclusion of anything else going on in the environment.

High levels of arousal interfere with information processing in all people, not just our students. Advocates in the fields of health and medicine today recommend that patients bring a friend or family member with them to the doctor's office when facing potentially life-threatening conditions. This is because we know how difficult it is for patients to process information while in a highly aroused state. Anyone who has faced this alone knows how little he or she remembered of what the doctor said. Only after getting into the safety of our own home, for instance, do we think of all the questions we had wanted to ask but forgot in the moment. As Perry (2003) and others have found, it is very difficult to process information while in an aroused state due to the altered functioning of the neocortex during such times.

The traumatized student, who has difficulty processing verbal information especially, also has trouble, by extension of that, with following directions, recalling what was heard, and making sense out of what was just said (Steele and Raider 2001). Focusing, attending, retaining, and recalling verbal information is difficult for these particular students. Cognitive deficits, such as poor problem solving, have also been associated with the experience of "early negative life events" or trauma (Yang and Clum 2000). Traumatized students are often unable to think things through clearly or make sense of what is happening, skills that are required in order to problem solve.

What should now be apparent is that the way the brain is changed by trauma greatly reduces the number of choices available to traumatized students. The kindling effect of the amygdala that leaves traumatized students in a state of terror limits the number of responses available to them. Essentially, they live in fight or flight. Fight, flight, or freeze responses are their repertoire of behaviors. This is a rigid and inflexible way of responding to the world, reflecting the rigidity and inflexibility of their brain and nervous system. They are unable to "go with the flow." Traumatized students, as we have seen in our classrooms, are unable to adapt to changes in routine or the environment without perceiving them as threatening. Perhaps now we understand better why this is.

For Review:

1. The brain mediates all processes related to school functioning.
2. Experience, including stress and trauma, changes the brain.
3. The brain's first and most important purpose is survival. The need for survival supercedes all other brain functions.
4. The brain is triune consisting of three parts:

   Neocortex: youngest brain
   involved in higher order functions
   words are its language

   Limbic: the seat of our emotions
   amygdala resides deep within
   emotions are its language

   Reptilian: oldest, most primitive
   involved in fight, flight, or freeze
   overrides the neocortex during stress/threat
   sensations are its language

5. Trauma causes the nervous system to get "stuck on high." Two trauma response patterns emerge:

Overaroused: hyperactivity, agitation, hypervigilance
Underaroused: shut down, spacey, dissociated

6. Being "stuck on high" means being out of balance and unregulated. Traumatized students lack the critical ability to self-regulate.

7. Trauma activates the subcortical areas of the brain and shuts down the more refined and sophisticated neocortex, causing "low-road" functioning.

8. We are all born with only the reptilian brain or brain stem and the sympathetic branch of the autonomic nervous system. This means that babies rely on their caregivers to modulate their arousal. When caregivers help regulate their babies' arousal, they set up the healthy conditions under which growing children can develop their own ability to self-regulate.

9. Self-regulation is essential to memory, learning, and successful educational performance.

10. Trauma, stress, or any highly aroused state interferes with the ability to retain information. Trauma causes deficits in short-term memory, verbal, explicit memory, and the transfer of long-term memory into permanent memory.

11. Trauma causes cognitive deficits, including poor attention, concentration, and problem solving, all critical to school performance.

III

TOOLS FOR TURBULENT TIMES

6

"Resourcing" (a Verb): What Schools Can Do to Intervene Effectively with Traumatized Students

> I do not understand how anyone can live without some small place of enchantment to turn to.
>
> —Marjorie Kinnan Rawlings in *Cross Creek*

According to Rollo May, in his now classic text *The Art of Counseling*, counseling is done everywhere: "At a football game, on the street car, during an evening walk across campus after a committee meeting—in short, everywhere that people meet" (1978, 120). This is true when we think about May's premise that "in every human contact some molding of personality occurs" (120). That is "after all, the fruit of counseling." Each of us, as educators, by virtue of coming into contact with our students, is participating in the molding of their personalities, and thereby, in some way, we are counseling them. What a responsibility we have, and what an honor.

Typically, we leave the job of counseling up to the mental health professionals provided to us on our campuses—school psychologists, counselors, social workers, behavior specialists, and school-based psychotherapists. According to May, however, "counseling is a matter of degree" (1978, 120). Some relationships can be strictly classified as counseling and others not. Counseling really is *not* an activity that is performed in an office somewhere and then left within the confines of that office at the end of an eight-hour workday. We are all counseling—molding each other's personalities—most of the time.

School psychologists and counselors are the mental health professionals in schools commonly responsible for utilizing counseling techniques within the confines of their offices. Their position in schools as mental health providers is unique. Their offices are in environments that are not quite the places early traditional psychological thinkers had in mind when they created their models of therapy. Contrary to common belief, therapy is something that most school psychologists and counselors are not trained to do. Therapy refers to specialized treatment, as in the cases of physical therapy or occupational therapy, the successful execution of which requires years of training and experience. Counseling is different from therapy. It is what most school psychologists and counselors are expected to be able to do, and what most educators are doing without even knowing it.

According to May, the field of the counselor lies somewhere between two professions: the consulting psychologist or psychotherapist and the educator. The consulting psychologist or psychotherapist is needed when someone suffers from personality problems that are psychological and not due to any physical cause. The educator is needed when someone is "immature or uninstructed" and needs schooling. The counselor deals with problems that are not so serious as to require the particular specialized services of a consulting psychologist, yet are too complicated to be solved incidentally in the ordinary course of educational procedure (May 1978). Consulting psychologists are relatively unavailable to schools for financial or geographical reasons, among others. Educators, on the contrary, are available, making it important for them to be prepared for counseling duties as they arise.

Traditionally, counseling implies a process that involves two people sitting together—a counselor and a counselee—discussing a problem or challenge until some kind of understanding of the issue is derived. As defined by May, counseling is "any deep understanding between persons which results in [change]" (1978, 120). The author wrote that the counselor seeks to understand people from the standpoint of appreciation, and that "there are few gifts that one person can give to another in this world as rich as understanding" (May 1978, 119). This may be considered by some as an oversimplification of the process but does consider the focus of counseling as a talking/listening/observing process between two people, one of whom takes on the responsible role of counselor or adviser.

In many instances, school administrators rely on school counselors and psychologists to be advisers to the students of their schools. From my observation and experience, counselors and psychologists vary to a large degree in their comfort level with that role. Some come from educational programs that readily equip them to take on counseling duties, and others come from institutions that provide little or no training for such a role. Classes offered by educational counseling programs may review theories and books on the subject, and the students may be required to write an exam on the topic, but many are not provided with the training required to provide counseling services in a practical sense with sound knowledge and comfort.

The result of this lack of rigorous training in counseling techniques has led to a dilemma in many school districts around the country. Legally mandated counseling services designated for special education students, for example, are not always being delivered. Some school personnel do not feel trained enough to do so well. A large number of special education students requiring counseling have such severe problems that even the most educated counselors and school psychologists are overwhelmed. Their college programs simply do not provide them with comprehensive enough training to know what to do and how to do it.

"RESOURCING": A VERB?

In my district, because of my clinical training and experience, I am asked for guidance on counseling issues. School professionals in different roles performing various duties ask me how to counsel our most troubled students. "What more can I do?" they say, "I don't know what to do anymore. Nothing works." To each of them, no matter how exasperated they are, I say, "Do not despair, resource. When in doubt, and at any other time, what you need to do is resource." The message is simple, the process is powerful, and the results are far-reaching for even the most difficult cases.

Resourcing is a new verb created to demonstrate the active process that it is. It has an important yet little known science behind it. Very simply, as we learned in chapters 4 and 5, every individual has what is called an autonomic nervous system. It is comprised of both a sympathetic and parasympathetic branch. The sympathetic branch is responsible for sensations of excitation, including increases in heart rate and blood pressure, and the latter is responsible for more relaxed sensations, including decreases in heart rate and blood pressure. Many of the daily struggles that any of us, including our students, contend with activate the sympathetic nervous system and can keep it elevated for extended periods of time. For our students, overactivated sympathetic nervous systems can contribute to a host of secondary challenges, from learning problems, hyperactivity, and inattentiveness to paranoia and attack.

While many regular students *without* numerous problems in life or difficult histories to overcome likely have balance in their system between the sympathetic and parasympathetic branches, other students are out of balance. The students who require more of our time and attention than our average students have an overactivated sympathetic nervous system that is not easily calmed down or soothed. Their parasympathetic nervous system, the part of them that helps calm and regulate powerful emotions, is not experienced by them readily. Through resourcing, however, we can help these students experience the physiological comfort that is their birthright. We can help these students begin to sense their body as a safe place as they begin to experience their parasympathetic nervous system in action. Through the active process of resourcing, students are taught when and how to resource themselves. They learn to identify the times when they need to access resources that will help them feel more relaxed sensations again.

At counseling in-services, I share my experience as someone who needed to surrender a counseling agenda as well as traditional ideas of what counseling should look like. What I have learned is that as long as we can *be* with students while actively applying the guiding principle of resourcing, students experience relief and become equipped with the tools they need to access relief at any given time. The relief is physiological and the result is balance—a palpable biological balance that is experienced in the body, an absolute must if healing and transformation is to take place.

BALANCING OUT THE SCALES

Consider the visual image of the scales of justice. Consider the fact that most of the students we are asked to work with are weighed down on one end of the scale by any number of stresses—the environment they live in, the family life they have or do not have, the personal challenges they face with learning disabilities or mood disorders. Many times we feel compelled to help reduce that load in some way by trying to change the student's circumstances. Unfortunately, that is how *we* burn out. We do not need to change or fix anything about a student's circumstances. Those givens are just that, and in many cases do not get better even with our best intentions and interventions. What we *can* do is bring the scales into balance, not by trying to eliminate problems from one side of the scale, but by piling resources on the other side of the scale. We have the power and ability to equip students to handle, manage, and tolerate both their internal and external challenges by helping them experience the comfort, the good, and the joy that resources bring to the nervous system.

This is the simple yet powerful guiding principle that I share with the school personnel I work with, in small meetings and large in-services, the guiding principle of resourcing. Helping students identify, access, and *experience* resources in their lives, both externally and internally, has proven to be an invaluable part of the work I do.

A resource is anything that is helpful to the student, anything that contributes to health, safety, comfort, balance, calm, and transformation. Resourcing is something that can be done, in different ways, by each and every educator who comes into contact with a student, no matter what their education, training, or experience. In addition to direct teaching, let us consider four strands that are part of the professional lives of many educators in our schools today, and how the principle of resourcing can be applied to each strand. They include *assessment*, *intervention*, *consultation*, and *counseling*.

Resourcing during Assessments

During the *assessment* process, taking an inventory of students' resources is a valuable way to spend time. During the process, students are helped to identify the resources they have in their lives, and the resources they are missing. A typical resource inventory might look like an eight-part grid that includes space to fill in lists of resources that are external, internal, short-term, long-term, past, present, imaginary, and missing. External resources for students may include nature, animals, people, places, and activities, such as places the students enjoy being (e.g., the park, the beach), and activities that make them feel competent and valued (e.g., a sport, subject, or game they are good at). Internal resources may include music (both an internal and external experience), faith, beliefs and values, personality characteristics (e.g., gregariousness, sociability), sense of humor, talent (e.g., artistic, athletic, academic), courage, and adaptability. Short-tem resources help students get through a crisis in the moment or shortly thereafter, such as a phone call to a grounding, safe person. Long-term resources help maintain the students thereafter, such as an ongoing therapeutic relationship or reliance on some form of belief system.

Past resources include what was helpful to the students as younger children in times of stress or challenge. Helping them remember how they coped with a difficult situation or in the face of a frightening event can itself be resourcing, and can help identify a missing resource in the present that needs to be restored. Imaginary resources can be as powerful as real ones, although what can be most useful to students is helping bring pieces of the imaginary into realization. Perhaps students imagine a place of safety and comfort and there are elements of that visual image that can be created in their actual life. That is worth exploring with students. Imaginary resources often include hopes and dreams that can act as motivators or mobilizing forces for students and are, therefore, an important part of the inventory. A space on the inventory should always be reserved for a list of resources that are missing and in need of being restored.

Going back to internal resources for a moment, it is critical to keep in mind the research reviewed on trauma and the nervous system, including the brain, in chapters 4 and 5. Considering the vital brain-body connection, and how readily the functioning of our students at school is impacted by stress and anxiety, we can see that the most far-reaching intervention we can engage in is *internal* resourcing. This is because the process of internal resourcing helps restore students' most powerful resource of all—their body—the balancing, soothing impact of their parasympathetic nervous system. When stressed and anxious, or when terrified from some previous traumatic event, our students no longer feel safe in their own body. They feel jumpy inside, afraid, as though something bad is about to happen. They feel as though the triggers that bring about these feelings and sensations are unpredictable and that they have no control over them. This causes them to panic and draw inaccurate cognitive conclusions that the feelings and sensations are not going to go away on their own. To quickly avoid feelings of discomfort and pain, the students *behave*, as Dr. Stewart explained (see chapter 2). They act *out*, they act *in*, and they self-medicate.

On January 23, 2003, the infamous Oprah Winfrey aired, on her popular television talk show, a program that examined the brutality of domestic violence. She questioned a perpetrator about what it would take to make violent criminals stop physically assaulting their loved ones. The perpetrator replied without hesitation. That was the easiest question she could have asked him, he said. "We need to be able to tolerate pain and manage emotions that don't feel good." *We need to tolerate pain and manage emotions that don't feel good.* What a revelation. The simplest of truths always are. In that very moment, Ms. Winfrey connected her own behavioral acting out, overeating, with the same process—as a way to avoid pain and discomfort. If those feelings and sensations that do not feel good could be tolerated, the need for the behavior, no matter what behavior, would cease. When we consider our students, we begin to understand that this is precisely what they need to do in order to stop acting out or acting in, in the ways they do. They need to be able to tolerate pain and manage emotions that do not feel good.

Tolerance within this context is not psychological, but physiological. It is not some kind of cognitive process that involves talking, analyzing, or digging for insights. The idea that such a process will create greater tolerance within us is simply not true. Holding on to this false belief is precisely why even the most enlightened, psychologically minded people continue to self-medicate in some way when uncomfortable feelings inevitably surface. Focusing on thoughts and feelings to the exclusion of sensations is where we go wrong. In fact, sensations often precede our thoughts and feelings. The tightness in the chest, the lump in the throat, the nausea in the stomach—

these are what need to be tolerated—whether or not the emotions of fear, guilt, or shame accompany the sensations.

The label—the interpretation of the sensations into feeling words—is a cognitive process that follows the experience of sensations. The famous psychologist and philosophical thinker William James wrote extensively about how it really is not that "I am afraid, therefore I run," but that "I run, therefore I am afraid." The bodily experience comes first and then we make a cognitive interpretation that gives it meaning. Once we begin to notice and observe our physical sensations—right in the moment they begin to surface—our labels and interpretations can change. We can more readily understand our experience and what we need to do to intervene in a positive, rather than self-destructive way. "There's that unpleasant sensation again. Let me do something to resource myself so I can tolerate this sensation until it changes." This is a simple yet powerful process.

We have to be able to tolerate feelings and sensations in our body if we are to have the capacity to contain them without needing to behave destructively. We must learn through guided experience that whatever sensations and feelings go up will also come down. This will happen. It is a natural, innate process. We do not need to resort to self-medication or harmful behavior. However, until we *experience* that truth internally, we do not believe it. We will learn more about how to help our students believe it by restoring their body as an invaluable internal resource in the text ahead.

Resourcing as an Intervention

Resource inventories help identify the persons, places, and activities that serve to balance out the nervous system and thereby enhance a student's ability to tolerate pain and manage negative emotions. They are completed during the assessment strand of our work as educators. At the strand of *intervention*, there is much we can do to resource our students. We can help them restore missing resources. We can help connect them with school, family, and community resources. We can help them reconnect with their body in a safe way that empowers them and restores their sense of strength and competence. Once we have aided in the process of identification of what is helpful, we can remind students of what they have experienced as helpful, teach them how to access what is helpful, and be with them for support as they reach out and ask for what they need to bring about positive change. Encouraging students to spend time doing the things that calm and soothe them, with the people who calm and soothe them, is a valuable part of any intervention process.

Psychoeducation is as far-reaching an intervention as any. Educating parents and other adults in the lives of our students, as well as the students themselves, about the importance of having a balanced life is powerful work. Parents need to learn the relevance of the principle of physiological balance in the lives of their children. Physiological balance, as we have learned, is in the body between pleasurable and unpleasurable sensations. It is the balance between, and natural regulation of, the sympathetic and parasympathetic nervous systems. Parents can give their children the opportunities they require to access resources that help them become more aware of what that balanced state feels like.

As an intervention, we can teach parents about what is particularly useful to their children. We can motivate them to support their children in accessing, and spending time doing, what is helpful to them. The secondary gain of that education to parents, we hope, is that they receive the message for themselves and teach their children how to live a balanced life by modeling one.

Resourcing during Consultations

Psychoeducation, the *intervention* process just described, is also a large part of the *consultation* strand of what we do as school personnel. Important to our work as consultants is a focus on the solutions and exceptions to the problems faced by our students. This helps us to empower students, as well as their teachers and families, so that everyone feels that he or she can handle whatever the problem involves. By the end of each consultation, parents and/ or teachers should have some direction to begin conquering the problem immediately. In *Today's School Psychologist*, Dr. John Murphy (1997), author of *Brief Intervention for School Problems*, highlights the importance of asking questions about what has worked to alleviate the problem before. He emphasizes how essential it is to ask about when and under what circumstances the problem has been absent or less noticeable. Identifying the times, places, people, and circumstances of success, or absence of the problem, are good first steps to change outcome in a positive way.

Mr. Murphy, in his article entitled "Turn Brief Interviews into Problem-Solving Opportunities," highlights the importance of resourcing. He encourages school personnel to consider the special talents and interests of students, teachers, or parents, as these may be useful in solving a problem. He encourages educators to examine the student's (and family's) coping skills, social supports, and heroes. Questions he suggests educators ask during problem-solving or solution-focused interviews include:

1. [Considering how difficult this problem has been for you], how have you managed to keep things from getting worse?

2. What do you think [insert hero's name] would do about this? Would you be willing to try something similar?
3. Who helps you most in your day-to-day life?

We can, through consultation, identify powerful resources that motivate students and their caregivers to ask for help, gain support, and create greater balance in their lives. We can also, through the consultation process, identify the times of day, particular settings, and specific people that are associated with the absence of the problem—when the problem is *not* occurring. If we can discover these elements, we can be part of establishing more opportunities for our students to be in a peaceful setting, for example, or be with a comforting or encouraging person. This is part of what balances out the nervous system. Physiological relief and restoration within the body is possible when our students experience more success than failure, more pleasure than pain.

Resourcing *Is* Counseling

A fourth strand of what many educators do is *counseling* and, in my experience, this best involves helping students experience the resources we are talking about. They need not talk about success, competence, safety, balance, comfort, and health but experience these internally. As "counselors" in the school setting, whether we are teachers, administrators, or psychologists, this is the most powerful and far-reaching activity we can engage in.

Physiology changes when people experience resources in their body in the here and now. The body stores the memory of what it was like to be in the present moment and feel safe, comfortable, and balanced. Once that is felt, even if just once, the body, in its infinite wisdom, begins to seek out more opportunities to feel that way. As such, sensory or body awareness in the present moment that is safe can be the greatest resource we give our students. Not another cognitive experience of discussing events from the past, or planning events in the future, but a being in the moment in the here and now. When grounded in the sensations of the body, these occurrences are palpable and therefore both transformative and lasting.

Eugene Gendlin, founder and author of *Focusing*, found that the difference between psychotherapy clients who got better and those who did not was body or sensory awareness (Gendlin 1981). His years of research concluded that the clients who healed their psychic wounds with psychotherapy were those who noticed and experienced their bodily sensations and were able to share them with the psychotherapist in the moment they became aware of them. They noticed when they were tight, tense, warm, cold, shaking, quivering, relaxed, or comfortable. They paid attention to where in their body they felt these and other sensations. They were able to notice the sensations, however uncomfortable, and focus on them until they shifted from less to more comfortable and tolerable. They had a palpable and total experience, involving both mind and body, of the physiological truth that "what goes up, must come down" (more on this in chapter 7).

The language of sensation cannot be ignored. Events are experienced and recalled not just by our cognitive mind but also by our brain and body. The longer we engage only the cognitive mind in the healing process is the longer that healing does not take place, not in a lasting way. The mind may develop new insights and begin to set new goals, but the body will not have the capacity to follow—especially not in the long term. This can actually create more damage than we ever imagined. New insights without the body's capacity to follow through can set up troubled students for feelings of greater failure, shame, and helplessness because they now *know* better but find that they still cannot *do* better. No matter what their cognitive mind thinks is possible, their body has not been engaged in the healing process and, therefore, cannot physically tolerate the feelings and sensations of pain and discomfort that their daily lives evoke.

SENSORY AWARENESS

Teachers understand the importance of involving sensations when they teach. They know that experiencing language at the level of sensation is vital to the learning process. For many students struggling to learn language, the whole person must be engaged, mind and body, in order for retention and recall. In many specialized reading programs, for instance, the Lindamood-Bell program, students are taught and encouraged to feel the sensations of their mouth, lips, and throat as they form and say the letters of the alphabet and their corresponding sounds (Lindamood, Bell, and Lindamood 1997). It is not unusual for many students to require this totality of experience. Sensory awareness not only helps psychotherapy clients achieve greater mental health and well-being but also helps our students learn to read.

As educators we must do everything we can to increase sensory awareness. However, we cannot teach what we do not have ourselves. We need to be the first focus of our own work. The language of sensation is not familiar to many. The more comfortable and aware we become with our own body and sensations, the more we will be able to help others become aware and comfortable. We will come to appreciate the enormous value of sensory awareness, as well as the power such integration of mind and body has over the healing process, once we experience it ourselves.

As one might expect, sensory awareness is not something that comes only from conversation. As stated earlier, it is not a cognitive process that involves much verbal language at all. Rather, sensory awareness is the result of experience, and the experiential is had through activity and resource. Many current authors recognize the importance of working with children at the level of sensation and provide descriptions of activities that help increase sensory awareness. For instance, in their book *Your Anxious Child*, John S. Dacey and Lisa B. Fiore wrote that children are constantly bombarded by stimuli from the external environment and have thus lost track of their inner environment—their heart and breathing rates, pain in their joints, and tension in their muscles (Dacey and Fiore 2002). Sensory awareness, according to the authors, is a way for children to discover what these inner experiences are and how they are affected by them. As children become aware of their inner worlds, they can be taught procedures to alleviate stress and strain and, therefore, better deal with problems presented in the outside world. Looking again to our metaphor of the scales of justice, as we pile on resources such as sensory awareness to the one side of the scales, students are better able to tolerate and overcome the challenges piled on the other side.

Although Dacey and Fiore mostly ascribe to a cognitive approach, the first step of their COPE program is relevant to this discussion. C stands for calming the nervous system. (O is for originating an imaginative plan, P is for persisting in the face of obstacles and failure, and E is for evaluating and adjusting the plan.) The authors recognize the effects of stress on the nervous system, and the involvement of body sensations in the stress response. They describe sensory activities that help increase children's awareness of breathing, heart rate, and comfort levels. For instance, one important exercise described involves an exploration and experience of supportive surfaces. Children are encouraged to begin noticing what surfaces they find most comfortable—an armless chair, an armed chair, a cushion, or the floor. The consideration that the authors make is an excellent start to an exercise that involves children noticing how and when and under what conditions they are most comfortable and supported. Paying attention to their inner environments—their bodily sensations—is required in order to arrive at an answer.

In her book *Relax*, author Catherine O'Neill helps children notice when they are feeling tense in their body by having them pay attention to the signals their body gives them, such as a "horrible feeling in [their] stomach" (1993, 12). She teaches children in her well-illustrated book that when they are stressed they may sweat, blush, or shake, clench their fists, bite their lips, or grind their teeth. The sympathetic nervous system is in full swing. Children learn about their body and its reactions in a way that is sensitive to the fact that there are times when they simply cannot think properly. O'Neill wrote, "Your mind goes into a spin. You can't get the words out. You stammer. You can't understand what people are saying. . . . [You] feel as though [you] are wound up like an elastic band, tighter and tighter, until [you] are ready to snap" (1993, 14). Is it not alarming to think that these are the very times we expect our students to take a deep breath, count to ten, and make a rational behavioral choice?

O'Neill included in her book a depiction of several different resources that help stimulate the parasympathetic nervous system—the opposite, more comfortable sensations than those just described. Just as with the image of the scales of justice, O'Neill wrote that sometimes we cannot make the things that make us tense go away. What we need to do is spend time doing things and being with people that balance out the tension. Resources that O'Neill described and depicted in her book include taking a bath, swinging on a hammock, cuddling up with a teddy bear, reading a book, and talking to someone trusted. These are not necessarily the things that will have a calming effect on all our students. Some of the above-mentioned activities may actually increase some students' anxiety depending on their personal history. The idea, however, is to help students identify and access the activities that will be soothing to them during times of need. The "secret key" to tolerance, healing, and self-regulation, according to O'Neill, is "keeping balance between tension and relaxation, sadness and happiness" (1993, 35).

THE POWER OF VISUALIZATION

Dr. Violet Oaklander's book *Windows to Our Children*, is also full of sensory-related activities, including various visualizations that help children become more aware of their inner worlds (Oaklander 1988). It is through these activities that children gain the experience of sensation and create body memories of what it is like to feel more relaxed and at peace. Visualization is especially valuable because of what research has revealed: When people visualize themselves engaged in an activity or being in a particular place, their brain fires neurons throughout their body as though they are actually having the experience. This can create implicit memory in the person— procedural or motoric memory of the visualized experience. When felt in the body and grounded in sensation even visualizations have lasting and transformative effects.

A now famous and well-known basketball study was done years ago to demonstrate the value of visualization (Wissel 1994). Three groups of "basketball players" (subjects) were involved in the study. One group practiced their free-throws from the free-throw line on an actual basketball court. Another group was instructed not to practice at all. The third group of players was taught specific visualization techniques and told to use those rather than actually physically practice. The third group was encouraged to see themselves at the free-throw line practicing their shots as though they were on the court doing it. The process of visualization involves more than sight. It involves all the senses to create more vivid images (Wissel 1994). The research proved, in Wissel's words, that "the brain does not distinguish between imagined thoughts and real actions. When you mentally feel yourself shooting, it is as though you are actually shooting. [The] mental images determine how well you actually do" (Wissel 1994, 2).

At the end of a specified practicing time frame, it was found that two of the three groups of players improved their free-throws substantially: The group that actually practiced and the group that only visualized practicing. The players who only saw themselves practicing experienced their neurons firing throughout their body just as the players who actually practiced. This is because "the mind is like a computer. What you put into it is what comes out. Sensory input determines motor output" (Wissel 1994, 2). Both groups of players created new body memory stores. They each developed an implicit memory—a procedural or motoric memory—of taking the free-throw shots over and over, thereby improving performance over time.

Visualization does not just improve athletic performance. A review of the research on the subject revealed the positive relationship between visualization and muscular relaxation, decreases in stress hormones, heart rate, galvanic skin response, breath frequency, and muscle tension (Gillis 2003). Imagery of sprinting was found to increase tachypnea considerably, demonstrating that visualization can work effectively either way, to increase or decrease sympathetic nervous system responses.

Although visualization is often used to help students feel more relaxed, it is important to note that some students become highly activated when "relaxation" exercises are introduced as such. Having an agenda of relaxation can create tension and anxiety in our students when they know that there is an end goal in mind. It becomes something that must be achieved—an outcome they must attain. Counseling sessions are safer experiences when goals are not introduced to the student directly. Students have enough goals to meet in the classroom. In my experience, students benefit more from counseling when they know there is no agenda, no right or wrong answer, no evaluation of their "performance." By the same token, when students begin experiencing either pleasant or unpleasant sensations in their body, they need to be taught that pleasant sensations are not necessarily "good" while unpleasant sensations are "bad." They need to be encouraged to *not* try to change any sensation but simply to notice without judgment. Sensations just *are*. They do not have to be positive or pleasant to have value.

EXAMPLES OF HOW TO RESOURCE STUDENTS

Important resources that we can help students experience in our work with them in schools include *safety, groundedness, connectedness, competence,* and *calm.* Activities that help lead to the experiences of these resources in the mind and body of our students are listed below.

Visualization and drawing: Once students are guided through a pleasant visualization, have them draw what they saw (e.g., a safe place, a caring community or circle of people, how they like to be comforted, what they are good at, their happiest memory). Then ask them about their drawing and what they notice inside their body as they look at it and remember the experience. They may report noticing pleasant sensations of warmth, flow, or gentle pulsating for example, that they can be encouraged to sit with and enjoy for a moment. They may report unpleasant sensations of tightness or tension that they can be encouraged to watch with curiosity to see how they may shift or what might happen next. Introducing the idea of movement or change is important when our students notice unpleasant sensations that seem to get stuck. They will learn through experience that unpleasant sensations naturally shift to more pleasant ones given a moment or two of focus (more on this in the next chapter).

Movement and rhythm: Music, especially drums, and dance serve to connect students to their own inner rhythms. Countless organic rhythms make up the biological drumbeat of life: "The bip-bip-bip of a tiny fetal heart, the muffled syncopation of a mother's pulse. Oscillating brain waves, the ebb and flow of hormones, the cadence of breath" (Weiss 1994, 1). Connecting to these natural rhythms of life through drumming and dance helps students to feel balance, connection, and support. When they are called to notice their feet planted on the ground as they move and sway, or the connection they have to the earth beneath them, or their own internal rhythms as they beat the drum, they are called to notice their part in the rhythm of life.

Students seem to instinctually know how much they benefit from drumming because they ask for it. Over and over again, I have witnessed that students do not tire of taking the drums out and making their own music. They enjoy hearing recorded music and following along with a drum, stomping their feet or marching to the beat. Several studies have documented decreases in stress hormones released in the brain and body as a result of listening to, and making, music (Gillis 2003). In the field of medicine, music has been shown to bring about great improvement in people with Alzheimer's, cerebral palsy, Parkinson's, traumatic brain injuries, and strokes. Veterans of World War II were soothed by community music groups that played for them in the hospitals where they recovered. "Nobody was quite sure what was going on, but many of the [veterans] seemed to perk up and get better" (Weiss 1994, 1).

Some of the most promising research on the benefits of rhythm and song has been done in the area of pain management (Gideonse 1998). A study done in Texas found that pregnant women who listen to music they enjoy during labor are only half as likely to need anesthesia. A Michigan cardiologist gave eight patients recovering from open-heart surgery a choice in pain medications: a morphine drip or a regimen of twenty minutes of low frequency humming. The patients preferred the vibrations to being drugged and their hospital stays decreased by four days.

Considering the levels of stress and pain endured by many of our students, exploring the usefulness of both visualization and music as powerful resources is worth our time and effort as educators. The decreases in sympathetic nervous system responses from visualization and music, as well as the experience of the more soothing parasympathetic nervous system, will increase the capacity of our students to tolerate and manage stress and pain without behaving in destructive ways.

Supportive exercises: These help students notice their feet planted on the ground, their body being supported in the chair they are sitting in, their company—the fact that they are not alone in the room but with someone who cares about them and is willing to listen and witness them compassionately. We can help our students notice how, where, with what, and with whom they feel most comfortable and supported (e.g., sitting on the ground, sitting in a chair, standing in a particular position or at a specific distance from the others in the room). It is important to have the student notice the cues inside their body that let them know when they need more or less support, lesser or greater distance.

Opportunities for competence: These are vital to the healing process and well researched. Students need to be encouraged to participate in, and to demonstrate, what they are good at and what they enjoy doing. Over the years, the students I have worked with, no matter how low functioning, have demonstrated numerous talents and personal strengths. By actively witnessing them and providing them with genuine praise, their body language shifted from collapsed and depressed to active and alive. Their facial expressions showed hope and pride and dignity, whether they played an instrument, danced, drew a picture, or played a sport. It did not matter what the activity was. Some students wrote poems, sang songs, or made objects out of clay or Play-Doh. Some even asked to take a spelling test. Some students felt great about the way they could trace an object with trace paper and other students felt great when they were able to hide well during a game of hide and seek. It is true that some students' strengths may not be readily apparent or expected but, as educators, it is our job to find areas of competence and provide opportunities for students to experience them in the present moment.

One important study conducted and reported by Dr. Judith Herman (1992) in her book *Trauma and Recovery* points to the need for a person to have resources of safety and competence in place before any kind of therapy or treatment can happen effectively. Dr. Bessel van der Kolk (2001) concluded after decades of research that symptoms can only be helped and managed when attending to day-to-day resources of safety, self-care, connections with other human beings, and competence. Like Herman, van der Kolk stated that "skills, hobbies, activities that calm the [person] down, give satisfaction and a sense of competence" must be in place before any intervention can happen successively (2001, 21). Developing a sense of bodily mastery and competence contradicts an identity of physical helplessness, according to van der Kolk. "Physical and sensate memories of mastery," important for management of anxiety and stress, are the results of both visualizing and actually experiencing competence.

Relaxation exercises: When they are not introduced as such, relaxation exercises help students notice their internal worlds, such as breathing and heart rates. Have students take deep breaths in through the nose and out through the mouth and notice the difference before and after such breaths. Have them breathe into their belly, making their stomach blow up like a balloon. While this may sound elementary, there is actually a science behind it. Millions of tiny nerve endings that cause a relaxation response line the inside of the stomach and are activated when we breathe air into that area. Have students place their hand on their belly to begin to feel and notice the expansion of the stomach during these deep breaths. Have them notice what is happening inside (e.g., breathing, heart rates, muscle tension) before and after at least five deep breaths.

With progressive or successive relaxation, another example of a relaxation exercise, students are asked to tense and relax each body part and notice the difference in their bodily experience when they are tense versus when they let go. Students may also be instructed to notice bodily changes when they participate in guided visualizations (e.g., have them imagine themselves as a melting candle or snowman, floating on the open sea, or swimming with the dolphins in the ocean).

By now, I hope you have come to notice how important *we* are in this process, how relevant it is for us to experience many or all of the above-mentioned resourcing activities. Not only is it imperative that we have a comfort with these exercises so that our students will be comfortable with them, but it is also true that we cannot help create internal and external balance in the lives of others when we do not have it for ourselves. If we are out of balance in our own lives, we do not have what it takes—the stamina, energy, endurance, health, and stability—to do *well* the very hard work we do.

7

Tools for Tolerance

The body knows things a long time before the mind catches up to them.

—Sue Monk Kidd in The Secret Lives of Bees

Based on our previous review of trauma and the brain, we now know how the body processes extreme experiences. In order to protect itself, the nervous system automatically does what it needs to do to keep from feeling terror, helplessness, and pain. It goes into fight, flight, or freeze. When the fight-or-flight responses are thwarted, or when the reptilian brain decides that freeze is the only option for survival, people become stuck both literally—in that moment—and figuratively—from that moment on. When our students, for example, are unable to successfully protect themselves from harm or the threat of harm, they become frozen in that time of terror and are unable thereafter to be present in the here and now.

Students who have experienced trauma become haunted by the past event(s) and worry constantly that danger is around the corner. Some become obsessed with completing the thwarted response, as evidenced by their reenactment of the trauma. Their frozen or demobilized defensive responses often repeatedly replay themselves as bodily symptoms, detached from their moment in history (Levine 2003). Traumatized students, for example, may continue to put themselves in dangerous situations against their better judgment in order to be forced to respond quickly and defend themselves. The impulses ignited by the traumatic event, left unable to complete their intent, become a driving force that will not let traumatized students rest. The painful by-products of this restless internal force include numbness, chronic fear, shame, and humiliation (Levine 2003).

Consider the many students who are identified as emotionally disturbed (ED) and placed in more restrictive environments (than regular classrooms) with other students who are similarly "disturbed." Many times, these are students who seem to have boundless amounts of energy, ready to use it up at any given time. They leap to defend themselves with little or no obvious provocation, at least nothing that would be considered life threatening or proportionate to their outburst. Teachers often attempt to help these students by scheduling regular running times throughout the day, hoping this will aid the students in using the energy up so they can be present in the classroom to learn more readily. This is an excellent idea. The spirit of it is exactly right. We need to help these students release the excessive energy they have stored in their body. Once they do, they will be able to be in the present moment with what they need to learn, how they need to behave, and where they can experience joy and freedom from what occurred in the past.

Students seem to use up their excessive energy during a run, and we think we see improvement in their behavior thereafter, at least for a time. It becomes clear quickly, however, that the effect of the intervention is minimal over time. To an extent running can be useful with students who are hyperactive, but with ED students who are often traumatized and *hypervigilant*, it simply does not work. Students who have experienced traumatization who just ran or played basketball to the point of physical exhaustion are soon back to jumping out of their seat, ready to attack a peer over the smallest incident. Teachers with the best ideas remain baffled by these students (more on interventions for ED students in chapter 8).

Turning to what the latest research indicates, and what our own eyes are telling us, we know that many of our most troubled students' internal states remain fundamentally unchanged after various kinds of interventions, including therapy. Traditional therapies and forms of counseling that attempt to change these students' perceptions of the world, and behaviors in the world, by means of reason and insight, using conditioning, behavior modification, and medication, simply do not work (Levine 2003). Dr. van der Kolk stated at a national conference November 15, 2002, therapists and their clients "may be having a nice time chatting" in a session of traditional therapy, "but they shouldn't be charging." Anyone who has been traumatized cannot be healed through the "talking cure." Brain science is now showing that our emotional states originate in the conditions of our *body* (van der Kolk 2002). Both research and best practice indicate that we must look to new techniques that incorporate the body in a very specific way in order to see lasting change.

There are new therapies in the world of mental health that heal traumatized children remarkably. They are generally referred to as "somatic" because they involve the integration of the body and its sensations into therapy. Leading researchers in the field of trauma and the brain, Drs. Bruce Perry, Bessel van der Kolk, and Allan Schore, all have concluded that the effects of trauma can be healed through somatic approaches.

One such approach is self-regulation therapy (SRT). Its goal is to decrease any excessive activation in the nervous system—the result of trauma—and bring the system back into balance. SRT recognizes that a dysregulation in the nervous system—an inability to modulate emotional and behavioral responses—is manifested in a whole host of disorders and symptoms, including hyperactivity, inattention, and learning problems. SRT works by providing a contained environment in which the individual can complete the thwarted responses of fight, flight, or freeze. Through resourcing, an important part of SRT, new neural pathways are developed in our students to help them flexibly manage daily challenges and stresses. Once the nervous system is better balanced, students are able to experience joy, closeness in relationships, and vitality and resiliency in the body, all necessary requisites for learning and age-appropriate behavior.

As the number of crises and traumas continue to escalate, and the number of students coming to school traumatized continues to increase, SRT may one day be as integral a part of some students' education as physical therapy (PT), speech therapy (ST), or occupational therapy (OT). For the purpose of this book, however, it is important for educators who are not therapists to know what invaluable measures they can take to make a difference to our students now. Many of the applications of SRT are modified and adapted in this book for educators to use effectively with their students (see chapter 9 for more).

THE PURPOSE OF SRT AND
OTHER TOOLS FOR TOLERANCE

In order for students to learn and behave as expected, they need to be helped to become unstuck in the past, unworried about the future, and in the moment to meet the demands of their present-day life with embodied exuberance. As educators we know that this is what is missing for our students. They cannot *be* and are not *being* in the present moment. Being in the present moment with mind and body requires an ability to regulate internally whatever is there. Learning and behaving in expected, age-appropriate ways requires the ability to *self-regulate* emotion and behavior. Autonomic dysregulation—the imbalance between the sympathetic and parasympathetic nervous systems reviewed in chapters 4 and 5 on trauma and the brain—is why traumatized students cannot concentrate, why they cannot learn, and why they leap out of their seats with little, if any, real provocation. A peer taking their pencil is not why they are out of their seat ready to pounce. They are out of their seat because the traumatic energy that is stuck in their body cannot be contained. It is too great, too overwhelming, and too intrusive. There is no room for anything else, not for any kind of input, not for joy or pleasure, not for academic demands, and certainly not for a talk with the teacher about how their behavior needs to change.

Any reason to pounce is important to students because it gives the energy focus and helps explain to them, albeit incorrectly, why the energy is there. Students do not understand why they are so jumpy. They look around and conclude that it must be because "He's looking at me—yeah—he's looking at me funny—I'm going to get him!" The energy is really about the past. Do not be confused that the energy is *in* the past, however. It is not. The energy may be *about* the past but is very much in the present, and it makes the student scared to death about the future. That is what trauma is all about.

CENTERING, GROUNDING, CONNECTION, AND BREATH

All the exercises reviewed in this chapter were designed to be utilized with students *who have already been traumatized.* It is possible and encouraged to use them at any time in the weeks, months, and years following the traumatic event(s). These exercises can be done with individuals, small groups, or large groups, although there are times when a small adult-to-student ratio is best. Crisis interventions, tools designed to be implemented *immediately* after a crisis event in order to *prevent* traumatization, are reviewed in chapters 10 and 11. At both stages of intervention, reestablishing ground, greater connectedness, and the student's center within his or her own body is very important to the prevention and healing of trauma.

Being grounded, centered, and connected to our own body as well as our own resources is a necessary prerequisite for any of the work we do with students. We need to be in our own bodies in a conscious way. We need to know what it feels like to be centered, grounded, and connected. We need to have these bodily experiences in order to give them to our students. Please review the previous chapter on resourcing to recall what we need to do for ourselves in order to help students experience their body in a safe and empowering way.

The importance of having students experience their body in a safe and empowering way is not new to education. As long ago as 1975, Gay Hendricks and Russell Wills published their book *The Centering Book: Awareness Activities for Children, Parents and Teachers.* In it they wrote that "centering is one of those things you must experience in order to understand" (11). In fact, all the exercises that will be reviewed in this chapter as well as those reviewed in the previous chapter on resourcing must also be experienced in order to be understood and appreciated for the restorative power they possess.

Five children quoted by Hendricks and Wills described the feeling of "centering" in different, but related ways: "Being lined up just right; feeling solid; not thinking, just feeling; being right on; being balanced" (1975, 15). The authors described several different relaxation and guided imagery exercises that help students, parents, and teachers become more present and clearly aware in the moment. Feeling centered in one's body, rooted, anchored, balanced, and secure is important not only to the successful performance of any task but also to healthy living. The centering exercises I do with students, sometimes outdoors in the grass, under a tree, or in the sun, are to help them feel more grounded and connected to both themselves and all of life, including Mother Nature.

In trauma, people lose their ground. It is as though the earth is ripped out from under their feet. Our traumatized students, like adults, feel less connected and more spacey, as though they are floating. An important part of healing is to reestablish ground with simple exercises developed by Dr. Peter Levine. For instance, encourage students to stand and feel their feet on the ground, feel the way their feet contact the ground. While they are slowly swaying back and forth, forward and back, encourage students to locate their center of gravity in the abdomen area. Have them place their hands on their lower belly and notice the energy that comes into that area through the legs and feet. Students may sit in a chair with their feet planted on the ground and notice how they are being supported by the chair and the earth, feeling their belly and the energy that is there.

During the grounding exercise, have students focus attention on their breathing. Encourage them, as they have their hands on their belly, to fill their tummy with air as they take a deep breath in through the nose. Trauma often restricts breathing patterns to the chest area, keeping oxygen from the rest of the body. Having students experience a fuller, deeper breath that nourishes a larger region of their body is a helpful intervention. Breathing in through the nose engages the parasympathetic nervous system, the part of the autonomic nervous system that helps to relax and calm. Breathing in through the mouth, on the other hand, engages the sympathetic nervous system responsible for accelerated heart rate and blood pressure. We can redirect our students' breathing very simply so they feel a greater sense of ease.

SCHOOLS AS COMMUNITIES

In *Waking the Tiger: Healing Trauma*, Dr. Levine reviews the importance of healing in community. He wrote that "deep interconnection, support, and social cohesion are necessary requirements for the healing of trauma" (1997, 59), and cited the 1994 Los Angeles earthquake as a time when the greatest healing took place in the people who camped, ate, and played together. Those who isolated themselves, obsessively watching replays of the event and listening to interviews, were "much more susceptible to traumatic effects than those who supported each other in community" (60). We also saw this after the attacks of 9/11. The people who gathered at Ground Zero in the days following the tragedy and lent themselves to the effort of taking care of the people there who needed help fared better than those who were isolated and obsessively watched the news. We heal in community, especially when we realize our purpose.

This means a great deal when thinking about the students who come to our schools. While schools, and classrooms in particular, are seemingly not the places where healing takes place—this is supposed to happen in hospitals or therapists' offices somewhere—that really is not true. In many cases, schools and classrooms are the safest, and can be the most grounding, centering places that students have access to. There is much we can do as educators to help in the healing of trauma, to bring our students back into the present moment to learn and have joy.

Schools can be the very communities that Dr. Levine referred to as instrumental in the healing of trauma. Schools have the power and resources to promote the transformation of even our most troubled students. The healing of our communities and the individuals within our communities is not just the job of mental health professionals. In schools, healing is not just the job of school counselors and psychologists. Our lives are too interrelated for that to be true. At every level, there is something that can be done, and with the right knowledge and understanding, it can be done effectively.

The following tools can be applied in any school setting. Some may be best left to a counseling office, but others are effective in the classroom. Teachers, nurses, counselors, and administrators are encouraged to consider how some of each of the tools presented may aid in the work they do with troubled students who have histories of trauma. Some exercises work well with groups of students while others are more effective in one-on-one situations. Individual educators need to decide how best to use the following tools, keeping in mind the importance of community in the healing process. Challenging as it may be to do group or classwide intervention, it is my hope that knowing the power of community in the healing process will inspire educators to overcome obstacles to the process.

GROUP INTERVENTION

The most impossible groups to run successively are groups with only one facilitator, especially when the groups are large or involve students with behavior problems. If teachers want to do a classwide intervention, they would be best advised to invite the school counselor or psychologist to help them. Administrators too often rely on *either* the counselor *or* psychologist to run most groups in schools and rarely provide additional support or the possibility of cofacilitation. When working with a group of troubled students, however, it is very important for two or more adults to provide containment for the energy. We all know how much energy many of these students have. It is excessive. It is only through the commitment of at least two adults that effective containment and management of the energy is possible.

Two adults who make worthy cofacilitators are the counselor and psychologist together, or one of them paired with the facilitator, social worker, behavior specialist, or school-based mental health provider. Psychologists can also "buddy up" with one another as an alternative, with one going to the other's school for group time and vice versa.

Whatever the arrangement, when working with emotionally and/or behaviorally disturbed students, it is important to do in-class groups with two adults coleading. Additionally, it is important to have the adult involvement and support of the teacher and teacher aides. The classroom is the community and the group process is to help the community relate to one another in healthy, healing ways. This requires the active participation of the teachers in order to communicate that as a class community everyone is part of something greater than themselves, and everyone is there to help each other. In other words, "We're in this together." As Martin Luther King Jr. so famously stated, we are all "caught in an inescapable network of mutuality, tied in a single garment of destiny. Whatever affects one directly affects all indirectly." King said that he could "never be what I ought to be until you are what you ought to be, and you can never be what you ought to be until I am what I ought to be. This is the interrelated structure of reality." This "reality," so well described by King, must be acknowledged and acted on right now if we are to make a necessary difference.

From interviews with the teachers I have worked with in group counseling situations, I learned what they found valuable about the process. One teacher said that the group brought about greater *connectedness*. "Giving the kids

someone else to connect to allowed them to be more free to express themselves." Another teacher stated that being able to "get things off their chest
put students *at ease.*" One teacher mentioned *relationship*, stating that group
counseling helped the students *tolerate* relationships, something very difficult
for them to do, he said. The students began to "see that it's okay to say thank
you." Their guards came down and the classroom had more of a "friendly
atmosphere," indicating a greater sense of *safety*. In fact, one teacher
reported a decrease in fighting overall. Another teacher reported greater sharing and consideration of one another. She gave examples of students saying
"I'll find that for you" or "You can have mine." Students began picking
things up off the ground for other students, and one student returned money
he had found to the teacher so it could be given back to the student who
lost it.

These may sound like normal and expected behaviors, nothing out of the
ordinary perhaps, and not worthy of great praise and recognition. For these
very troubled students, however, who have suffered terrifying experiences,
these outcomes were very encouraging. The students in these groups had had
such overwhelming experiences in earlier years it was remarkable that they
were functioning at all. One boy had witnessed his father shot and killed in
front of him when he was just two years old. He continued to talk about the
event and his father seven years later, as a nine-year-old boy. He spoke obsessively at times of wanting to find whoever did it so he could kill him. He did
not have reading, writing, and arithmetic on his mind. He had death on his
mind. Death was on his mind and in his body, rendering him incapable of
being in the present moment to learn and behave as expected. Rather than
attend to the lesson at hand, this boy obsessively drew pictures of guns. He
formed his hands into the shape of a gun and ran around the school threatening others. He was stuck in the past of the trauma he experienced. He was
occupied with energy in the present moment that made him think of the past
in which the event happened, and the future in which he imagined he could
avenge the death of his father.

Another student in one of the groups I co-led had spent three days alone in
his trailer home with the dead body of his grandfather. His grandfather had
died while the young boy lived with him. The boy was so frozen from shock,
he did not do anything or go anywhere for help. Rather, he stayed in the
trailer, numb and alone, until they were found. When help finally came, the
boy was found drinking out of the toilet bowl.

Another student had a gender change operation. She was born a hermaph-
rodite in a small town in South America. Without knowing what to do, the
family raised her as a boy only to find that things were not developing as
hoped. The family was able to obtain the help of American doctors so they

moved to the United States and followed the recommendations of the doctors here. It was decided that the student was a girl and the operation took care of the anatomy of that decision. The student, as well as her family, suffered an enormous amount of stress throughout her abnormal development, as well as the major, invasive surgery.

Before beginning a group with such troubled students, it is important to conduct a pregroup meeting with all the adults who will participate. Include the group's coleader (usually a counselor, school psychologist, behavior specialist, social worker, or school-based mental health professional), as well as the teacher and teacher aides. At the meeting, discuss the importance of safety and containment. Each adult is there to help the students feel more safe and contained within the group community. Discuss the impact of trauma on these students' lives and the fact that what often becomes destroyed in that process is the student's sense of safety, knowing and accepting boundaries, feeling connected to themselves, to others, to nature, and experiencing groundedness or centeredness. These important senses and feelings are gone. As previously mentioned, trauma is like having the ground taken away from underneath the feet. Nothing is secure, safe, or predictable. Nothing can be controlled or planned for. It is important for the adults, therefore, to go into the group knowing that this is what needs to be restored in these students.

During the pregroup meeting, discuss the importance of everyone's involvement, participation, and sharing. This is not a time for the teachers to take a break while the group is conducted without them. Rather, this is an opportunity for everyone to work together to heal whatever needs to be healed. When our students see our participation and hear us sharing, they come to understand that they are not alone and indeed we are all in this together.

The pregroup meeting is a good time to review some of the important points from chapter 6 on resourcing. Discuss the "scales of justice" that are out of balance and the need for us to help students remember and access their resources. Introduce resourcing as a general guiding principle for the group activities.

In the feedback I have received from schools where group was conducted for ten weeks, I learned that this is not nearly enough time for the students to benefit. Knowing that trauma leads to such disconnection and difficulty with trust and relationship, it takes at least that long to gain the students' comfort and to establish a sense of safety within the group.

At my own schools, where I do these groups all year long (for approximately thirty weeks) with ED students, it has become clear that such long-term counseling is needed for more observable results. With less troubled students this is not the case. Shorter-term groups may be just as sufficient. It is important to consider the severity of the difficulties and the experiences of the students, as well as how well resourced they are in their lives. Some students are in safe homes and communities where their nervous system can be at ease. Others do not have that important sense of safety in their lives and will therefore require more time to begin to feel that way in school.

Students who live in our most dangerous neighborhoods may never come to feel more at ease. It is not adaptive for them to let their guard down. If they are being retraumatized on a daily, weekly, or even monthly basis when they are in their homes or on the streets, there may be little we can do to balance that out. The little we are able to do, however, *understanding* them better, for example, may make all the difference in the world to individual students.

GUIDING PRINCIPLES FOR INTERVENTIONS

Time-Out/Time-Away

Time-out is a tool that requires a complete paradigm shift in our thinking. If this tool continues to be used in a punitive way, we will perpetuate and exacerbate the symptoms of trauma. This often misunderstood and poorly implemented tool can actually be an excellent way to help students (and adults!) de-escalate their nervous system in a safe, nonjudgmental way. In order to use this tool effectively, we need to teach ourselves first and then our students to connect with bodily sensations in order to use them as signals. Just as we learned in the educational video *Think First*, developed by Jim Larson and Dr. Judith McBride, our sensations are valuable cues that communicate to us (Larson 2005). Coming up with a list of these with our students can be instrumental in helping them make the connection between their sensations and their impulses to behave in a certain way. The direct and powerful relationship between our students' sensations and what it is they need in order to tolerate them is the heart of the matter. When students can tolerate uncomfortable and painful sensations, they will no longer need to engage in maladaptive behaviors.

Bodily sensations of heat, rapid heart rate, tightness, or tension, for example, may signal the need for a time away in a safe, nonpunitive place. Having such a place to go to as a resource—without being banished there punitively—can help the nervous system do what it needs to do to calm and return to balance. While taking a "time-away," the use of calming visualization exercises, soothing self-statements, or focusing techniques (to be discussed later in the chapter) can be very helpful to our students, when taught and practiced with adult guidance. With these tools, our students learn that "what goes up must come down." Because the parasympathetic nervous system works to relax and balance out the heightened responses of the sympathetic nervous system, the body naturally begins to calm down given enough quiet time to do so. This is the best use of time-out or time-away with traumatized students.

Repair

Dr. John Stewart (1998) discussed the importance of repair at a presentation of his work with acting-out students. When our nervous system is activated, triggered, or set off in any way, we say and do things we regret. This is the nature of trauma. When we perceive a threat, real or imagined, we automatically go into fight or flight. It is in our biological makeup to do whatever it takes to protect ourselves and survive the threat. Because of this innate biology, our students say and do things before they have the chance to think and make a choice. As a result, there is a great deal they wish they could take back on a daily basis. Overwhelming emotions of guilt, shame, and humiliation ensue, feelings they work very hard to keep from consciousness, and from being obvious to others.

As the adults in these students' lives, it can be an important part of the work we do to help them repair the damage done by their words and deeds. We cannot take away the natural consequences of their behavior, nor should we, Dr. Stewart cautions, but we can help them manage the consequences. If we show them how they can undo some of the damage they have caused, they have a better chance of tolerating their feelings of regret and shame. This is how we can interrupt a vicious cycle of problematic behavior.

Once our students have calmed down, we can communicate to them with words, actions or gestures that we know they did not mean to do what they did, or say what they said. We can let them know that we understand how upset or hurt they feel—that we know that when they are upset they have difficulty thinking rationally and making good choices. We can help them by first understanding what it is like to be them—to be in their skin with all that bound up traumatic energy just waiting for an opportunity to discharge. We can aid them by demonstrating and/or guiding them in how they can apologize to the person they hurt or do something constructive to make up for what they did—not in a punitive way, but with compassion and caring.

Structure

Containment, boundaries, and safety for our students is what we are working to provide. Predictability helps to create these conditions. Structure provides predictability. Therefore, with the aim of enhancing predictability and a sense of safety, every intervention is best provided with an overriding structure.

I find it effective to begin and end each intervention session, whether group or individual, with a resource, an activity that is helpful, positive, and strengthening. The middle part of each session can focus on thematic content, but overall, the content is best contained within resource. The deeper and richer the resource, the deeper and richer the work, the safer and more grounded the students are to process their sensations and feelings in a way that is healing and transformative.

A helpful way to enhance both structure and predictability in the process of "group" is to begin the first session by giving each participant, including adults, a manila folder. The folder becomes the place where each participant keeps the work he or she does during group. At the end of group, they are encouraged to take their folders home with them to share with their loved ones if they choose to. The first session can be an opportunity for all the participants to make their folders special by decorating them in their own unique ways.

Having the students come up with rules for the group is a useful way to spend the first session also, emphasizing the importance of respecting each other by not making fun of, or laughing at, anything anyone chooses to share in group. Laughter may occur when students are uncomfortable so there needs to be room for, and discussion of, that. Otherwise, it is important to protect the safety of the group by being firm in not giving that behavior attention and thereby reinforcement.

Reestablishing Safety

I like to use Violet Oaklander's very first visualization in her book *Windows to Our Children* during the second session of group or individual work to help establish within each of the participants their own safe place, whether real or imagined (Oaklander 1988). I change the visualization somewhat to keep it positive and to introduce the idea of safety—finding a place behind a visualized door that is safe for them. After the visualization, I have the students draw what they saw. Then, the most important step in the process is having the participants notice what they feel inside their body as they look at or think about their safe place. Do they notice any pleasurable sensations, such as warmth, flow, calm, relaxation. If so, where? Can they describe it? Does it have a shape or color? Have them spend time experiencing the pleasurable sensations that come from seeing, thinking about, and describing their safe place.

Once students begin to feel sensations of safety and pleasure in their body, new neural pathways start to develop that later support the students in tolerating and managing daily stresses and challenges. Their internal experiences become more balanced between pleasure and discomfort, as opposed to being overloaded with discomfort only.

If the students do not feel pleasurable but unpleasurable sensations after any of the resourcing activities, including the safe place exercise, do not panic. The more of this work you do with yourself, the less you will worry when this happens. You will already know from experience in your own body that the uncomfortable sensations will settle over time just by giving them your attention. Simply use the following focusing technique (Gendlin 1981): Have students notice the unpleasurable sensation, such as tightness or tension, and as you support them with your presence, have them observe it. Have the student watch the sensation with curiosity until something happens. You can direct them by stating, "I'm right here with you. Just focus your attention on the tightness and see what happens next."

Inevitably something will happen because that is how our nervous system is made. With only a moment's focus on the unpleasurable sensation, something will shift. A breath will come, a wave of warmth, or a lessening or spreading of the tension. This is the parasympathetic nervous system doing its job of calming the system when it becomes agitated or excited. Rarely do we take the time to notice that this process happens naturally without our needing to will it to happen. Rarely do we get to experience in a palpable embodied way that it is our birthright for this to happen. The body is built to heal itself, only we must give it our attention in order to notice that this healing can happen. Once we come to see that our body can be trusted and can experience relief without having to do anything but focus, we begin to heal.

We cannot give what we do not have. We cannot model or teach what we do not know. This is why our students' teachers and all the adults providing containment for the group participate as any other group member. If our students are to become more aware of their inner landscapes, so must we. If we are to support them in becoming more connected with their own wholeness in order to heal, so must we.

When one school principal saw the resourcing activities I do with students, she stated with excitement, "This is exactly what these kids need! This is what we need to be focusing on!" Having them remember their external resources—the people they have in their lives and what they can do to get help—is a great place to start. The best resources we can give them, however, are internal, in their body. Their body is just that—*theirs*. They need no one and nothing but themselves to have it, notice it, use it, and benefit from it. Focusing our efforts on experiencing our own internal resources first, and then helping our students to experience theirs is more than a worthwhile effort. It is precisely what is needed in order to increase our students' capacities to self-regulate, and ultimately, to learn.

SPECIFIC INTERVENTION EXERCISES

So far we have reviewed a number of overriding guiding principles that inform and guide the intervention process. In addition to centering, grounding, connection, breath, and community, we discussed the value of time-out/ time-away, repair, structure, and safety/safe place. Keeping these overriding principles in mind, the following are examples of thematic content activities that can be done in classrooms, group counseling settings, or one-on-one situations. The activities are designed to facilitate, for each benefactor of the intervention, a greater sense of containment, balance, and calm.

Caring Circle

The caring circle was developed by Marge Heegaard (1993) and is part of her excellent series of books for children. To conduct the exercise, have students draw themselves as a small circle in the center of the page and then draw a larger circle around that circle, then a larger circle around that, and a larger circle around that. The circles represent the people that surround the student in a loving, supportive way. Have the student identify who is in the circle closest to them, for example, the family members who take care of them. The next circle that is closest to them may contain their friends and classmates. The next circle may include their community of neighbors, teachers or other adults that help them. Have the students make a list of all the names they come up with and see just how many people they have in their lives to call upon for help when they need it.

The caring circle is a valuable exercise not just to see whom the students have in their lives, but also whom they do not have. It is always good to learn about missing resources so that we can help fill in the gaps and restore for the student what is needed. Perhaps a female mentor or "big sister" would help a student who has no female family members to rely on. Connecting that student with a caring female teacher or counselor on campus to check in with each day may make the difference. Without knowing that this is a missing resource, however, we cannot do something that simple and far-reaching.

Hot Seat

The hot seat activity is something my colleague Kathryn Goria taught me. Kathryn is a talented psychiatric occupational therapist who also worked as a school behavior specialist. She and I co-led groups together and used this activity with excellent results. This is how it works: Each student has a turn to sit in the "hot seat" at the head of a table that everyone else in the group sits around. When the students are ready to receive—and must sense and feel into the body in order to know when they are ready—each person in the group has a chance to say what they like about the person in the hot seat, or what they are good at. Some students find that they cannot do the exercise unless they turn around and have their back facing the group. It is too difficult for them to hear positive things said about them. They sense the overwhelm in their nervous system. The input feels like too much to contain. The important thing is that they notice their bodily discomfort and renegotiate their position until they find one that is more comfortable—one that will allow their nervous system to tolerate the input.

Trauma has the power to occupy so much of our body, nervous system, and energy that we have little or no room for pleasure. We cannot contain joy with comfort and ease. We are left with such humiliation, shame, and fear that we do not believe that pleasure can be ours, that it can last, or that we deserve it. Hence, our traumatized students turn away from compliments, find a quick way to discount praise, or sabotage a moment that seemed to bring them some peace or pride. It is important to recall that this is not a cognitive process. This is about the body's capacity to contain and tolerate the excitation that arises in the nervous system when noticed and complimented by others.

It is also important to remember that for any and each of these exercises, meaningful change is brought about only when the exercises are embodied. That is, the students must be taught, encouraged, and supported to bring their awareness to their bodily sensations as the exercises are done—to notice that they can contain both pleasure and pain. What goes up *will* come down.

In order to do these exercises, students must be given the language of sensation. It has been my experience that children are less in need of coaching on this point than adults are. The students I have worked with have readily noticed their bodily sensations and have been able to put them into words. Nonetheless, it is good to come up with a list of sensation words. The list may include such words as tight, tense, soft, loose, flowing, hot, cold, warm, cool, icy, tingly, prickly, pinchy, itchy, numb, open, spacious, expanded, constricted, jumpy, strong, solid, weak, tired, heavy, light, shaky, quivery, bouncy, and so forth. These are all words used to help students express verbally what is happening internally. When they do, they create awareness of their inner landscape, get connected to it, and ultimately become more whole.

Noticing

This activity is a good introduction to the inner world of sensations. First, students are encouraged to notice what is outside; then, notice what is inside. The first time I did this exercise, I brought into the class two framed pictures from my home. The first picture was an outdoor landscape in Louisiana, full of lush, green trees and grass. The second was a picture of two young girls, my nieces, basking in the sun as they walked up the path of a wooded area carrying the fish they had caught that day. Kathryn and I passed the pictures around the room and asked each of the group members to notice what they saw, simply to take note of the details or overall impression of the pictures—to notice. Then we talked about the things they notice when they walk outside. "Do you notice the sun warming your skin, birds chirping, or flowers blooming? When you eat, do you notice the colors, the smell, and the taste of the food?" First we talked about noticing things on the outside of us, things that involve our five senses (we reviewed these), and then we talked about noticing things on the inside.

The importance of noticing what is going on outside of us has to do with mobilizing an important adaptive response—orienting. When we experience something terrifying or threatening and our body goes into a freeze, we become fixed into a rigid pattern of responding and lose sight of our options and choices. This has to do with, among other things, the narrow focus of our eyes as we hone in on the threat of danger before us. Our physiology, for the sake of our survival, has us narrowly focus on what we need to defend against. When we get stuck in that place of readiness, we lose our ability to orient to the world around us. We are caught in the narrow world of trauma, the constricted pattern of reenactment of the traumatic event. When we have students begin to orient to the world around them in a way that is sensory based, we begin to loosen that constricted energy by connecting the student to the expansiveness of the outside world and all it has to offer.

For the latter half of the noticing activity, Kathryn and I introduced the idea that there is a whole other world that exists in addition to what is around us on the outside. It is the world that is on the inside of us that we rarely pay much attention to—our inner landscape of sensations. We asked the group members, "What do you notice happening inside of you right at this moment? Is anyone hungry, for example? How do you know? Are your stomachs growling? Does anyone have a headache? How do you know? Is anyone's head tight, tense, pounding, hot, or cold? If so, where? Does anyone feel good right now? How do you know? Do your muscles feel relaxed? Is your belly soft and warm?"

After we asked these questions, we gave group members a handout with the silhouette of a body on it, as well as a grid indicating which color matched what sensation. The students were given crayons to color and asked to shade in the silhouettes of their body where they were feeling particular sensations. We all did the activity together and then whoever wanted to share did so.

During group counseling, I always give group members a choice in sharing. They are welcome to share only when they want to. It is another opportunity to connect sensation to feeling and behavior. "How do you know you want to share? Do you feel excited? How do you know you are excited? Where do you feel those sensations? In your stomach? In your chest? Is it pleasurable or unpleasurable? How does your body tell you that you do not want to share?" Getting people connected to their body connects them to the whole of who they are and gives them the most important tool they need to manage their experiences.

Occupational therapists (OTs) have always known that sensory awareness is the necessary prerequisite to self-regulation of behavior and affect. This is what their work is all about. They reconnect students to their bodily sensations in order to help them begin to regulate their experiences. Hence, the development by two OTs of the intervention program "How Does Your Engine Run?/The Alert Program for Self-Regulation" (Williams and Shellenberger 1996) (see chapter 9 for more).

Progressive Relaxation

If students have a difficult time getting into their body and noticing the sensations there, one way to back up and help them connect is with progressive relaxation. This is a common relaxation exercise that involves, first, tensing each muscle group; second, relaxing each muscle group; and third, noticing the difference. As mentioned in chapter 6, I caution against introducing this exercise as one of relaxation per se because that word or agenda can be activating. Simply encourage each student to tense their muscles, beginning with their toes or feet, then relax their muscles, notice the difference between those two states, and continue.

There is often a difference in how students feel before and after each of these exercises. I have students rate on a scale of one to ten how tight or tense they feel before the exercise, and then again when the exercise is over. When they do, they often report feeling less tight or tense at the end of the exercises. This was true when Kathryn and I had students participate in what we call fine-point coloring.

Fine-Point Coloring

With fine-point markers, Kathryn and I had students color advanced, intricately detailed coloring books. As Kathryn explained to me based on her years utilizing this activity with psychiatric patients, this exercise gives people a focus for their fragmented energy, parameters that aid in organizing their more disorganized internal experiences. The structure of the exercise provides containment for excessive energy. It is soothing to our students because of their inability to regulate their emotions on their own. They need help from the outside—safe, calm, and quiet containment—to structure and hold their internal experiences in order to regulate them.

Having students rate their inner experiences before and after each exercise helps to identify the most effective exercises for a particular individual so they can then be used during difficult times. For instance, once the most calming activities have been identified through the rating system, those particular exercises may be used to calm an individual or whole class when highly activated before a lesson or exam, for example, or after a frightening event. There are many times, as educators, we wish we could think of an effective calming technique that would get our students back on track when aroused. I have experienced firsthand how many of these exercises are just what is needed for students to achieve that calm.

I See, I Hear, I Sense

"I see, I hear, I sense" is another way to introduce both adults and our students to the world of sensations. It is a game I was introduced to by one of my teachers, Steve Hoskinson. Students are encouraged to report something they see in the room or around them, then something they hear, then something they sense in their bodies, such as hot, cold, tight, tense, or something else most noticeable to them in the present moment. If they report a headache, for instance, then I help them describe the headache with sensation words, like pounding or throbbing or stabbing. Then I help them use the simple tool of focusing to watch the sensation until it changes. It always does. Gendlin wrote, "The most exciting characteristic of all is the fact that a 'felt sense' [sensation], when you focus on it well, has the power to change. You can actually feel this change happening in your body. It is a well-defined physical sensation of something moving or shifting. It is invariably a pleasant sensation, a feeling of something coming unstuck" (1981, 37).

There is a simple scientific explanation for this phenomenon that has been described in previous chapters. Sensations shift as they do in a noticeable way when we focus on them because while noticing and focusing on sensation, we become aware of the natural built-in job of the parasympathetic nervous system. As we now know, the sympathetic branch of the nervous system is responsible for the usually unpleasant, often frightening sensations of accelerated heart rate, elevated blood pressure, flushing of the face, and shortness of breath. The parasympathetic is responsible for the slowing down of these responses to restore the body back to its more relaxed state. This latter system always kicks in and does its job. It is simply a matter of taking the time and space to notice it so that we can come to trust it. As Gendlin wrote, "When people have this [body shift] even once, they no longer helplessly wonder for years whether they are changing or not" (1981, 7).

It is important to remember that focusing is not something that needs to be taught by therapists or counselors. Gendlin's research indicated that "this crucial internal act can be taught, and is not taught by therapy. People need not be therapy patients to learn it. . . . People can do it for themselves and with each other" (Gendlin 1981, 6). This has implications for our work in schools. We know from the research Gendlin conducted at the University of Chicago in the 1970s that the people who get better in therapy are those who experience their bodily sensations, those who can connect with that part of themselves. We also know that we can teach each other and our students to utilize this important skill. What are we waiting for?

Gratitude

This is an activity that involves having each student recall and record five things they have been grateful for so far that day. The importance of gratitude as a tool for healing was written about by Sarah ban Breathnach (1995). The idea is to encourage and support students in orienting to their worlds, seeing what is in front of them, appreciating what beauty and comfort, however little, may be around them. At first, anyone beginning this exercise may think only of the big things in life—loved ones, health, shelter, or food. Over time, however, as one is continually required to come up with five things in a day, one begins to notice the smaller things in life—the details of the bigger things. For instance, one may begin to notice such things as an unexpected phone call from a family member, the taste of chocolate, the smell of hot cocoa cooking, the sound of birds chirping outside the window, the warmth of the sun, or getting to sleep in a comfortable bed. As the students recall and record, they are encouraged to notice what is happening in their body, what sensations are there, as they think of the things they are grateful for.

Discovery

This is a collage exercise also written about by Sarah ban Breathnach (1995). The exercise requires students to bring in a picture of themselves. They paste the picture in the center of a blank page and begin to cut out from magazines the things they would like to have more of in their lives. They may wish to have more family time, play time at the park, privacy in their own room, time to talk on the telephone with a friend, trips to theme parks, or camping in the outdoors. As they select their items and create their collage, they are encouraged to imagine themselves doing more of what they love and to notice their internal experience as they imagine those things.

Friendship

This activity is an opportunity for students to talk about what they think makes a person a good friend. They have a chance to state who their friends are and why, and what about them makes them a good friend to others. During times of stress or overwhelm, students may be helped by being encouraged to imagine their best friend is with them, to see all the details of that person and to notice their sensations and emotions as they imagine the support of that person. This is an effective tool to use when a student is feeling emotional, afraid, or alone.

Balancing

This is a physical activity that has students stand on their feet and rock back and forth, noticing where and how they feel most balanced. Students are encouraged to notice their feet being supported by the ground, to notice how they are connected to the earth beneath them. This is best done slowly so that at each junction of the rocking motion students can be asked what they notice inside. When leaning to the left, for instance, what do they notice happens? When more centered over their feet, what do they notice? This is to help them become more aware of when they feel in and out of balance and more or less centered.

Gifts

This is a lesson that involves students telling about a gift they have given and a gift they have received. The focus is on noticing how they feel in the present moment as they share and are reminded of giving or receiving a gift. This is a useful time to provide the student with a silhouette and colored crayons.

The silhouette may have a grid of options to choose from, or may be blank so they can decide for themselves what sensations get what colors.

The silhouettes are useful to use to check in with students at the beginning of the day, at the beginning of group process, or at the beginning of individual work. Have them color in what they notice they are feeling in their body right then and there. Always work in the present moment. Have them color "red" in the places they feel hot, tight, tense, or other angry sensations; "blue" in the places they feel the sensations of sadness, such as tired, achy, or sore; "yellow" in the places that feel warm, flowing, loose, relaxed, or happy; and "brown" where they feel strong and solid.

THE IMPORTANCE OF SLOWING DOWN

Oftentimes, students will color red in their hands and feet. They do not hesitate. They know that this is exactly what they feel inside those areas—hot, tight, tense, and angry. They speak of wanting to kick or hit. They feel the energy in their body, energy that wants to complete itself. This is the thwarted traumatic energy that was mobilized during threat in order that they may protect themselves. Because they were unable to protect themselves and use up the mobilized energy, it did not discharge. It remained, and remains, stuck in the body.

The best thing we can do for students in that moment of noticing the sensations and impulses, is what I call very simply, slowing down. While the student is noticing their experience, without judgment say, "That's right. You feel like you want to hit or kick. What else do you notice? Do you feel hot, tight, or tense? Where in your body do you feel that?" Once they describe their experience, simply say, "That's right. Just notice what your body wants to do. I'm right here with you." It is important to pause between statements to allow time for the body and mind to integrate what is happening. Then I may say, "Now very slowly, inside your mind, picture yourself doing what your body wants to do right now. Keep the movements slow. Can you see yourself doing that?" I simply continue to support the student with my calm presence as the body's own self-healing mechanism is at work completing the response. I may continue to speak quietly saying, "I'm right here with you. Let yourself, inside your mind, do what your body needs to do *very slowly*. That's it."

Slowing down students' actions and impulses helps to prevent them from going into overwhelm or feeling out of control and afraid of their own responses and energy. We become overwhelmed and afraid when things happen too fast, when we are unable to think as we act. Slowing things down helps the body reorganize itself and create the new neural pathways that are needed to feel more balanced and tolerant of both pleasure and discomfort. When students move quickly and give into the rapid impulses that up to that point have been governing their lives, they continue to feel like they have no control over them. When we instruct students in their mind's eye to move more slowly, and support them as they slow things down, we give their systems an opportunity to make connections between all their parts. The movements of the body—behaviors—are able to connect with thoughts and emotions when we slow things down, giving everything a chance to integrate.

When we have students imagine themselves acting out their impulses, and we ask them to do so slowly, this is an entirely different process than what we see with cathartic approaches. Cathartic approaches, such as having individuals punch a pillow or punching bag as they feel their anger and do not hold back, are ineffective and harmful to traumatized students. Such approaches are not soothing to the nervous system. They can be so activating, in fact, that they can cause retraumatization and intensification of symptoms. Short-term gains were originally found with cathartic types of exercises, which is how they became popular decades ago, but we now know better that for long-term gains and healing, discharge of bound-up energy in the body must happen slowly through conscious connection with sensation.

When students imagine themselves acting out their impulses, watch for any physiological changes in the body. The most obvious changes are a deep breath, flushing of the face caused by an increase in body temperature, or relaxation of the muscles. Then ask, "What do you notice now?" There is an excellent chance that what the student will notice is more calm, relaxation, warmth, or flow. Something will shift; a movement or "unstuckness" will occur and this will create an overall sense of greater balance in the system. Slowly and over time, this is how the energy will discharge and the body will have greater capacity for containment of other experiences, including pleasure.

Allowing the defensive responses of running, kicking, or hitting to come to the surface and be moved through the body in the present moment in a slow and conscious way is critical to the healing of trauma. This is how all the various chemicals, including adrenaline and cortisol that are released at the time of the trauma, are finally discharged from the body leading to a marked decrease in the problems we see both in classrooms and on the playground.

When we resource our students in their body in the present moment we prepare the way for discharge to take place. Once the foundational work of resourcing is done, it is possible to work with the defensive responses as they begin to surface. Resourcing within the context of group sets the stage for smaller group or individual work that focuses on completing the thwarted defensive responses. When several adults are committed to the process and a structure is developed that provides safe containment, the possibilities for our students' healing and learning become endless.

CONCLUSION

We have discussed important paradigm shifts in this chapter—recognizing the need to develop a language and appreciation for sensations, for example, as well as understanding time-out or time-away as a nonpunitive technique that allows the nervous system to settle into greater balance. Another important paradigm shift in our thinking is necessary in order to help our students heal, and that is to pay the emotion of anger the appreciation it is due.

Anger is a necessary feeling. It helps the body mobilize the energy it needs to protect itself. Without anger, we could not take care of ourselves at crucial times. Our students have needed their anger and have good reason for their anger. Until we recognize this and accept it as necessary and valuable, too much energy will continue to be spent trying to suppress a natural response to threat.

The American Psychological Association featured the topic of anger as a misunderstood emotion in the *Monitor on Psychology*. The need for, and benefits of, anger were highlighted in an article entitled "When Anger's a Plus." A number of the studies reviewed indicated that "everyday episodes of anger as opposed to more dramatic ones" help strengthen relationships, give people a sense of control during uncertain times, and serve an important alerting function that leads to deeper understanding of the person and the problem (DeAngeles 2003). Anger "gets a bad rap," according to one author, partly because it is often erroneously associated with violence, when in fact, anger seems to be followed by aggression only about 10 percent of the time (DeAngeles 2003). Another author who argued that anger is the misunderstood emotion paraphrased Malcolm X stating, "There's a time and a place for anger, where nothing else will do" (Tavris 1989, 3).

Helpful Anger

This is an activity that gives participants an opportunity to accept their anger as a natural part of who they are, and to thank it for helping them in a time of need. Participants are asked to share a time when their anger helped them do something they needed to do. Often, students will share that it helped them to get someone to stop treating them badly, to stop hitting them or hurting them in some way. This opens the conversation up to help students understand when anger is helpful and when it is not, when there is an important use for it and when we need to let it go so it does not hurt us more deeply than we have already been hurt. If we can help students understand that there are times for anger, then perhaps we will be able to help them understand that there are times to let it go. Anger is not going anywhere. We will always have it, need it, and use it. We must stop focusing on it as evil and something to be ashamed of. I witness daily how this is crippling our students.

Standing Up

This is an activity related to helpful anger that gives participants an opportunity to share their memories of when they stood up for someone and when someone stood up for them. One year, at the suggestion of a colleague, and with his help, I did this exercise around Memorial Day and had students begin by sharing who they knew that had served in the armed forces—someone they knew who had chosen to stand up for his or her country. As they recalled a time they stood up for someone, or a time someone stood up for them, they were encouraged to notice the sensations evoked by their memories in the here and now.

What I hope is clear from this review is how these activities are related. They are simple yet empowering exercises that are done using art and movement to help participants access and experience the sensations of their body. Experiencing the body as a resource helps discharge tightness and "stuckness" in a safe way. The purpose is to help create new neural pathways that build the nervous system's resilience and help balance it out. The purpose is not to make uncomfortable or painful sensations go away. The fact that they naturally diminish when we focus on them is what we are hoping for, but it is not desirable to try and make this happen. We need to follow the body as it heals and regulates itself. We simply *aid* in this process by calling attention to our sensations and how they change. Balancing out discomfort with more pleasurable sensations reminds us of how flexible and tolerant our body can be.

In a review of recent brain research, the neuroscientist Antonio Damasio confirmed that the body does not work well physiologically in the presence of so-called negative emotions, but works exceptionally well when emotions are positive. Knowing that we need our students to learn and behave according to strict standards and expectations, it seems to me that we must, as educators, find a way to help our students access more pleasurable sensations and emotions in order to have both body and mind working exceptionally well.

8

Understanding and Intervening
with Emotionally Disturbed Students

WHO IS THE EMOTIONALLY
DISTURBED (ED) STUDENT?

Not all students who experience a traumatic event will become traumatized or emotionally disturbed. The presence of well-established and readily utilized resources, whether internal or external, before, during, and after a terrifying event can offset its potential negative impact. Trauma need not be "traumatizing" unless, as defined in the DSM-IV-TR, it elicits a behavioral response of fear, helplessness, or horror, a state suggestive of elements of the freeze/immobility response (Scaer 2001) discussed in previous chapters.

Although not all experiences of trauma lead to traumatization, there is no doubt, following a review of hundreds of ED cases over several years, that a common feature of ED students is that they have been traumatized. Their histories indicate the experience of not just one but many traumatic events. Their symptomatic behaviors involve several of the characteristic features of those associated with posttraumatic stress disorder (PTSD). This should not be surprising. Considering the low level of functioning of these troubled students across domains, it is understandable that their extreme difficulties were preceded by something that shocked or terrified them, often repeatedly or over a prolonged period of time. It is the experience of trauma, when left unresolved, that has the power to alter people's realities and distort their identities; trauma has the power to fragment and ultimately disconnect people from themselves and others (Levine 1997).

The ED student is characterized by extreme disturbances in functioning in one or more areas. Defining features include an inability to build and maintain relationships with peers and adults, as well as the expression of abnormal emotional and behavioral responses under normal circumstances (see chapter 1 for more). These students have histories of depression, anxiety, and/or destructive behaviors that have been resistant to intervention over time. Their difficulties can many times be traced as far back as conception. Caregivers of ED students have reported, for example, that their troubled child was the product of a rape and/or was unwanted from the beginning, a product of an abusive relationship that they want to forget. Several studies have linked unwanted pregnancies and babies with increased rates of both suicide and juvenile criminality in the children who were unwanted (Karr-Morse and Wiley 1997).

Caregivers of ED students have also reported that during infancy and toddlerhood, their troubled child was more sensitive and difficult to soothe than their other children. As toddlers, ED children were often overly active and aggressive toward siblings and playmates. Many did not outgrow tantrum behaviors and continued to wet and/or soil the bed after being potty trained. After entering preschool, these students often have great difficulty because of classroom requirements to interact with peers and comply with teacher demands. This is typically when ED students begin to get noticed.

Depending upon the severity of the students' behaviors among other circumstances, documented interventions usually start in kindergarten with parent conferences and referrals for parenting classes. Positive behavior contracts may be tried and continued when they are effective. Some students benefit from such interventions while others do not. As a result of resistance to intervention over time, a number of these behaviorally challenged students become formally identified and begin receiving a modified educational program through special education. One common scenario leads to formal identification—when students have become a danger to themselves or others by physically attacking or hurting, in some way, themselves or another.

A number of troubled students are helped tremendously by interventions developed specifically for them. Those who benefit may never require identification and support through special education. When identified early as requiring assistance, and when support is received in a timely fashion from both school and home, students with problematic histories sometimes go on to develop normally thereafter. Others benefit only to a degree from intervention and continue to display behaviors on occasion that most educators do not tolerate, such as threats or assaults against them. Despite improvement, when physical assaults continue, most educators consider such progress "limited." Disciplinary transfers to other schools for "fresh starts" may occur before formal assessments are considered. However, if violent behavior persists, such students are likely identified and served in contained classrooms with similarly aggressive students.

The following list includes the signs and symptoms of the ED student. The signs and symptoms listed must be present for a prolonged period of time before they would be considered abnormal, especially if the student has experienced a traumatic event or loss of a loved one within a six-month time frame. The signs and symptoms listed below can often be *normal* responses to abnormal, often unexpected, events. They may dissipate over time with the help of a loving family, a good support network, or some other powerful resource. The signs of ED are as follows:

- lability, volatility, abrupt shifting between emotional states
- anxiety, fear, phobia, paranoia, panic
- infantile behaviors (e.g., tantrums, wetting, or soiling the bed)
- numb, spacey, disoriented, dazed ("emotional anesthesia or deadening" [Terr 1990, 79])
- frenzied, undirected, disorganized behavior
- excessively sad, cries easily
- easily overwhelmed, helpless, gives up
- withdraws, "closes up," "shuts down"
- psychosomatic complaints (e.g., headaches, sore tummies)
- easily startled, hypervigilant
- irritable, low frustration tolerance, sudden rages
- bullies, verbally abuses, physically abuses
- lies, engages in criminal behaviors
- self-destructive, self-mutilates, suicidal ideation
- abuses substances
- "exquisitely sensitive to small insults" (Terr 1990, 64) and being controlled
- preoccupied with death, dying, violence, revenge
- difficulties with speaking, attending, concentrating, remembering, learning
- utterly passive, hopeless
- dissociated, unable to feel pain, attracted to danger and pain
- paranormal thinking, odd behaviors
- excessively angry, guilty, plagued by shame
- sexual acting out

These signs are often evident in ED students from very early ages and progressively get worse with increasing demands and the accumulation of stress over time, especially when not intervened with consistently across settings.

With appropriate and reliable assistance across school and home settings, however, these symptoms can improve and students with early developmental difficulties can lead normal lives.

IMPROVING THE ED ASSESSMENT PROCESS

During the review of hundreds of files of ED students over several years, most striking was the lack of early developmental information provided by assessors in their reports. While a good job was usually done gathering background information and medical information, such facts were often limited to what schools the students attended, and what their vision and hearing was at the time of the assessment. While some psychoeducational reports included a general statement referring to the need to read the nurse's report for developmental information, the nurse's report was often not found in the students' files. In most cases, the reports of the school psychologist and nurse were not combined or attached in any way.

Most frustrating about the lack of inclusion of early developmental information was that, by the end of the report, it was still unclear how the student came to be so troubled. Long descriptions of destructive behaviors displayed by students as young as six years of age were reported, yet there was no sense of why the behaviors were being exhibited. Not knowing how, when, or why their difficulties began translated into not knowing what to do to intervene effectively. Standard practices applied to most students with success were not working with these students. Despite a "full psychoeducational assessment," there still was no sense of what could be done that would work.

In the reports of ED students that *did* include information regarding early development, there was *always* mention of early trauma. School psychologists rarely mentioned the trauma, despite the fact that they are often the professionals who formally identify these students. It was in either the nurse's report or the report from a mental health agency where facts related to early traumas in the lives of these students were provided. This vital information regarding early development belongs in the reports of school psychologists as well (see chapter 3 for more).

Once I learned of the students' histories beginning with conception, not only did I end up with a clear sense of how they became so troubled, but I also knew that certain interventions were going to be more or less effective and more or less harmful. Sharing this information with the students' teachers, administrators, and parents became key in the development of interventions that worked.

THE TRAUMA HISTORIES OF ED STUDENTS

From my extensive review, traumatic events in the histories of ED students included:

- prenatal exposure to drugs, alcohol, and/or cigarettes
- stressful conception and pregnancy involving rape, domestic violence, or death of a loved one
- stressful birth process involving frightening emergency C-section, elevated blood pressure, reduced heart rate, umbilical cord wrapped around the infant's neck, and so on.
- lack of bonding with, and love for, the child (e.g., a number of mothers admitted to hating their sons from the moment they were born because they reminded them of their fathers)
- physical neglect and/or abuse
- witnessing the death of a family member (e.g., numerous ED students I have worked with have seen their family members die of natural causes or violent causes, including being shot in their own home)
- surgeries and other medical procedures with or without general anesthesia and restraint (e.g., enemas and other invasive forms of treatment)
- accidents, falls, and injuries (e.g., an alarming number of students have fallen from second-story balconies between the ages of one and three)
- childhood illnesses (e.g., one parent of an ED student reported that his premature son—born weighing less than two pounds—was "constantly sick" as an infant)
- witnessing street violence (e.g., many students have reported seeing people shot on the street)
- hospitalizations, especially extended stays that involved periods of time when, or specific procedures during which, no loved one could be present
- near-drowning experiences
- marital separation and divorce
- being attacked by an animal

CASE STUDY: EARLY SIGNS OF POTENTIAL ED DUE TO UNRESOLVED TRAUMA

Recall Shante, the eight-year-old third-grade student who had been given a disciplinary transfer to one of my schools due to her repeated problems with teachers and administrators (see chapter 2). According to her previous school,

Shante had a "bad attitude." She was a "master manipulator" and used physical violence to get her way. At my school, Shante's teacher described her as defiant and stubborn on a daily basis. She was out of her seat "constantly" and often "glued" to another student in the class. If the teacher remained at her desk and stood "right there" beside Shante, she could stay in her seat and get her work done. Otherwise, she would avoid class work with psychosomatic complaints. The nurse reported, for instance, that Shante made frequent visits to her office complaining of a sore head or upset tummy.

According to both Shante's teacher and baby-sitter, Shante liked to boss people around. She loved to be praised, hated to feel embarrassed, and engaged in "any power struggle to the end." The teacher also noted that if someone upset Shante, it was as if "the whole world has to come to an end."

I asked the teacher about Shante's resources and strengths and encouraged her to focus on these with Shante in class. She loved to sing and was a good reader. She liked to read aloud in front of the class. I asked the teacher to give Shante opportunities to do so.

The principal let me, as well as Shante's mother, Ms. Brown, know that she would not hesitate to give Shante another disciplinary transfer should the circumstances call for it. This was unacceptable to Ms. Brown. She came to see me, wanting to do whatever she could to prevent any further disruptions to Shante's education.

When I met with Ms. Brown, she told me that her daughter began having behavior problems at the age of two. The problems were so great that she was "kicked out" of her YWCA play school. When she was three and four years of age, Shante had a "rough time" at the Child Development Center she attended. By first and second grade, Ms. Brown reported that Shante was doing "awful." She said that Shante could be doing "fine one minute, the next I don't know what's going on." Two to three times per week, Shante was "throwing tantrums" at home. Ms. Brown stated that "minor things set her off big."

I asked Ms. Brown whether or not Shante had ever experienced a fall, accident, injury, or hospitalization while growing up. Right away, Ms. Brown's face changed. She said, "No one has asked me that before. Yes. Something terrible happened. When Shante was two, she fell from the top bunk of a bunk bed and broke her elbow." Ms. Brown recounted the horror she experienced that day. She said she tried to put a coat on her daughter to be ready for transport to the hospital. When she tried to do so, Shante let out an excruciating scream. She looked down and saw that her two-year-old daughter's elbow was the "size of a lemon." Shante passed out from the pain. Ms. Brown shook her daughter trying to wake her but Shante would not stay conscious for more than seconds at a time. The fire department came and took them to

the hospital. Ms. Brown reported that rather than the firemen being a powerful resource to her and her daughter, they made them feel more afraid than
they already were.

I spoke with Ms. Brown about trauma and its impact on the nervous system. I let her know that it did not just happen to her daughter; it happened to
her too. I helped her understand that she too may have unresolved trauma
reactions easily triggered by minor events. She told me she knew exactly
what I was talking about. I encouraged her to seek the support of her family
and friends in trying to deal with her thoughts, feelings, and sensations
related to what happened. I gave Ms. Brown a handout that would help her
better understand her daughter's needs as a traumatized student. She looked
relieved to have this information and asked why no one had ever talked to her
about this before.

Ms. Brown remembered one more incident she wanted to share with me.
She said that when Shante was three or four years of age, she "went on a
rage" and "attacked" another girl. She specifically remembered how hot
Shante was, how much she was sweating, and how "full of rage" she was.
She said she would never forget seeing her daughter that way. It was Shante's
grandmother who was able to calm Shante down. She simply "held her and
held her until [much later] Shante took a deep breath" and was calm again. I
let Ms. Brown know that that was exactly the right thing to do and that she
could also help Shante in that way when the situation called for it. No unnecessary talking, no trying to stop the tears, just holding until that deep breath
comes and the nervous system settles once again.

Ms. Brown went home with a better understanding of her daughter. The
handout was something she could read at her own pace as many times as she
needed in order to know how best to help Shante. I reassured her that I would
work with Shante at school to help resolve the early trauma she had experienced.

I met with Shante three times on an individual basis. The first time I saw
her I picked her up from the nurse's office where she was complaining of the
front of her head hurting. I brought her to my office and focused on building
her internal resources through grounding and centering exercises. First, I had
her stand in front of me and pretend, like me, that she was a tree. I directed
her to feel her feet planted in the ground like roots of a tree connecting to the
earth. I asked her to stretch her arms into the sky like branches reaching for
the sunshine and swaying in the breeze. As we swayed back and forth like
trees in the wind, strongly connected to the earth, I asked her what she
noticed inside her body. She said her "tummy" was like a "giggly melon."
"That's it," I said, "Just notice how your tummy feels like a giggly melon.

Is that a pleasant feeling or an unpleasant feeling?" She smiled and said it was a "beautiful feeling."

As Shante and I stood face to face, after a few moments of allowing time for her to enjoy the "beautiful feeling," I taught her how to take full deep breaths. I took a deep breath in through my nose and filled my belly up with air. I had her watch my belly so she could see how it filled up when I inhaled. I held the breath for a few seconds and then let it out slowly through my mouth. Shante practiced a few and got better each time.

We moved to the table where I had her draw a picture of what it was like to be a tree planted in the ground with branches stretching up to the sunshine. She drew a picture of an apple tree with flowers and grass, sunshine and clouds, and a bird flying. I asked her where she felt something inside her body when she looked into her picture. She said her "tummy." I asked her what she felt there and she said it felt "smooth." I had her put her hand on her belly for a few minutes and asked her to attend to that smooth feeling. She left my office after about forty-five minutes, smiling and skipping.

I saw Shante six days later. I had her start by drawing a picture of something she was good at. She drew a picture of herself skipping rope. I had her look at the picture and notice what she felt inside her body. She said, "My tummy hurts." I asked her to tell me more about her tummy and how it hurt. "What does the hurt feel like?" I asked. "A rock," she answered. I asked for details about the rock to help her stay with what was happening in her stomach. "Does it have a color or a size?" "Yes," she said, "It's big and gray." "I see. It's big and gray," I said. "That's it. I'm right here with you. Just notice how your tummy feels like there's a big gray rock inside."

I allowed a few moments for Shante to be with the hurt in her tummy reminding her that I was right there with her. After a few moments, her tummy still hurt so I asked her to remember how she was a tree with her feet planted in the ground. I reminded her of the sunshine on her face. Then I asked her what else she noticed in her body. She said she felt "strong." I asked her where and she said in her "legs." "That's it," I said, "Notice how strong you feel in your legs." I allowed time for her to be with that feeling. When I asked her again about the rock in her stomach, she said it was smaller and did not hurt as much.

After a few moments, I gave Shante a picture of a silhouette of a body with a grid on it. She colored in the silhouette according to the grid what she was feeling. She felt "soft" in her head and face and "flowing" in her tummy with the exception of one small black circle that she drew in the center of her stomach. The "gray rock" was still there but it was now very small. I did some deep breathing with Shante for a few moments and then had her draw another picture. This time it was a picture of how she liked to be comforted.

Shante drew a picture of two things. She drew herself at home taking a bath, and then one of her vacuuming. I reminded Shante of how she could take deep breaths in class or on the playground before she got upset and how she could remember her roots planted in the earth with the sun shining on her face.

Four days later I checked with the nurse who reported that Shante was doing "much better" and not going to her office as frequently. After another five days, I learned from the teacher that the main residual issue was defiance. The mother was helping with that, however, and it was getting better. I saw Shante one last time.

Shante and I reviewed the grounding and breathing exercises we had done together before. She drew a picture of a happy time in her life. She drew herself playing ball with a friend. I had Shante look at the picture she drew and notice what she felt inside her body as she looked at it. Then I gave her a silhouette and asked her to color in what she felt inside. She drew orange on her face and head, reporting that she felt warm there. I allowed time for Shante to feel into her sensations and as she did, something very important happened. Her head started to move back and forth slowly and her eyes began rolling into the back of her head. I did not interrupt what was happening. I simply stated quietly, "That's it, Shante. I'm right here with you."

As I watched Shante's head move very specifically, I was struck with a sense that this was how her head and eyes must have moved when she went in and out of consciousness during the accident. After a few moments of Shante looking like she could pass out, although she remained conscious and seated at the table, she yawned widely. I kept my hand on her upper midback and said, "That's it. You're doing great, Shante." She took several short breaths and then one large deep breath seemed to take her. She became more alert and oriented back to the room. I asked her if she was okay. She said yes. I had her rest a few moments. Then I reviewed with her all the beautiful pictures she drew and acknowledged her hard work. I told her she could come back and see me anytime.

Shante stopped going to the nurse's office completely. I referred her and her mother to a community agency to help with some of the bad habits that had been formed over the years they struggled to understand the situation. It took awhile for those services to commence but in the meantime, Shante did not report any more psychosomatic complaints and was doing much better in class and on the playground. Well over a year after Shante and I worked together, the nurse remarked what a different girl she was. She said that Shante had become a pleasure to talk to and be around. The community agency involved with Shante and her mother reported that, after a year of counseling involving play and art work, their services were being decreased due to excellent progress.

Shante was a student who had been well on her way to becoming identified as ED. She had a history of behavior problems commencing at the age of two that had been resistant to the interventions commonly put into place for "difficult" students. Parent conferences were held at the play school, the Child Development Center, and Shante's schools when she was in kindergarten and first grade. She was put on behavior contracts and counseled by her teachers and school counselors. She was given "fresh starts" at new schools. Without taking a history of trauma with the mother, however, we did not know how to intervene in the best way possible. We did not understand who Shante was and what her specific needs were. One meeting with the parent, one meeting with the teacher, and three individual sessions with Shante helped to turn her life around. The support of counseling from a community agency assisted Shante not only in maintaining her physiological gains of a more balanced nervous system but also in achieving the additional goal of decreasing defiance.

Not everyone is as fortunate as Shante. We often get to students too late. We fail to ask the right questions. We continue to misunderstand. We do not yet appreciate that our interventions need to take into account trauma's impact on the nervous system. From years of working with ED students closely, I have learned that they are traumatized, they are misunderstood, and they are being harmed by some of the practices we have put into place on their account.

HOW WE MISUNDERSTAND THE ED STUDENT

A Physiological, Not Psychological Problem

We tend to think of the problems of ED students as "psychological," "non-physiological," or "functional," requiring psychological intervention in the form of talk therapy or traditional counseling, anger management being the most common—and most inadequate—approach for these students. To believe that anger is their primary problem is to completely miss the mark. Anger is most glaring, certainly. It is most bothersome to us as educators probably. However, it is only symptomatic of what is actually ailing these students and is not a wise focus of intervention (more on this later). A review of the histories of these students helps to correct this common misunderstanding.

The developmental histories of ED students tell us that the primary source of their problems is the significant trauma and loss they have experienced.

Trauma is not a psychological but a physiological event that can result in demonstrable and dynamic neurophysiological changes in the brain. As we accumulate more and more evidence verifying the physiological implications of trauma, we come to understand that many of the chronic, unexplained diseases that we treat so ineffectively are based on a variation of autonomic dysregulation based on cumulative life trauma (Scaer 2001). As Dr. Scaer noted in his work *The Body Bears the Burden: Trauma, Dissociation, and Disease*, a whole new paradigm for prevention and intervention based on this growing body of evidence is called for.

In accordance with educational law, educators list all the ways in which students were intervened with, within general education, before consideration of special education. In order to designate students as ED, we must first demonstrate that we made multiple attempts to assist them, and that the help failed. What we know by virtue of the designation is that what we did for the students over time—and what we continue to do routinely—did not work. Without understanding them, without knowing their trauma histories and the impact of trauma on their neurophysiology, we cannot help them. Research on trauma and the developing brain over the past ten to fifteen years, however, is changing this. Educators not only deserve to have, but also need, this important information. With it, we can understand and know what to do. Without it, we cannot be efficacious with the students who need us the most.

ED Not LD (Learning Disabled)

I recently had a conversation with a special education facilitator who was concerned that school psychologists do not habitually test students for learning disabilities when they assess for ED. He argued for the need to rule out cognitive and learning deficits as root causes of behavioral and emotional problems. Perhaps a better placement for behaviorally acting-out students with learning difficulties is a contained classroom for students with learning disabilities as opposed to a contained classroom for students with ED, he stated. While I agreed with him that it is important to rule out mental retardation and borderline intellectual development as contributing factors to behavior problems when assessing for ED, which school psychologists routinely do, it is dangerous to conclude that delays in academic achievement cause acting out (or acting in) of such proportions.

For school psychologists assessing students who are potentially ED, it is a matter of recognizing the severity of the behaviors and prioritizing the intervention. While I agreed with the facilitator that learning problems may contribute to behavior problems, I disagreed with him about the need to consider these the priority of our interventions, which is what we do when we consider placing acting-out students in classrooms for students with cognitive and learning deficits. Learning disabilities are not the root cause of the extremes of the behaviors we see with ED students. Such "chicken and egg" debates are quickly settled when detailed developmental histories of these students are taken. Failing to do so is how we become subject to confusion about which behaviors preceded others.

A detailed developmental history always reveals the presence or absence of early problems with the physiological mechanism of self-regulation so important to the management of both behavior and learning over time. Lack of self-regulation in students commencing in infancy and toddlerhood is precisely what interferes with the development and expression of age-appropriate behavior and ultimately, in some cases, with learning.

During our conversation, I reminded the facilitator that it is unethical to assess a student in an area that is not an "area of suspected disability." In my experience, school psychologists inquire at the onset of their assessment whether or not academics are an additional concern to the behaviors of a potential ED student. What we find is that a great number of ED students are smart, capable learners with relatively well-developed reading, writing, and math skills. Those with delays in academic achievement are often not learning disabled. They have delays because their behaviors consistently interfered with their ability to access their academic program across time. Their inability to self-regulate their behavior and affect interfered with their learning.

When we see a history of extreme disturbances in behavior and affect that remained resistant to intervention over time, we intervene with the behaviors first. This is best practice. Behavioral, social, and emotional stabilization will only aid students in accessing their educational program, bridging the gap between their intellect and achievement when such a gap exists.

Conduct Disorder Is ED

Students with conduct disorders are not "truly" emotionally disturbed and do not benefit from interventions developed for ED students. This statement has been made liberally for all the years I have been a school psychologist and is a disservice to the students we serve. We are educators, not clinicians. Students are either in need of intervention for extreme behaviors or they are not.

In handbooks on the practice of school psychology all over the country, we are given an outline of the criteria for ED eligibility that is based on educational law. We need only follow this outline to determine whether or not a student is ED and in need of the interventions designed to help ED students. If the unlawful and destructive behaviors of conduct disordered students do not warrant consideration of ED eligibility and services, then I do not know which behaviors do.

As we saw from the review of the histories of ED students, early developmental information gathered on conduct disordered students reveals that they were toddlers and young students who were unregulated in their behavior, often with a clinical picture that started with and/or progressed to ADHD, ODD, and depression. Such behavioral profiles easily meet the criteria for ED we are given as educational assessors. It is unlawful to deny them both the assessment and the designation. A "truly" ED student is one who meets the criteria set forth by state and federal educational law, and conduct-disordered students certainly do.

Gas on a Fire

It is a common belief that antidepressant and/or stimulant medication will ease ED symptoms of ADHD, anger/rage, depression, and anxiety. While some medications help some ED students, there are students who get worse with psychotropic drugs. For example, studies have revealed that some students become suicidal, sometimes homicidal, in the early stages of treatment with antidepressant medication. Depending upon the makeup of the students, side effects of some medications can cause further and unnecessary suffering. What often happens with ED students, as well as with general education students who are traumatized, is that their symptoms of anxiety and hypervigilance are hastily interpreted by psychiatrists as hyperactivity and paranoia. When the latter symptoms are treated rather than the former, the medications typically prescribed do not lead to relief of the actual ailment and in many cases exacerbate the problem.

While DSM-IV-TR diagnoses are not required to become designated as an ED student, educators rely on the help of psychiatrists and psychologists with this population of students. As a community, we need to do a better job of recognizing the difference between similar-looking symptoms, like those just described (anxiety and hypervigilance versus hyperactivity and paranoia). Taking a detailed developmental history helps us to understand symptoms within their context. Without context, grave errors are made. Many of our students, ED or not, suffer from some degree of posttraumatic stress and are not being treated for it.

There are many reasons ED students are misdiagnosed. Many medical and mental health professionals do not yet know about the significant impact of trauma on the brain and nervous system. They often do not ask about history and simply want to know about current symptoms. Some do not yet know what can be potentially traumatizing to children in particular. Even when trauma is recognized by practitioners, children must meet the exact criteria for PTSD in order to be diagnosed and treated for posttraumatic stress. If children have many but not all of the symptoms of PTSD, another diagnosis and treatment regimen is provided, usually for ADHD, ODD, or depression. Their hypervigilance is mistaken for hyperactivity, their freeze responses are mistaken for defiance, and their grief from the traumatic losses they have experienced is mistaken for depression. As educators, we feel helpless as we watch the medication cocktails these students receive do more harm than good.

ADHD is passed on genetically in at least 50 percent of all cases (Karr-Morse and Wiley 1997). It is one hypothesis that these are the students who are helped most readily by traditional forms of medication treatment for the condition. In the other 50 percent of cases involving pre- and perinatal stress and trauma, such traditional medications may not only be ineffective but also harmful. As a community of professionals working for children, we need to work together carefully to gather detailed developmental information and provide feedback about how students are responding to various medications. Currently, it is a rare event for a physician or psychiatrist to communicate with the school about how a student is behaving before and after commencing a medication. It is rare that they consider trauma histories and therefore alternative medications to psychostimulants or antidepressants for what may only *appear* as ADHD.

Psychostimulants are generally for students who are overly active. Antidepressants are typically for students who are on the opposite end of that spectrum (although agitated depression is common in children). Traumatized students often fluctuate between these two states. They shift rapidly from one state to another, from overly active to shut down and withdrawn. Medications that treat a nervous system dysregulation, an inability to self-regulate internally between states, may be a better alternative for our ED students than either psychostimulants or antidepressants.

When the medical assessments of these students are thorough and accurate, including a consideration of their trauma histories, medication treatment can be tailored with greater accuracy. As more and more evidence that makes clear the neurophysiological impact of trauma is distributed to the medical community, it is my steadfast hope that doctors and mental health practitioners alike will adjust their treatments accordingly. Our students as well as the field of education will benefit greatly from such an adjustment.

WHAT DOES *NOT* WORK WITH ED STUDENTS

Anger Management

Anger management is a cognitive approach that does not intervene with the whole student. It requires students to use their rational minds to overpower their instinctual drives for survival and "make better choices." Students are encouraged to think about the ABCs of anger—the antecedents or triggers of anger, the behaviors that stem from anger, and the consequences of those behaviors. Anger-management training encourages students to understand the myriad of emotions that underlie the "tip of the iceberg" that anger is. Students are helped to recognize how disproportionate their responses to a trigger are. They are taught to scale their reactions from one to ten and find just the right match between how angry they get and how radically they respond. Numerous cognitive calculations are required in the heat of the moment in order for students to successfully manage their problems with anger, and once they have received anger management training they are expected to do so with efficiency.

By the time ED students have been formally identified, they know the anger-management curriculum by heart. In fact, I have seen firsthand how they humor school psychologists and counselors alike by regurgitating the curriculum back to them. They know what their group leaders expect, just as they do when participating in social skills training. It is not that anger management and social skills training programs do not have value. They simply do not work with these particular students.

No single cognitive approach to teaching self-management skills comes close to understanding the power of the energy alive in students who frequently feel as though their very survival is being threatened. Until we get that about ED students, we will not intervene with much effect. The fears of ED students, whether rational or not, are residuals left in the nervous system from traumatic experiences that, on a daily basis, continue to be triggered. They are led by their hyperarousal to reenact what they heard, saw, or experienced that was so shocking. Only a psychophysiological approach that recognizes the need to balance out the nervous system will help these students modulate arousal levels so that they are both tolerable and manageable.

Reasoning

Just as anger management is too cognitive for ED students, reasoning with these students also appeals to the cognitive part of their brain. Not only do we try to reason with them but we also try to reason with them in the heat of the moment. When there has just been an incident and students' nervous systems are in overwhelm, we remind them that we told them this would happen. We seize the opportunity to scold and demand answers to our questions because this is, after all, a teaching moment. "Don't you know what you did is wrong? Don't you want to do things differently? Didn't we talk about this? Didn't you say you would turn your day around?" Or we say things like,

"Why did you do it? You know you need to make better choices. If you would just make better choices, you would have a better day." It makes sense to us to say these things. We want to seize the teaching moments of our day, but once we know how the brain works, we realize that this kind of responding does not make sense after all.

Our logic actually defies our work with these students. We think that because students were upset over an incident earlier in the day and seemed genuinely sorry about it they naturally would not cause a similar incident to happen later in the day. Logically, it is true that we would not expect the regretful student to repeat his or her reprimanded behavior. Why would they continue to make the same mistakes right after they felt such genuine shame about them in the first place? The answer is trauma. Reenactment is a powerful part of the physiology of our traumatized students.

Power Struggles

ED teachers who become triggered by their students' words and deeds fare poorly over time, and so do their students. It happens. Teachers' buttons get pushed, naturally. We are human after all. We are tired, frustrated, and fresh out of ideas. Our own nervous system revs high. That is what happens in a room full of troubled students. ED teachers, not unlike most other professionals, do not yet understand how what we are taught on airplanes needs to be applied to everyday life. We need to first put on our own oxygen masks before trying to assist others.

Like many of us, ED teachers do not fully appreciate the importance of drawing from their own well of resources so they can function with their students from a healthy, balanced place. The volume gets high in ED classrooms. Teachers engage in power struggles with their students, yelling, threatening, and waving their finger. We think this is going to get us somewhere, or at least we try to reassure ourselves of that, when in fact we are simply out of control.

ED students are harmed by power struggles. Yelling at them, threatening or provoking them, raises their arousal and anxiety levels to such a degree that their brain and nervous system become further entrenched in fight or flight. The times we think we have made progress because we have yelled and threatened are times of wishful thinking. Our threat may quiet a student for a moment but that moment may actually be the student in "freeze." We now know that students freeze or dissociate when arousal becomes too great. They develop a spacey quality or have a dazed look on their face. It is temporary. Students come out of freeze eventually, and when they do, the fight or flight energy is not only still there but magnified.

Time-Out

Time-out is currently being used as a punitive measure that can serve to humiliate students and send them deeper into a state of shame, not just a psychological state of shame but also a physiological one. Drs. Bruce Perry and Dan Siegel talk about this state as a collapse in the nervous system that feeds into an overall state of general helplessness and hopelessness. We tell ourselves that shame is good because it helps us teach right from wrong, and this can be true for young toddlers. In our ED students, however, and traumatized students in general, shame acts as a catalyst for greater despair and more acting out.

In older students, and in adults, shame feeds the cycle of aggression. Students come to feel so innately and deeply "bad" about themselves that they give up. They act in ways that are consistent with their poor self-image. As educators, we need to offset their negative beliefs about themselves by reminding them of their healthy side, by nurturing their healthy side.

Time-out, the way we are currently and most commonly using it, reminds students of their now well-worn label of "bad" boy or "bad" girl. They come to accept that they are banished to time-out because they *are* "bad," "bad" is who they are. They do not deserve the goodness others enjoy. Deeply rooted shame lives inside ED students and drives them to act out in various ways in order not to feel anything anymore. Of course, this only leaves them feeling a greater sense of shame because of the acts they continue to commit that contribute to those feelings. The process defies logic, but that is just the point. Logic does not explain these students. Logic does not work with these students. Their rational mind is on hiatus when their instinctive mind is working overtime. We must meet these students where they are.

Loss of Points/Privileges

Once ED students—and other behaviorally troubled students—earn something, it should never be taken away. They do not possess the self-regulation it requires to learn or recover from such a loss. They are not readily able to bounce back and earn again what was lost. It is a big deal when they earn something. Once lost, that which was earned actually becomes a source of great fury, further shame, and degradation. We have to let them have something. I am not suggesting that we freely give rewards and honors away. Of course they must earn them. Once earned, however, it is vital to their sense of worth to be allowed to keep them.

We have to get off the bandwagon that wants to shame these students, teach them a lesson, and make them accountable like everybody else. If we have not yet noticed, these students are not like everybody else. They require an immense amount of compassion, our immediate forgiveness, and the right to keep what they have earned fairly and squarely. Obviously, the natural consequence for inappropriate behavior is the loss of the potential to earn something more by acting more appropriately. The disappointment of a loving teacher is a consequence. The shame that already lives and breathes deeply and securely within them is a consequence. Consequences are important for these students. It is not helpful to remove them. However, there are other ways to provide consequences without taking from them what they have already earned.

Talking

Talking at students when they are having a "meltdown" is destructive. It keeps students highly aroused and in fight or flight longer than necessary. Talking at them during these fragile times prolongs and intensifies the agony for everyone involved. When ED students are kicking and screaming and requiring restraint, that is *not* the time to be talking into their ear, reminding them of how they were warned this would happen. "I told you if you didn't calm down I would have to do this. This is what happens when you do not follow the rules. Hitting and kicking is not tolerated. I am going to have to call your mother now. Just relax. Calm down and I'll let you go." Words, words, words.

Words are processed and understood by the cognitive brain. The cognitive brain is shut down during "meltdowns." Students in this fragmented state, much like the everyday state of traumatized students, are operating largely from the instinctive, reptilian brain. They cannot process language in these moments, or cognitively reason, or "use better judgment," even though this is precisely what we like to require them to do. We have to change our ways. We must understand these students better and find more effective ways to intervene.

Punching a Pillow

I recently read a book that was written for parents and educators about anxious students who can, at times, take their frustration out on others, a quality of many ED students. In fact, several authors have written about ED students without knowing it necessarily. Authors have written about the anxious child, the hyperactive child, the inattentive child, the explosive child—also known by one author as the "easily frustrated, chronically inflexible" child—the bipolar child, the depressed child, the scared child, the list goes on. In their descriptions, the authors frequently capture at least some part of ED students. That is because ED students can be any or all of these things depending upon the time of day, how they slept the night before, what happened in their families recently, or what is being expected of them in any given moment.

While the specific symptoms may vary day to day, moment to moment, what these students have in most common as a group is their alternation between periods of overactivity and periods of exhaustion as their body suffers the effects of traumatic hyperarousal of the autonomic nervous system (Rothschild 2000). When students alternate in this way, they exhibit behaviors that look like hyperactivity, depression, and inattentiveness, but are they best conceptualized as students with ADHD or depression? Are they best treated as students with ADHD or depression? With all the new knowledge we now have of who these students are, don't our interventions need to change accordingly?

The author of the book on the anxious student encouraged parents and educators to allow their students to take their anxiety and frustration out on a pillow. We have heard of such advice for decades. The approach is supposed to have a cathartic effect relieving students of the built-up energy they experience in their body, but it does not. In fact, the approach can be dangerous. It can reinforce the cycles between hyperarousal and exhaustion as described in *The Body Remembers: The Psychophysiology of Trauma and Trauma Treatment* (Rothschild 2000). When these cycles are reinforced, the neural patterns in the brain that support them become further entrenched and embedded and therefore more difficult to change.

While students may look like they have experienced some relief from punching a pillow, look more closely. They are likely spacey or dazed as a result of dissociating from such a high level of arousal. Their nervous system has likely collapsed with exhaustion. Such physiological scenarios do not promote lasting change. Any apparent gains are short-lived as students become drawn to punching the pillow over and over again to experience that brief moment of "relief"—when, in fact, they are reenacting previous traumas, thereby strengthening maladaptive circuitry in the brain.

WHAT WORKS WITH ED STUDENTS

A Quiet Safe Place

Whether it is in the classroom or the school psychologist's office, it is important for all students, especially ED students, to feel safe and to experience quiet, compassionate space. Loud music or voices, especially yelling, can keep the arousal levels of ED students high. Even though the students themselves may get loud and yell at others, it is important that the adults who surround them do not contribute to this increase in volume. We need to model for our students that everyone will have a chance to be heard even when we are speaking quietly.

In my years visiting numerous ED classrooms, I have always been struck by the difference in volume in different rooms. I have never witnessed a loud teacher with quiet students or loud students with a quiet teacher. In my experience, I have seen students match their teachers over time. I have witnessed quiet rooms with calm teachers (despite expected loud outbursts from specific incidents) and loud rooms with highly aroused students and teachers who raise their voice frequently. It was obvious which students were getting more work done.

Compassionate Containment

Many times ED students benefit from physical proximity to an adult, especially when the adult is calm and contained. In fact, before they were identified as ED, these were the students described by teachers as needing someone to stand right there next to them in order to behave appropriately and get work done. The highly aroused nervous system of traumatized students is calmed and contained by the boundaries provided by another person's physical closeness. There is a calm and a balance that is palpable to them when they experience the presence of another.

Bruce Perry has done extensive research illustrating what happens in the brain when we are in close physical proximity to others. The brain and nervous system are soothed by social, interpersonal experiences (Perry 2003). This is one way to differentiate between the ADHD and traumatized student. I have found that ADHD students will often continue to have difficulty managing themselves even when an adult is right beside them, whereas traumatized students are almost immediately soothed by such a presence.

Caring, *Calm* Teachers

"A quiet safe place" and "compassionate containment" can only be provided by adults who successfully manage their own stress levels. Teachers need to balance their own nervous system with resources and experiences that increase rather than diminish their energy and well-being. This is one of the biggest pieces missing for many ED students. Especially in ED classrooms do we have teachers who are extremely challenged by not just one or a few of our most difficult students, but up to eighteen of them in one room. Resources for these teachers are few compared to the needs of the students.

We do not do enough to support and train them, not only on how to help their students but also on how to help themselves.

A balanced life is a balanced nervous system. When I have provided in-service training to special education teachers and teacher aides, this is the topic that interests them the most. They ask numerous questions about how to stay balanced and how to resource themselves in order to do a better job with their students. They line up to say how rare and important such a discussion is. They want support for their own self-care because of its direct impact on students.

Students, especially those who are ED, rely on experiencing balance in others in order to have even a glimpse of it for themselves. Educators who continue to believe that what they feel inside will not have an impact on their students, especially because they think they hide it so well, are kidding themselves and ultimately doing a disservice to their students. When we stand before an upset student and counsel them and get frustrated that they are not getting it and listening and calming down, it may be best during those moments to ask ourselves how well we are getting it and listening and calming down.

Community and Belonging

Building a family in the ED classroom, and reminding students that each of them is an invaluable member of that family, has been one of my most positive experiences with these students. Over time, and it does take time, when consistently reminded that they are part of something, they begin to respond in positive ways.

Speaking to students from the time they enter the classroom about being a community in which everyone helps everyone else, where people take care of each other, and where we build each other up instead of tear each other down is very important. They are reminded that their community or family stands for compassion, forgiveness, fresh starts, and chances to repair whatever damage gets done. Students need to be shown how they belong to something important and special, to a group of people who see their value and reinforce their goodness.

Boundaries, Rules, Regulations, and Predictable Consequences

All students need healthy limits and boundaries. ED students, with their high levels of arousal, require firm yet flexible boundaries that allow them a certain amount of room to move. Although they will test these boundaries, whining, complaining, negotiating, throwing tantrums, even resorting to physical violence to get away with breaking the rules and regulations, what they really crave is the containment that limits provide.

Every ED room needs an "if-then" chart posted in everyone's view. The chart can outline exactly what will happen as a consequence whenever a listed unacceptable behavior is performed. It cannot matter who performed it, when they performed it, or how much they whine and manipulate after they perform it. The listed consequence that corresponds to the listed behavior must happen each and every time with 100 percent predictability. We cannot create safe environments that compassionately contain troubled students without this. The more ED students can predict their environment, the safer they feel.

Opportunities to Earn Rewards That Will Not Be Taken Away

Developing a sense of competency, value, worth, pride, satisfaction, self-efficacy, strength, and resilience all depend upon the ability to earn positive recognition. Taking away the very things that represent for students the fact that they have been positively acknowledged is to tip the scales of balance of the nervous system not in the needed direction of greater resource, but in the direction of greater trauma. ED students can completely decompensate in frightening ways when both their deep sense of shame and impulse to collapse are triggered by the loss of what they have earned.

Time-Away

Time-outs are important for ED students (and the adults who care for them). They need to be provided as a resource in a compassionate rather than punitive way. We need to normalize their need for assistance with calming and soothing, and then provide them with the opportunity to calm and soothe in a caring and sympathetic way.

Few Words

When the nervous system is aroused or overactivated, one of the best things we can do to help decompress the situation is to say very few words. The few words we use should simply remind students that they are okay and that everything will be all right. We can gently tell them to take their time and rest, that they are not alone, and that someone who cares about them is right

there with them. Other than that, no words should be spoken, especially con-
demning words, critical words, or statements of frustration and reprimand.

TISHA

One kindergartner I worked with briefly years ago had a difficult time transitioning from recess back into the classroom, usually as the result of having
perceived a threat on the playground. Small things, such as having to share
a ball, caused meltdowns. Once upset, Tisha simply could not move from
outside to inside when required. She often clung to the fence with all of
her might so that no one could carry her inside against her will.

When I was notified that this had been happening, and went to the
playground to intervene, Tisha was clinging to the fence with streams of
tears running down her face. I went to her calmly and quietly and held
her. I said very little except, "It's okay to cry, Tisha. It's good to cry sometimes. Just let it all out. You don't have to stop. I'll be right here with you
until you don't need me anymore." I paused at length between my statements. I spoke calmly and quietly. I did not try to stop the process she was
in. The stress Tisha was experiencing needed to be released. I provided
her with containment, reassurance, and time. I reminded her that she
could take the time she needed. I had her notice what she felt inside her
body, if she felt hot or stiff (I could feel how hot and stiff she was). I let her
know her body was doing what it needed to do and we would stay
together until it was done.

It took approximately fifteen minutes before a huge breath came over
her and a great settling happened. I stayed with my own body taking deep
grounding breaths as I waited for her to pull away from me rather than
taking away my physical containment before she was ready. When she
was ready, she let go of me and looked up into my eyes. I smiled at her
and she smiled back. She took my hand and said she was ready to go back
to class. I went with her and watched her settle back comfortably.

After speaking with the teachers about Tisha's need for quiet time and
space with few words during meltdowns, they never needed to call me
again. A few months later, I was in the class to check on other students.
She saw me and waved, flashing her big beautiful smile. According to her
teachers, she had been transitioning easily from recess to the classroom for
several weeks.

Chances to Start Over

Repair is an important concept that needs to be put into action in an ED classroom. Once an incident is over and students have had the opportunity to

decompress, they need help to repair the damage done by their words or actions. They need to be helped to see that they made a mistake, that mistakes happen, and that there is a way to make up for them.

Students can be supported and reinforced as they apologize or share a valued object, or extend kindness in some other way. Students need help to see that their mistakes, although not always intentional, hurt other people's feelings, and make everyone involved feel embarrassed, ashamed, afraid, sad, guilty, or angry. This is a time to reinforce what the classroom community stands for and to remind the members of the community that it is not okay to make people feel that way. The community stands for building people up, supporting, forgiving, extending kindness, and treating people with respect.

Once the repair is complete, ED students need chances to start over and start fresh. Not in a different classroom or different school but in the same classroom at the same school. They need to be reminded that they belong, they have a "home," and they will be supported and encouraged as they continue to do the best they can from that point forward.

Positive Acknowledgment and Encouragement

As much as teachers believe in the need for positively acknowledging their students, this is one principle that many admit to failing to do often enough. I recently had a meeting with a teacher who said that it was so good to hear again the importance of not just ignoring minor irritations in the classroom but also actively pointing out and reinforcing appropriate and desired behaviors. She said that she had not heard about that "approach" since she had been in college and had forgotten its importance. Later, she shared with me that her relationship with the troubled student we met about radically changed after that meeting, beginning in the hours of the first day she put the approach into practice.

Success and Competency

Drs. Judith Herman and Bessel van der Kolk have extensively documented the need traumatized individuals have for both safety and competence in order to offset the impact of trauma. According to many researchers, the need for resources is biological (Perry 2003; Schore 2003; Siegel 2003). Traumatic events cannot be renegotiated or resolved without the neurophysiological support that comes from safety and competence. They change the brain.

As educators, we have a unique and powerful chance to help students feel safe and competent. We can create safe environments that provide plentiful opportunities for success for our students, even if it is for just six hours a day.

Six hours a day every day for 180 days a year means something. That can translate into something powerful for our students. When we hold the intention daily to create safety and the opportunity for the development of competence in our classrooms, we will see our ED students shine.

Building Resources, External and Internal

Safety and competency are resources. They are something students can feel on the outside, and most importantly on the inside. As we get to know our students better, we develop a sense of what resources they have access to and what resources they need but are missing. Taking a resource inventory on each ED student can be helpful. What strengths do they possess and draw upon when they need to? Who do they have in their lives that they can count on? What do they do daily that they are good at and feel good about? Part of our jobs in ED classrooms is to help students access their resources and develop others that are not so readily available. This is how we tip the scales of their nervous system in the healing direction, toward greater calm, balance, and optimal alertness.

Bodily Sensations as Resources

Rarely are students educated about, or reminded of, the comfort that can come from inside their physical body, from connecting with their body. Introducing to them the language of sensations can get them connected to this rich internal world. This is not easy. Some students (like adults) do everything they can to *not* feel their body because it can be a source of such pain and discomfort. However, when we help students access and experience comfortable sensations, they come to learn that the body is not only less frightening than they thought, but also a great source of safety and strength.

Communication with Parents that Emphasizes Strengths

Conversations with parents of ED students need to be positive as much as possible. Often, these parents are called to hear complaints about their child, how their child acted up again and did poorly somehow. We damage the potential for parents to be a resource to us as well as to their children when our calls emphasize problems rather than solutions, weaknesses rather than strengths, and failures rather than successes. The simple phrase "what we focus on expands" may serve us well to keep in mind as we work with these students and their families. The healthy side of ED students may only be a seed when they first enter the classroom—but if that seed is watered and nurtured, it will grow.

9

Self-Regulation Therapy

Whether ED or not, many of our most troubled students will benefit from the suggestions of the previous chapter as well as self-regulation therapy (SRT).

SELF-REGULATION DEFINED

Self-regulation involves the shifting from one bodily state to another. For example, students may get anxious or excited about an event or situation, and then experience a natural relaxation response that calms them and keeps their arousal levels within a manageable range. Arousal levels involve both sensations and feelings. The ability to tolerate them is important to every task involved in education, including attention, learning, and behavior.

In order to attend, concentrate, and perform tasks in a manner suitable to situational demands, the nervous system must be in an optimal state of arousal (Mercer and Snell 1977). It is only within an optimal state that the assimilation and integration of information is possible.

When we are too anxious, nervous, or afraid, we cannot focus, retain, or perform at our best, just as we cannot when our arousal levels are too low. Like any of us, students perform optimally when moderately aroused. Self-regulation is what keeps students within this manageable and motivating range of arousal.

Self-regulation is driven and mediated by the right hemisphere of the brain. The right orbitofrontal or prefrontal cortex in particular has been identified as responsible for coordinating the two branches of the autonomic nervous system (ANS) (Schore 2003) involved in self-regulation. It is between these two ANS branches, the sympathetic and parasympathetic, that regulation occurs. As mediated by the right brain, the body shifts naturally between more or less relaxed states and more or less excited states depending on how the environment has been, and is, experienced.

In students with a history of relatively normal development there is a natural ebb and flow between the two ANS branches. They may hear an alarming sound that revs the autonomic branch of the ANS, but their orbitofrontal cortex likely identifies the source of the noise as unthreatening and signals the parasympathetic branch to commence a relaxation response. Self-regulation is the ability of the brain-body to work in concert in this way enabling adaptive responses to the environment.

Mary Sue Williams and Sherry Shellenberger, creators of the "Alert Program for Self-Regulation," define self-regulation as the ability to attain, maintain, and change arousal appropriately for a task or situation (Williams and Shellenberger 1996). This is such a critical ability that experts across fields are now recognizing it as what allows us to perform effectively in society. Two such experts have emphasized its importance by stating that in one sense we can consider the whole of child development to be the enhancement of self-regulation (Fonagy and Target 2002).

THE DEVELOPMENT OF SELF-REGULATION

There is a right-brain growth spurt from the last trimester of pregnancy through to the end of the second year of life. The right brain is deeply connected with the limbic system, and, in fact, drives its functioning. The limbic system has three key structures, each important to our understanding of the development of self-regulation: the amygdala, the cingulate, and the orbitofrontal cortex.

At birth, we have only our amygdalas. This is why we are entirely dependent on our caregivers to modulate and regulate our arousal levels in order for our brain to develop normally. The cingulate and orbitofrontal cortex, among other important brain structures, help us to regulate independently of our caregivers, but these only develop later. The attachment relationship and the quality of the interactions that occur between infant and caregiver are vital to normal, healthy development of these and all brain structures.

The volume of the brain increases rapidly during the first two years of life. All major fiber tracts connecting brain regions to support their efficient communication are developed by the age of three. With this amount of brain growth occurring within the first few years of life, it is as essential to healthy development what happens during these years as what happens during pregnancy.

In past decades, we have been educated about the importance of taking care of ourselves during pregnancy in order to prevent harm to the developing infant. We now know, however, that it is as important what we do in the first few years after birth as during gestation. All brain development that occurs during the first years of life is heavily dependent on the quality of transactions between caregiver and infant. Whereas the proliferation of cells in the brain is genetically driven, the pruning of cells (sculpting or thinning down of cells) is environmentally driven. This pruning process, so readily impacted by trauma, is hypothesized to have a direct impact on the development of self-regulation, determining whether or not it will function normally (Schore 2003).

At ten to twelve months of age, the development of the right orbitofrontal cortex begins and continues until the end of the second year of life. This higher cortical structure comes to regulate the already existing and operating lower structure, the amygdala, moving infants over time from a dependency status for regulation to more of an independent status. With appropriate attachment and support from their caregivers immediately after birth and during the critical period of development of the orbitofrontal cortex, infants come to possess the capacity to regulate themselves. This is what happens when the axons connecting the amygdala to the orbitofrontal cortex are sufficiently pruned or thinned down.

The pruning, sculpting, or thinning down of neural networks in the postnatal brain is negatively impacted by early traumatic environments (Schore 2003). When infants experience repeated or prolonged fear, over time their amygdala stops ceasing to fire the neural signal of danger to the rest of the body. When it is "turned on" repeatedly, it eventually fails to "turn off" producing the kindling effect discussed in chapter 5. Kindling is thought to cause excessive pruning. The axons from the orbitofrontal cortex going down to the amygdala become too thinned down. As a result, the amygdala does not come under the control of the higher cortical system as intended, thereby reducing the infants' capacities to self-regulate.

There is support for the hypothesis that "relational trauma," or the occurrence of repeatedly poor attachment and interaction behaviors between caregiver and infant, has a negative impact on the development of the right brain, and ultimately self-regulation. Dr. Allan Schore, author of *Affect Regulation and the Origin of the Self*, summarizes the evidence. Both maltreated children diagnosed with PTSD, as well as children diagnosed with other severe anxiety disorders, show right metabolic limbic abnormalities (Schore 2003).

Dr. Schore cites a study that found that adults who were abused as children and later diagnosed with PTSD showed reduced right hemisphere activation in working memory. Additionally, brain-imaging studies have shown heightened activity in the right hemisphere when traumatic emotional memories are recalled, when reexperiencing visual imagery of traumatic material, and when experiencing panic or terror states involving intense somatic symptoms (Schore 2003).

Trauma has the potential to negatively impact brain development and later self-regulatory function. However, as we know, not all students who experience trauma will become traumatized. Those in generally nurturing, securely attached relationships with at least one effective caregiver fare better than those in insecurely attached, especially "disorganized" or abusive relationships. Their significant relationship with another can be the much-needed resource before, during, and/or after a trauma that gets them through the event without traumatization. It is the students without such a resource that are most at risk. Developmental traumatology studies indicate that it is often not the specific trauma that disrupts brain functioning but the context in which it occurs. When the context itself is the source of the trauma, such as in the case of authoritarian or abusive parenting, these students can be at greatest risk for traumatization.

It needs to be noted that even in the best parenting situations, traumatization can happen and does. Any event that causes terror in students has the potential to debilitate depending upon the sensitivity of the student and the resources available to the student directly before, during, or after the event.

Now that we know the importance of self-regulation to learning and behavior and how this is impacted by trauma, it is important to consider the application of SRT.

SELF-REGULATION THERAPY (SRT): A PROPOSAL

The purpose of SRT is to help students develop or restore the ability to self-regulate between states of arousal so they can successfully meet the demands of the educational environment. The goal is to help students operate within a "window of tolerance" or optimal range of arousal that promotes assimilation and integration of information. Within the window of tolerance, students are better able to attend, focus, concentrate, retain, and recall information, behave appropriately, and learn.

SRT is appropriate for any student at any age that has problems regulating learning and behavior although, as with most approaches, the earlier we intervene, the better. It is especially necessary for students who are ED or who are at risk of being identified as ED. As we know, these are students with histories of problematic arousal levels, who are easily upset and difficult to soothe. Their reactions are often out of proportion to the situation. Slight challenges, minor changes, or minute disruptions are often intolerable to them, causing tantrum or "shut down" behaviors.

SRT is not a cognitive approach. It recognizes that behaviors that seem out of proportion to a situation may actually be automatic, protective responses of the brain that are elicited without cognitive thought (Williams and Shellenberger 1996), often the result of traumatization. The approach recognizes that it is critical to engage the reptilian brain, utilizing a more "bottom-up" approach to attaining optimum arousal, rather than an ineffective "top-down" approach such as verbally reminding the student to "get in control," for example (Williams and Shellenberger 1996). Some cognitive elements, such as psychoeducation, are a part of SRT and will be reviewed later.

Anyone trained to do so can provide SRT, which brings into question who would be the best people to train. Currently, a number of occupational therapists (OTs) working in education have been trained to use the sensory integration program, "How Does Your Engine Run? The Alert Program for Self-Regulation," which utilizes sensory-motor strategies to help keep students within an optimal state of arousal. When the nervous system of students is set up with a "sensory diet" (Wilbarger and Wilbarger 1991) of proprioceptive input (proprioception being the ability to sense the position and movement of the limbs) as well as sensory-motor input (vision, hearing, motion, and touch), it has the best chance of functioning optimally (Williams and Shellenberger 1996).

Unfortunately, the Alert Program is mostly used with students with autism and rarely used with ED and other behaviorally troubled students who desperately need the intervention. While it includes some elements of SRT and is similar to the "resourcing" phase of SRT, the Alert Program on its own is not comprehensive enough to meet the unique needs of traumatized students.

Various professionals working in schools, including OTs with their wealth of knowledge regarding the importance of sensory awareness, would benefit from cross training. We can teach one another the importance of intervening at the level of sensation and then inspire and support one another to do so utilizing the tools of SRT. Learning to speak the language of the reptilian brain is the beginning of the promotion of optimal levels of arousal in the nervous system. Optimal levels of arousal and a healthy capacity to self-regulate are needed to support learning and adaptive behavior in our students. As we learn more about the prevalence of trauma, the impact of trauma on the brain, and the effective somatic approaches that are healing trauma, a sound model of SRT will crystallize and could become as important to our students as any other designated instructional service.

THE NECESSARY ELEMENTS OF SRT

Developing Resources

The most important resource for students that needs to be developed in the first stages of SRT is safety. The relationship between SRT providers and students will be one of the most powerful ways to establish a sense of safety. Not only do providers need to be reliable, trustworthy people in a safe environment during the SRT process but they also need to work with students' teachers and administrators to develop a greater sense of security in the classroom and on the campus.

One way of providing safety is to first, understand students, and second, let them know they are understood. We need to communicate to them that we know they would control their behaviors better if they could; we need to let them know that we know they feel badly about their behavior afterward. Reminding students of their goodness and their healthy side, speaking to those parts, focusing on and amplifying those parts of students goes a long way in establishing the safety needed in order to do this important work.

Providing students with opportunities to feel competent is also important to establishing the necessary conditions for SRT. As we now know, many of these students have deeply imbedded shame states rooted in both their psyche and their physiology. They feel hopeless, helpless, ignorant, incapable, and/ or out of control. It is our job to find what they can do well, in what circumstances or with whom they *are* well, and highlight and encourage these conditions in a genuine and consistent way. When students feel both safe and competent within the context of a trusting relationship with an SRT provider the healing benefits of SRT will be experienced.

Utilizing the Body as a Resource

In order to resolve the effects of trauma on the nervous system, we have to learn to communicate with the nervous system. This is done through the language of sensations, the language of the reptilian brain or brain stem. Students need to be taught sensation words and how they can use these to describe their inner landscape. They need to be encouraged to notice in the moment what is happening inside their body as they have different experiences. This connects and integrates students with their more primitive brain where the secrets to resolving trauma lie. It is within the body's implicit procedural memory that unresolved trauma is "hidden" and where it is ready to be activated (Schore 2003) in order to be resolved.

Once students begin to experience their bodily sensations in a more conscious way, they will come to notice that sometimes they have comfortable or pleasant sensations and other times they have uncomfortable or unpleasant sensations. By teaching them to focus their attention on the sensations without trying to change them they will come to notice that inevitably they change on their own. They may change from pleasant to unpleasant or vice versa but they do not stay fixed, stuck, or the same. There is an ebb and flow that students will come to experience more readily through SRT. This will allow them to begin to understand at a physiological as well as psychological or cognitive level that the body will take care of itself when we do not interfere with it.

When unpleasant sensations seem to be taking over and do not appear to be shifting quickly enough (always wait at least two minutes), introduce resources to students in order to help create a change. We know, for instance, that mental representations of positive experiences have an impact on physiology causing the release of oxytocin, one of the body's natural opioids (Schore 2003). Having students think of, and describe, their best friend or safe place or a pet they love can help the nervous system regulate in those moments when it does not seem to be doing so on its own. This is how we teach students to self-regulate, through *experiences* with their body that teach them it can be trusted and it can mend.

Completing the Incomplete Behavior

As students begin to experience their bodies, they will notice more than sensations; they will notice impulses to do something. They may feel the impulse to run, kick, hit, move their limbs in a particular direction, such as raise their hands in front of their face, fall to the floor, or roll to one side. The possibilities are endless. These are the body's implicit memories coming to life. The body remembers its responses to the trauma because they were left incomplete.

Students who undergo medical procedures, for example, are often so afraid of what is happening to them that their body attempts to engage in defensive responses, such as running away from the hospital or fighting off the doctors. These impulses to defend are thwarted when they are restrained or placed under anesthesia. Under such conditions, students are unable to complete their impulses to run or fight. Their defensive energy and corresponding impulses are left in their body until completion is possible.

Many of our students are easily provoked by any kind of reminder of the particular trauma they experienced, big or small, because when the energy or impulses are triggered, it is a chance for the body to reenact what happened in order to complete the response. What we know as educators, however, because we have witnessed it in our students, is that completion of the behavior, thus resolution of trauma, does not happen through reenactment. The repetitive behaviors involved in reenactment are disconnected, dissociated, and harmful, and leave our students feeling worse not better.

Reenactment more deeply entrenches the maladaptive circuitry in the brain of our traumatized students perpetuating the dysregulation of the nervous system as well as problematic behaviors. Once the language of sensation is spoken, however, the incomplete behavior or unresolved trauma that is waiting to resolve can be completed. With the SRT provider's gentle support and quiet encouragement, students may be helped to finish the response.

Completion of the thwarted behavior must happen slowly within the context of the safe relationship. It is very important that, despite students wanting to act on the impulse quickly and with vigor, they are slowed down and encouraged at first to imagine themselves completing the behavior, seeing it in their mind's eye while noticing the sensations in their body and how they change. A physiological discharge may occur when students imagine the completion of the response. They may get hot, red, or begin to perspire. They may tremble or shake. They may yawn widely and repeatedly. They may laugh or cry. These are all signs of discharge indicating the completion of something powerful that was left undone.

One student I worked with to complete an incomplete behavior had been diagnosed with both ADHD and OCD, rather than the posttraumatic stress that I believed was a more appropriate way to conceptualize his anxiety and "hyperactivity" (really hypervigilance). He was molested at the age of four by his stepmother. At the time he and I worked together, he was seven.

COOPER

In our fourth session over an eight-week period, Cooper and I continued our work together building resources of relationship, competency, and safety. A visualization activity was utilized to help Cooper establish a safe place. Once the exercise was complete and he was asked to draw the safe place he saw, he drew scribbles all over the page with a black crayon. When I asked him what he drew he said it was "her," his stepmother, and when I asked him about it further, he said he saw her "all the time."

I suggested Cooper notice what he was feeling inside his body as he looked at the picture and he said he wanted to run. I encouraged him to allow that impulse to surface and notice where in his body it was. He said his legs. "Feel your legs wanting to run," I said. "Now without actually running, I want you to picture the place you want to run to. Can you see it?" "Yes," he said, "It's a tree. I want to run to that tree." "That's it,

Cooper. Now I want you to see yourself running to that tree. Run and don't stop until you are safe in that tree." Cooper's face became very flush and I could feel the heat emanating from his body. Once he was up in the tree, I encouraged him to rest there, to take his time, and notice how he felt inside now that he was in the tree and safe. Within minutes, Cooper became more settled and relaxed.

At that point, I let Cooper know he could do to the picture he drew whatever he wanted. Without hesitation, he scrunched it up into a tight little ball, stomped on it, threw it into the trashcan, and shut the trashcan outside the door of my office.

The next time I saw Cooper, two weeks later, was the first time I had seen him in over two months without a large red circle of dry, flaky skin around his lips from compulsively licking them. He looked more vibrant and alive. In fact, he looked completely normal. I was struck by the difference in him, and sensed he had made tremendous progress.

Sadly, Cooper lived with his biological mother who admitted to me that she hated Cooper. She told me that she hated men because of what they had done to her and that when she looked at Cooper all she could see was a "little man." Cooper's progress was eventually lost, as I was unable to reach his mother well enough to get her to seek her own intervention.

Integration

As we have seen from our review of current brain research, experiences have the power to promote either neural integration or disintegration. Brain structures either work well in concert with one another as intended or become deficient in their ability to communicate and thereby regulate states of arousal. For instance, recent studies of brain anatomy in abused children demonstrate not only an associated reduction in overall brain size but also impairments in the development of the corpus callosum (DeBellis, Baum et al. 1999; DeBellis, Keshavan et al. 1999).

It is the corpus callosum composed of bands of neural tissue that allows for the transfer of information between the two halves of the brain. Dr. Dan Siegel, author of *The Developing Mind*, has proposed that impairment in neural integration between the right and left hemispheres of the brain is a core deficit in unresolved trauma and is related to autonomic dysregulation. He proposed further that intervention efforts that enhance neural integration may be especially helpful to resolve traumatic states and enhance self-regulatory capacities. According to Siegel, it is possible to promote reintegration through activation of the right hemisphere from where regulation is driven and mediated.

Activation of the right hemisphere, like the reptilian brain, requires that we speak its language. While the left hemisphere analyzes words, the right hemisphere analyzes sensations. It is centrally involved in the analysis of direct information received from the body and is more closely connected with direct sensation than verbally logical codes (Schore 2003). Thus, in order to reintegrate left and right hemispheres, sensations must be accessed along with images, feelings, and behaviors. It is only when the whole person and the whole brain is communicated and intervened with that integration, and therefore coherence, is possible.

The SRT provider can help students cluster all elements—sensations, images, behaviors, and emotions—together, reintegrate them, and thus create a "unique state of mind" that enables new directions of information processing to occur (Siegel 2003). According to Siegel, resolution occurs when traumatic memories are processed in a new way through the integration of the left and right hemispheres.

Integration of disconnected parts into a reconnected whole is most important. Different researchers and clinicians use different terms depending on their orientation, such as sensory integration or neural integration. The integration that is required for the resolution of trauma and the enhancement of self-regulatory capacity is all of these things and more. SRT intervenes to retrieve what was lost, a sense of wholeness and connection to self and others. By intervening at all levels, including the level of sensation and brain stem, we reintegrate all of what it means to be human and all of what is required to learn and behave successfully as a member of the school community. Intervening in this holistic way is how students will come to be functionally whole.

> To resolve trauma we must re-integrate the functions of our triune brain. We must learn to move fluidly between instinct, emotion, and rational thought. When these three sources are in harmony, communicating sensation, feeling, and cognition, our organisms operate as they were designed to. . . . Without a clear connection to our instincts and feelings, we cannot feel a connection and sense of belonging to anything else. . . . If we do not sense our connection with all things, then it is easier to destroy or ignore them. . . . In the process of healing trauma we integrate our triune brains . . . and become fully human . . . fierce warriors, gentle nurturers, and everything in between. (Levine 1997, 265–66)

Psychoeducation and Support

An important part of SRT is educating students, when developmentally appropriate, as well as their parents, teachers, and administrators about their unique needs. Understanding students better *is* an intervention. With greater understanding, parents, teachers, and administrators may be more willing to implement alternative more appropriate ways of responding and intervening. Psychoeducation, the more cognitive part of SRT, can never be left out of the process if it is to have long-term efficacy. Otherwise, the changes we work so hard to promote will not be maintained in the classroom and at home. What SRT does to improve students' self-regulation can be undone when their unique needs are misunderstood. Relationships can serve either to further engrain trauma patterns in the brain or to promote their healthy resolution.

IV

PREVENTION OF TRAUMATIZATION

Crisis Intervention: A Critique

Of course there is the otherness,
right away inside you when
the doe steps carefully down
the embankment. Then clatter
of hoof and the dappled water
with leaf shade. The otherness
and the invisible until you came.

—Linda Gregg

Thus far, we have reviewed the traumatized, misunderstood student, what trauma is for children, how it impacts brain development, and what we can do as educators to intervene effectively with students *who have already been traumatized*. We now turn to an important responsibility of schools—crisis intervention. Crisis events are not only associated with adverse mental health conditions for our students but also with significant learning difficulties (Nader and Muni 2002; Silverman and LaGreca 2002; Vogel and Vernberg 1993). In the two chapters ahead, we will learn what we can do immediately following a crisis event in order to *prevent* the traumatization that contributes to these negative outcomes.

Crisis intervention in schools today is still in its infancy. No single model has been adopted because of the lack of scientific research indicating a reason to do so. We simply do not yet know what works with students in schools.

Linda Gregg's poem, cited at the top of the chapter, refers to the "otherness" that happens "right away *inside* you" when startled, in one interpretation, or perceiving potential threat. According to this interpretation, the "otherness" is what we are largely ignoring in the field of crisis intervention today. We grapple with what will work most effectively with students in the face of crises, as we continue to rely on talking cures that ignore the physiology of trauma. Recent scientific research has not supported the use of what is still the most widely adopted crisis intervention model: Jeffrey T. Mitchell's model of critical-incident stress debriefing (CISD). Several studies have found Mitchell's model to be no more effective than no intervention at all (Christner 2003; van Emmerik, Kamphuis, Hulsbosch, and Emmelkamp 2002), and in some cases, found it actually increased posttraumatic stress symptoms in a number of the recipients (Christner 2003; Gist, Lubin, and Redburn 1998).

Within approximately forty-five minutes, with up to thirty individuals at a time, CISD involves a "fact phase" during which basic information is provided to inform those involved of what to expect. Facts disseminated include common stress reactions and other more debilitating symptoms. This is followed by a "feeling phase" during which the up-to-thirty participants are encouraged to answer such questions as "What was the worst part of the incident for you personally?" This phase is followed by suggestions for coping with stress and then "reentry" into the world.

At a presentation Mitchell made of his model that I attended with school district personnel and state department mental health workers, I was most struck by how uncomfortable the audience was as they listened to his proposal. The body language of the audience members indicated that their own stress levels were increased when only *watching* the video shown of a debriefing session. Many audience members actually rose and left the presentation visibly shaking their heads. During the video, we watched several people delve into the worst part of the trauma for them, clearly becoming aroused physiologically and emotionally, yet within moments, the time was up and the group was left with one last caution. "Be careful driving home," they were warned, "as you may still be upset" after leaving the intervention.

Individuals have spoken out about their experiences participating in debriefing sessions. After 9/11, for example, many participants indicated that the intervention was not helpful. One participant said that he was "numb" throughout the session and that, weeks later, he was still having nightmares and often felt as though he were choking (Groopman 2004). Another participant said that hearing other victims describe what they saw and what they suffered was too much. He had to flee the session when another participant described seeing a body part roll down a sidewalk (Begley 2003). After an earthquake in Turkey, a recipient said, "It was as if the debriefers opened me up as in surgery and didn't stitch me back up" (Begley 2003, 1).

Cognitive approaches, such as Mitchell's, that ignore the body's physiology have the potential to create hysteria because of how readily the body experiences overwhelm. When the body goes through a flooding of stress and emotion, which often happens as one recalls the worst part of the trauma, it protects itself by creating another reality or dissociated state. Hysteria is a form of dissociation. Participants who become hysterical during debriefing sessions are removed from the group so they do not distract other group members (Mitchell and Everly 1996). Rather than accept this as an expected outcome of crisis intervention, however, we can bring our new knowledge of the brain and body to the work we do to prevent such responses.

Adaptations of Mitchell's model are what many educators in the field of crisis intervention rely upon. Some hesitate to make broad conclusions that the model is not helpful (Brock and Jimerson 2002), despite the growing number of studies that support abandoning debriefing approaches (Gist and Devilly 2002). Practitioners "remain committed to the principle of debriefing" because "clinical experience" suggests value in the "opportunity to express feelings" (Deahl, Gillham, Thomas, Searle, and Srinivasan 1994, 64). Others consider economic reasons for the continued use of the approach (Arendt and Elklit 2001). We need *something*, and it seems we lack any other efficient model to work from. Why else would we continue to use debriefing techniques when calls for caution and restraint have been heard from so many responsible scientists and practitioners (Gist and Devilly 2002)?

Instead of heeding the many warnings to abandon, debriefers continue their work by creating adaptations of their model. The concern with that response, however, is that without careful consideration of how crises impact the brain and body's physiology, intervention models continue to be developed and implemented that have the potential to cause the harm described by too many recipients.

In a review of recent developments in the field of crisis intervention, I was alarmed to find how little discussion there was of how the brain and body are impacted by trauma. Crises are repeatedly referred to as psychological events that have to be intervened with psychologically, as though trauma happens to the mind alone. We seem to be determined that our cognitive mind is the most powerful tool we have for healing, when in fact, it is the body, mediated by the ancient reptilian brain, that has the wisdom to know how to naturally recover from trauma and heal itself.

Most people recover from catastrophic events naturally and spontaneously over time. In fact, any "abnormal" behavior witnessed in the aftermath of trauma is actually part of a healthy process of recovery (Groopman 2004) during which the body does what it knows how to do to process stress to its natural completion. Recall the impala that takes moments to shake off the stress from its attack and then carries on (see chapter 4). Whether we are aware of it or not, in most cases, our body naturally finds a way to do the same. It is only a small percentage of people who experience a catastrophic event that will require formal intervention. This small percentage is comprised mostly of individuals with previous histories of trauma, with "fragile emotional profiles and few available resources" (Torem and DePalma 2003, 12). For example, we know that students with previous exposure to traumatic events are more at risk due to the accumulation effect of stress on the nervous system. "The new [traumatic] energy necessitates the formation of more symptoms . . . [so that the traumatic] response not only becomes chronic, it intensifies" (Levine 1997, 105).

More vulnerable students will likely need formal assistance in recovering from a crisis at school. For the majority, however, we know that the body has the capacity to heal itself, and that healing from stress and trauma is possible simply by being in community with others. These are important points to keep in mind when creating an effective crisis intervention model for schools. Dr. Steven Hyman, the provost of Harvard University, reminds us that the rituals we have adopted through our various cultures can be supportive in our healing and recovery from crisis events. He makes note of shivahs in Jewish cultures and wakes among Catholics. Dr. Hyman stated that, "No one should have to tell anyone anything! Particularly not in the scripted way of a debriefing." Dr. Hyman has argued that when facing crises it is the power of our social networks that helps us create a sense of meaning and safety in our lives (Groopman 2004).

Dr. Hyman is not the only responsible academic making statements that "no one should have to tell anyone anything." A panel of eminent researchers assembled by the American Psychological Society—Richard McNally of Harvard University, Richard Bryant of the University of New South Wales, and Anke Ehlers of King's College London—has reached a clear conclusion: "Pushing people to talk about their feelings and thoughts very soon after a trauma may not be beneficial. . . . For scientific and ethical reasons, professionals should cease compulsory debriefing of trauma-exposed people" (Begley 2003, 2).

With a growing number of studies cautioning us to abandon debriefing approaches, why is telling the story and verbally going over the details of a crisis still considered helpful? Why are cognitive and narrative approaches to crisis intervention gaining support in some professional circles? This trend may be part of a prevailing cultural bias that we can talk our way out of anything. Talking is, for most counselors, the best-known and most comfortable mode of operation. However, no explanation seems to warrant that, as ethical professionals, we ignore a striking body of evidence. Exposure techniques used in cognitive approaches to trauma are "not good for people with brains and not good for people with bodies;" telling the "story will re-traumatize and make things worse" (van der Kolk 2002).

Dr. van der Kolk, when recently speaking at a professional conference, was open about the fact that like most counselors, he did not know how to pace the work he did with trauma survivors. Like most counselors today, he said he hadn't been "mindful about the effect of having people talk about these very scary things." Learning about trauma's impact on the brain is what prompted him to speak around the world, educating professionals about the dangers of retelling the story and the so-called talking cure. Crisis intervention specialists working in schools are beginning to acknowledge the dangers. School crisis management research summaries provided in the official newspaper of the National Association of School Psychologists (NASP) stated that early crisis interventions involving detailed verbal recollections of events may not be helpful and may place those with high arousal at greater risk (Brock and Jimerson 2002).

What seems to be most helpful about current approaches in managing crises is meeting in a group and disseminating information. Litz and colleagues published a study comparing the CISD model with cognitive-behavioral therapy (CBT) (Litz, Gray, Bryant, and Adler 2002). Common between the approaches was education on typical reactions and instruction in coping skills for stress and anxiety. Results indicated that meeting in a group is what helped to maintain morale and cohesion. Group interventions seemed to serve as an opportunity for those in the group to feel less stigmatized, more validated and empowered. Psychoeducation or dissemination of information regarding what to expect was also cited as a helpful part of these crisis approaches. Even single sessions when they were supportive rather than therapeutic were helpful when they (a) assessed for the need for sustained treatment, (b) provided psychological first aid, and (c) offered education about trauma and treatment resources.

Some group interventions have been found to reduce anxiety, improve self-efficacy, and enhance group cohesion (Shalev, Peri, Rogel-Fuchs, Ursano, and Marlowe 1998). They have also been found to play a role in reducing alcohol misuse (Deahl, Srinivasan, Jones, Thomas, Neblett, and Jolly 2000). However, it has also been found that single-session group crisis interventions are insufficient for high-risk trauma survivors, those with poor pretrauma mental health (Larsson, Michel, and Lundin 2000). Individuals with previous traumas, such as burns, accidents, or violent crime, may actually be harmed by single-session group crisis intervention (Bisson, Jenkins, Alexander, and Bannister 1997; Mayou, Ehlers, and Hobbs 2000). This information is invaluable as we continue to work together as educators to develop an effective crisis intervention model.

COMMON MYTHS ABOUT CRISES

It is important to address some of the myths that persist today regarding the impact of trauma on our students. These myths are pervasive and stem from outdated beliefs about children that we now have the brain research to refute.

Some Events Are More Traumatic Than Others

I have witnessed professionals in the field of crisis intervention delve into lengthy presentations about certain events being more traumatic than others. For the most part, these discussions are not helpful. I listened to one presenter talk extensively about a broken arm from a physical assault being more traumatic than a broken arm from a car accident, and about war being more traumatic than an earthquake. It is not a matter of some events being more traumatic than others. Trauma is not in the event; it is in the nervous system (Levine 1997). Depending on the condition of the individual's nervous system and available resources before, during, and after the event, what may seem benign to some can be very debilitating to another. Believing that some events can be objectively judged for everyone as more or less traumatic leads to very dangerous assumptions about individual students. We cannot expect that some students will be less traumatized by what we have judged as a less frightening event. This is how we misunderstand students and fail to see their trauma-related symptoms after an event that was terrifying *to them*.

Trauma Causes Psychological Injury

While it is true that trauma has the potential to induce psychological injury, such a statement does not reflect the whole truth concerning the damage caused by traumatization. When people who are traumatized learn that crises are not simply psychological events but physiological ones, they experience relief. What they are going through is not "in their head"; it is the natural response of the body. People suffer years of anguish following a car accident, for example, or a surgery, believing that they must be going crazy. Their medical doctors tell them that there is nothing physically wrong with them, that there is no reason for their suffering. No one talks to them about what their brain and body have gone through so they conclude that the problem must be in their head. With that conclusion comes the belief that they must be in need of some form of talk therapy. I have seen firsthand how this conclusion leads to hopelessness, as traumatized people make numerous attempts at various forms of therapy with little or no success. They know they do not feel the same inside. They know they have applied all the cognitive techniques they were taught by their well-meaning therapists. They simply do not get better.

Medical tests cannot detect the problem and psychological approaches that do not intervene with the body's response to trauma leave traumatized people feeling like they are going crazy. When we look at physiology, however, we find answers. We learn that, among other physiological changes, traumatization increases resting heart rates and decreases cortisol levels. Hormones and neurotransmitters are altered in the short term or long term, depending upon previous history and resources. Physiological symptoms require a physiological approach. This is what is missing from the crisis intervention programs used today.

Children Look to Adults to Determine How Threatening an Event Is

No matter how young children are, preverbal or verbal, they have their own nervous system, their own brain, their own body and mind, and they experience life and its events as much as anyone else. They may not have words for their experiences, and they may look to adults for comfort and understanding in the face of a frightening event, but they do not need to be guided when to feel fear. We cannot tell a student that they are fine and what happened is "no big deal" if, in fact, it was a big deal to them. We stand the risk of shutting down their body's natural healing mechanism when we do so. There are ways to support the natural process of healing and there are ways to undermine it. Telling students how to feel is an example of how our cognitive mind can interfere with the body's capacity to heal.

A colleague of mine once shared that when she was a young girl she fell from her bicycle and badly hurt her knee. She was so stunned from the fall that she could not cry. She realized as an adult looking back on the event that she must have been in a state of shock because all she felt was numb. When she arrived at the door of her home and her mother saw that she had been injured but was not crying she was praised for being such a brave girl. "Look at what a good girl you are," her mother said. "You are not even crying." After that incident, my colleague said that she made sure she did not cry no matter what else came her way. She used her words, the power of her cognitive mind, to shut down her body's natural responses so that she would be regarded as brave and strong.

Adults have no way of knowing how threatening or frightening an event is to a child. If we think we can decide objectively what a student's subjective experience will be, we have no chance of understanding or intervening with students in crisis.

Developmental Immaturity Can Be Protective

Some believe that the younger a student is, the less the student will experience fear and terror. This is not supported by scientific evidence. One nationally certificated school psychologist (NCSP) made a presentation at my school district encouraging us to utilize his crisis intervention model. As part of the introduction to his work, he said that both developmentally mature and gifted students are more vulnerable and impacted by crises than their less well-developed peers. Smarter students can be more traumatized than less intelligent students because they realize the event was threatening, he said. They realize the event was traumatic because they are cognitively sophisticated enough to judge the event as threatening. According to this presenter, "Developmentally immature students don't understand the event, so it is not traumatic for them."

Trauma is a physiological event that impacts everyone in its wake (to varying degrees) regardless of level of intellect. The school psychologist's statements demonstrate a dangerous ignorance of science and what the brain and body experience in the face of threat.

CURRENT ATTEMPTS AT CRISIS INTERVENTION IN SCHOOLS

Several educational professionals from various areas of expertise have attempted to develop crisis intervention models that will meet the needs of schools. Three different men, each of whom had developed his own approach, presented to my school district on three separate occasions. I will review each of their proposals: (1) Bill Saltzman from the National Center for Child Traumatic Stress, (2) Michael Hass from Chapman University in Orange County, California, and (3) Stephen Brock, a nationally accredited school psychologist and coordinator of the Crisis Management in the Schools Interest Group.

Dr. Bill Saltzman

Dr. Saltzman's approach emphasizes the need to tailor crisis intervention to the developmental level of the students being served (Saltzman 2003). He reminds us that students' responses may be specific to their age and stage of development. For instance, preschoolers may display cognitive confusion. They may not know that the danger is over when a crisis event ends and may need to be given repeated concrete clarifications for anticipated confusions. Older, school-age students may display specific fears triggered by traumatic reminders. They may require help in identifying and articulating those reminders as well as associated anxieties. They may benefit from being encouraged not to generalize, according to Saltzman. Adolescents, on the other hand, may begin to exhibit posttraumatic acting-out behavior such as drug use, delinquency, or sexual activity. Saltzman postulates that helping adolescents understand the acting-out behavior as an effort to numb their response to, or to voice their anger over, the event may be of benefit.

Importance is placed on family and friendship. Maintaining and nurturing relationships is critical after a crisis event for students at every stage of development. Saltzman points out that sometimes crisis events cause physical relocations that can abruptly interrupt usual daily contact with loved ones. When this happens, it is helpful to make the effort to keep relational ties, regardless of physical separation, in order to be comforted by them.

Saltzman makes clear that it is always important to reintegrate students back into the school and classroom environment as soon as possible. Somatic complaints and specific fears related to school or loss of a loved one may make it difficult for a student to want to enter back into school. The family and the school need to work together to make sure students' fears are resolved and attendance in school is maintained.

Saltzman's model includes an initial interview protocol that asks crisis survivors questions in seven stages. The first step is to gather factual information about where the student was during the event, what the student was exposed to, and how the student knew the people involved. One important question to ask at this stage is whether or not the student has ever experienced any other kind of crisis or trauma, including subjection to violence, serious illness, or sudden, unexpected loss. The next four stages of questions have to do with the students' responses to the crisis. What was their subjective response to the event? Are they exhibiting new behaviors or new concerns since the event? What type of grief responses are they displaying? Finally, in the sixth stage of the interview, students are asked about their coping mechanisms before the final stage of closing the interview is done.

Saltzman's approach is useful. Awareness and consideration of the different expressions and needs of students at varying developmental levels is helpful. Caution should be made, however, that during times of crises, students may easily and quickly regress back to earlier stages of development so that even adolescents display the behaviors of preschool children. Saltzman highlighted "anxious attachment" as a possible preschool response that may involve clinging and not wanting to be away from the parent or worrying about when the parent is coming back. This can happen with teenagers. Like preschool students, adolescents may also greatly benefit from being reassured about "consistent caretaking" of being picked up after school and always knowing where their caretakers are.

In a review of all of Saltzman's hypothesized responses of students at different ages, it was easy to see that any one of these responses could come from a student at any developmental level. We do not want to make assumptions about how a student will act, given the student's age. If we have expectations, we may not see what we need to. Nonetheless, it is useful to be aware of the possibility of age and stage differences. Especially in teenagers should we expect to see such age-specific behaviors as "premature entrance into adulthood." Certainly that is something specific to adolescence. However, behaviors attributed to adolescence in Saltzman's approach, such as "life threatening reenactment, self-destructive or accident-prone behavior, abrupt shifts in interpersonal relationships, and desires and plans to take revenge," are readily seen in some younger school-age children after a crisis event.

Saltzman's approach, like most, is cognitive and emphasizes the use of verbal language and asking questions. It is unclear how soon after a crisis event all of the questions from the initial interview protocol are to be asked. Like other cognitive approaches, including the debriefing model, Saltzman asks crisis survivors to talk about their "most disturbing moment" and "worst fear." We need to learn from the examples we now have available to us that this kind of questioning may increase suffering.

Dr. Michael Hass

Dr. Hass has attempted to help schools develop a crisis intervention model utilizing the principles of solution-focused brief counseling (Hass 2002). His emphasis, like most others, is on interviewing the crisis survivor. The stages of crisis interviewing in his approach include role clarification, a description of the problem, an exploration of current coping efforts, "scaling" of coping progress, formulation of the "next step," and closure. The focus of this approach is on the establishment of helpful coping skills. Questions during the interview are intended to facilitate coping in order to empower students to take action on their own behalf.

Examples of coping questions include: What are you doing to take care of yourself in this situation? Who do you think would be most helpful to you at this time? What about that person would be most helpful? Have you been through a frightening situation before? How did you get through it then? Developing resources for the student to draw upon during difficult times is key. "Scaling" questions are also related to coping. They help students rate how much better or worse they think they are doing and give a gauge to crisis counselors of how much progress has been made. Together, the counselors and students problem solve to arrive at solutions for moving the scale in the desired direction.

During Hass's presentation, he highlighted the importance of telling the story of what happened during the crisis. He stated that researchers have found that putting a traumatic incident into language is a critical feature of the healing process—the idea being that language helps the images and feelings we have about a frightening event become more organized, understood and resolved.

The studies that Hass was referring to were led by Dr. Edna Foa, a professor of psychology at the University of Pennsylvania who, twenty years ago, began studying rape victims. She found that most rape victims spontaneously recovered without the need for formal intervention, but that 15 percent developed symptoms of posttraumatic stress (Groopman 2004). Foa devised a technique of storytelling to restore resilience in those who continued to suffer. The women were asked to tell their story into a tape recorder and listen to it, then retell it and listen to it, and so on. Within approximately twenty sessions, Foa found that twenty-nine of the thirty participants experienced a marked improvement in their symptoms and ability to function. She attributed their improvement to the changing of the story over time. It became more organized, with a beginning, a middle, and an end. It was hypothesized that because they were able to give such a well-developed account of the incident, they were more likely to develop perspective on the event, create a sense of distance from it, feel a sense of closure about it, and feel more hopeful about the future.

Hass's overall focus on strengthening and empowering students to cope after a traumatic event is very helpful. It is important to create a balance in the nervous system between the alarm response triggered by the event and whatever will be soothing to that sense of alarm. However, it is dangerous to recommend a technique to professionals who work with school-aged children when the few studies that support such an approach have been done with adult women who experienced sexual assault. The appropriateness of using such an approach with students may be suspect, especially when other eminent professionals in the field have seen that telling the story can retraumatize the victim (van der Kolk 2002). It is true that when trauma survivors can tell their story in an organized, fluid way without becoming overwhelmed by it, this can be a sign that they are recovering from the experience. Telling the story at some point in a trauma survivors' treatment may be relevant. However, we are not talking about adults receiving therapy. We are talking about crisis intervention for school-aged students. Now that so many responsible scientists and practitioners are warning us that telling the story can cause hysteria and retraumatization, it is best not to endorse such an approach to schools.

Dr. Stephen Brock

Dr. Brock developed a model of crisis intervention for schools that takes into account the different stages of the event (Brock and Jimerson 2002). The first stage is the impact, or when the crisis occurs. The next stage is the first phase of the school's response to the event, which he calls "recoil." Immediately after the event, the students involved receive "psychological first aid" and, in some cases, medical intervention. Support systems need to be enlisted during this phase, ensuring that loved ones are located and reunited. Psychoeducation groups, caregiver training, and informational flyers are also important at this time, as are risk screening and referral for students who may require more intense intervention.

The "postimpact" phase occurs in the days and weeks after the event. This is the time that Brock suggests that group crisis debriefings occur, as well as ongoing psychological first aid, psychotherapy, and crisis prevention/preparedness for the future. Rituals and memorials may be helpful at this time, as well as in the next phase of "recovery/reconstruction."

Recovery/reconstruction, the final stage of the approach, involves anniversary preparedness. Anniversary reactions have been found to be as intense as initial ones (Gabriel 1992).

Brock recommends that, before the school responds in the recoil phase, all pertinent staff members meet as a team, clarify their roles, and decide who will do what. There will be a different part to play for school psychologists, nurses, counselors, and administrators.

The psychological first aid approach developed by Brock specifically for schools is called group crisis intervention (GCI). It is designed to work with large groups of students who experienced a common crisis. Such large groups are typically classrooms. The approach is not intended for use with severely traumatized students, whose crisis reactions are thought to interfere with GCI (Brock 2002). Like in Mitchell's model, these students are removed from the group and referred to mental health professionals. It is suggested that GCI occur at the start of the first full school day following resolution of the event to ensure that participants are psychologically ready to talk about the crisis (Brock 2002).

The six-step model includes an introduction, provision of facts and dispelling of rumors, sharing stories, sharing reactions, empowerment, and closing. GCI is ideally completed in one session lasting one to three hours, depending on the developmental level of the classroom of students. Similar to other approaches, group facilitators introduce themselves and define their roles. Opportunities are provided for students to share their stories, their reactions, and become "empowered" through a focus on coping and stress management. Unique to this approach is the second step of the model that involves providing facts about the crisis and dispelling rumors that the students may have heard about the event. The final step involves the development of creative projects or memorials, as well as opportunities for students to discuss what they learned and what coping skills they are committed to implementing.

Brock's approach includes many helpful elements, especially his identification of the different phases of a crisis and the need to do different things at each phase. Psychological or emotional first aid is necessary immediately after the event, according to the model, before any kind of student interview, debriefing, or cognitive, narrative approach should be considered. When reviewing the process of Brock's psychological first aid, however, it becomes clear that it is actually very similar to debriefing. The GCI approach, called "psychological first aid," is more of a debriefing process. Yet debriefing, according to Brock's own model, should not occur before first aid has been completed.

Brock's approach is beneficial for students who are relatively healthy before a crisis event, who have resources that are effective and available to them, and who have not been seriously impacted by the crisis. The approach is not useful for (as is also the case with most other approaches) the students who have been more severely impacted. These students are appropriately removed from groups like Brock's and Mitchell's. They are referred to mental health professionals who, we hope, can help them quickly. However, many such students come back to our campuses having received some, little, or no help from mental health professionals or anyone else. They display various problems and behaviors related to their experience of the event and need our help. As educators, with these vulnerable students on our campuses up to six hours a day, we are the ones who are in the position to help them. Many of our public school students do not have access to services outside of our campuses. We need to be responsible for knowing how we can at least do no further harm to the students in our care. We must, first, understand them, and second, intervene with them in ways that we know are specific to their needs.

When impacted students are removed from groups like Brock's and Mitchell's, they need to be referred to a person on the school campus who knows what to do to help. We help when we know the physiological effect the event has had on our students' nervous system. We help when we know the most effective way to, at least, return the nervous system back to its previous level of functioning.

Psychophysiological first aid is how we can respond to the needs of our students following a crisis event in a way that reflects an understanding of how the brain and body are impacted by trauma. The approach is an alternative to psychological first aid and/or debriefing that emphasizes verbal language and a questioning process that many researchers believe can complicate natural resolution (Gist and Devilly 2002), interfere with the natural processing of a traumatic event (van Emmerik et al. 2002), and inhibit natural recovery by creating unnecessary fears (Winston, Kassam-Adams, Garcia-Espana, Ittenbach, and Cnaan 2003). Psychophysiological first aid, as with medical first aid, involves keeping students warm and calm with a reassuring presence that provides the space and containment necessary for the body to naturally bring itself back into balance. This alternative approach will be reviewed in the next chapter.

11

First, Do No Harm: Psychophysiological First Aid

Psychophysiological first aid is a response to, and an alternative for, psychological first aid. It is based on our new knowledge of how the brain and body are impacted by crises. The approach engages the oldest, wisest part of our brain, the brain stem, otherwise known as the reptilian brain, through the language of sensation for two reasons: first, because the core of the crisis experience is processed by the reptilian brain, and second, because the language of this more primitive brain is sensation.

After a crisis event, activity of the brain stem needs to be brought into greater balance with the rest of the triune brain—the limbic midbrain and neocortex. Once all three parts of the brain are realigned with one another and the nervous system is brought back into greater balance through a process of gentle discharge, the likelihood of problematic reactions emerging later is greatly decreased (Levine 1997). Self-regulation remains intact. Students retain their physiological capacity to move through frightening situations without becoming debilitated by them. The nervous system naturally moves in and out of stress unburdened by an ongoing, sometimes accumulating amount of stress.

Psychophysiological first aid is intended for use immediately after a crisis event. It does not require the waiting period of other approaches of up to seventy-two hours. Students do not have to be "ready to talk" about the event because discussing what happened is not required. Students do not have to be out of shock or no longer numb from the experience—a stipulation of other interventions—because those feelings and sensations are what get worked through and resolved with psychophysiological first aid. With other approaches, resolution of shock and numbness is needed before implementation can begin. However, for some people, shock and numbness do not go away in the hours, days, or even weeks after a crisis. Without psychophysiological first aid, these natural responses to trauma can last for weeks or months, even years.

Although psychophysiological first aid is a unique response to crises, it includes elements from other programs that are useful and empirically supported. For instance, from the research conducted examining Mitchell's model, we learned that intervention that occurred without delay resulted in fewer and less severe symptoms (Campfield and Hill 2001). We also learned that debriefing reduced distress when it was lengthened for up to 300 minutes and combined with either postgroup psychoeducation (Chemtob, Thomas, Law, and Cremniter 1997) or an integrated stress management system with individual support (Richards 2001).

From Saltzman's approach (see chapter 10), it is helpful to retain an understanding of the developmental age and stage of the students we serve knowing that regressive states will also appear. Meeting students where they are is the challenge. If adolescents present behaviors more commonly seen in preschoolers, we need to intervene with them at that level, and reassure them as we would a preschooler.

From Hass's solution-focused approach (see chapter 10), it is useful to highlight students' strengths and abilities, what is working, and how they can manage and cope with stress. Brock's approach (see chapter 10) emphasized the need to consider the different phases of the crisis and intervene at each phase accordingly. His GCI model is cost-efficient and productive overall because of the number of students that can be served at one time. Relatively healthy students with available resources and little or no remarkable history of trauma may be well suited to such a groupwide approach.

Each of these valuable contributions to crisis intervention has been included in the development of the model of psychophysiological first aid. Additionally, recent research has informed us that the best approach to crisis intervention and trauma resolution is one that understands and intervenes with physiology. In the *International Journal of Emergency Mental Health*, for example, in a study of the use of mental health services following 9/11, the authors stated that peri-event physiological reactions, and psychological perceptions of physiological responses, were important factors determining subsequent psychopathology (Boscarino, Galea, Ahern, Resnick, and Vlahov 2002). It is psychophysiological first aid, uniquely, that provides a model in which such reactions and responses can be understood and quickly resolved.

PHASES OF PSYCHOPHYSIOLOGICAL FIRST AID

While useful and empirically supported elements of other crisis intervention approaches are included, much of the model being proposed here is the result of the work of Dr. Peter Levine. Over the past three decades, Dr. Levine has traveled the world in response to global crises, studying and healing children and adults who have experienced life-altering events.

Psychophysiological first aid involves four phases: *needs assessment, intervention (small group, large group, individual), psychoeducation,* and *follow-up.*

Needs Assessment

This first phase is invaluable. The school's crisis response team meets as a group, clarifies their roles, and determines who will do what. The team gathers as many of the facts as possible regarding what went on during the event. Knowing the magnitude of the crisis helps the team decide how to intervene first. If the scope of the event was relatively small and a whole class or large group of students was not involved or impacted, then groupwide models would not be needed, nor would they be helpful. Group crisis interventions are reserved for homogeneous groups (Brock and Jimerson 2002; Mitchell and Everly 1996) of students who have all been exposed to the event to about the same degree, and who display a manageable amount of difficulty due to the event.

Homogeneity of groups is a difficult qualifier in the case of trauma. Most students will each have their own individual responses based on their own previous experiences with trauma, their closeness to the event and/or victim, and their available resources before, during, and after the event. The crisis response team may find that, unless a significant number of affected students make a large group intervention necessary, small groups and individual support are more appropriate.

The goal of the first phase of psychophysiological first aid is to decide what the needs are—large group, small group, or individual intervention—and which team member will respond to what need. If a large group intervention is needed, then Brock's GCI model may be helpful when the team is committed to spotting those in the group who need immediate removal and individual intervention in the form of psychophysiological first aid. A trained eye is needed to observe any early signs of physiological or emotional overwhelm in order to prevent such responses. Education and training is required in order to readily see these signs.

Should the large group approach be necessary, there would likely be a delay in the crisis response due to the time it takes to assemble the group's participants. At such times, it is helpful for certain members of the team to immediately seek out the students directly involved or impacted by the event due to exposure or closeness to the victim. Rather than wait for the larger intervention with these particular students, it is best to administer psychophysiological first aid with each of them on an individual basis as soon as possible.

If we are not able to be at the scene right away or help the students involved immediately after the event, we need not be overly concerned. The energy mobilized by the trauma is always there. It is in the body waiting to be discharged. As Dr. Peter Levine discovered through his research, trauma is an interrupted process naturally inclined to complete itself whenever possible. As soon as we create the opportunity, students will complete the healing process and avoid the debilitating effects of trauma (Levine 1997).

The needs assessment includes attention to what the crisis counselors themselves may need before offering their assistance to students. Our own physical and emotional responses require acknowledgment. Just as we are instructed to do on an airplane in times of crisis, we must assist ourselves first. We must sense the feelings going on inside our own body, and utilize stress management skills and the camaraderie of our colleagues to calm ourselves before we try to do anything else. If we feel upset, we need to ground and center through deep breaths, connection with the floor, the room, and the people around us. If we do not take the time necessary to calm ourselves, students will pick up on, and react to, our fear or confusion. Students are very sensitive to the physical and emotional states of their teachers and other adults.

There are three possible outcomes of the needs assessment: large group, small group, or individual psychophysiological first aid.

Intervention

Large Group Intervention

Like with other approaches, dissemination of facts, dispelling of rumors, and psychoeducation involving normalization of responses are important steps to take at the intervention phase of psychophysiological first aid. Unique to this approach is an emphasis on normalizing physiological responses, taking into account that crises happen to the whole person, body as well as mind. Students should be made aware that their body may respond to the event through involuntary trembling, shaking, heat, cold, and/or crying. They need to know that not only are these responses normal, they are important. Such responses are the body's way of moving through the experience. Allowing the natural physical expression of distress to continue until it stops or levels out on its own is the key to preventing residual problems later.

An emphasis on resources is important. Unique to this approach is a greater focus on resources than on sharing stories or reactions to the event.

Doing so in the large group particularly can cause unnecessary arousal for the person telling the story as well as for the people hearing it. In fact, if students begin to tell their story in the large group, they should be stopped gently and encouraged to notice their feet planted on the ground as they look around the room and see the people there supporting them.

Do not be concerned that you are stopping a process when you distract students from engaging in narrative about the event and instead have them focus on something around them that helps them feel more grounded and centered. This is an important protective service you are providing that will prevent the students from an experience of overwhelm in the nervous system. Some students may not be easily discouraged from telling the story. They may seem to have a compulsion to speak out about what they saw or what happened to them. These are the students to refer for individual support. At later stages of the process, students will have a chance to tell their story. The first concern, however, is to ground and center students, allowing their body to naturally move through the initial physiological reactions of the experience. Once the nervous system is balanced, telling the story will not have the same power to retraumatize.

Containment must be provided. In a large group situation, it is important to have as many calm adults as possible in and around the room, so that students feel a strong sense of support. We know from Dr. Bruce Perry's research on the brain that relationship and close physical proximity actually changes neural activity (Perry 2003). Studies have found greater neural activity, a healthy indicator, when people are in the presence of, and connected to, others as opposed to when they are alone. Elevated levels of heart rate and blood pressure decrease when we are in physical proximity to others and feel the containment and support of their presence.

Students benefit from becoming involved in creative activities as a group. Have them draw pictures, write letters, read poems, or design murals that help them express their thoughts and feelings about the event.

Educate students about the need to focus on their resources when they leave the group. Direct them to connect with friends, family, pets, and nature as much as possible. Let them know that it is important for them *not* to get together with friends or family to talk about the event, especially repeatedly or in a ruminating way. Rather, they need simply to feel the support of their loved ones and enjoy their company through games, rituals, or activities.

Make sure students know to turn the television off, especially the news or any shows or commercials that are frightening or violent. We are learning more and more about the impact television viewing has on the nervous system. One study completed after the Oklahoma City bombing indicated that simply viewing the images of the explosion on television accounted for more variance of posttraumatic stress responses than knowing someone who experienced the crisis or actually seeing or hearing the blast (Pefferbaum et al. 2001). Have students instead get involved with, or return to, sports, a martial art, or a creative activity that helps them express themselves.

Reassure students that they are not alone, that we are right here with them and for them. Encourage students to seek out the help of school personnel anytime they need to.

Small Group Intervention

Whether meeting in a large or small group, the above steps are necessary to bring the students' nervous system back into balance. In both groups, it is important to keep a vigilant eye on who may be becoming too physiologically aroused to be in the group. Some will likely need to be seen individually and provided with first aid.

Small group exercises that are helpful during times of crisis involve grounding. This is especially important for students who are too upset to stay in the large group. To help these overwhelmed students become calmer and better balanced internally, encourage them to remain seated, and guide them verbally to feel their feet planted on the ground. Have them sense the connection they have to the earth as well as the people around them. Encourage them to look around the room, see the others there with them, and feel their presence and support. Guide them to feel the support of the chair behind their back and underneath them. Have them really sink into the chair and sense that it is holding them. Have students call out the colors they see as they look around the room, blues, reds, and yellows. Have them describe something they see outside the window or in the room. This is how we call in external resources to develop an inner resource, a greater sense of calm and balance in the nervous system.

Without using the word "relax" with students, conduct a progressive relaxation exercise for grounding. Encourage the students to move their attention from their toes all the way up to the top of their head, tightening each small muscle group, holding it for a few seconds, and then gently releasing it.

Individual Psychophysiological First Aid

Create a sense of safety for students by keeping things quiet and calm. Keep students as still and warm as possible and simply encourage them to rest. This is important when students show signs of shock, such as pale complexion, shallow or rapid breathing, glazed eyes, shaking or trembling, or looking disoriented, as though they are walking through a dream. They may have a dazed or spacey quality about them. They may seem shut down or frozen. On the other end of the spectrum, students may be overly emotional. Whatever their state, it is our job as crisis counselors to provide them with a safe environment, monitoring our own internal responses as well as theirs. By taking full, deep breaths, grounding ourselves, and staying as calm as possible, we are better able to help students settle and rest.

Provide physical connection and support by gently putting your hand in the center of the student's upper back, behind the heart (I ask permission from them to do so). As good as our intentions may be when we excessively rock or pat students when they are in distress, this is actually a disruptive response and not helpful. Simply placing a hand on the back in a gentle way can be soothing as it gives the student a sense of connection and containment. Allow time for that glazed look or excessive emotion to dissipate. Gently remind students they are not alone and you are right there with them.

Gently guide the students' attention to the physical experiences they are having in their body by asking them about sensations. Speak quietly and calmly allowing a moment between each question. Reflect the students' answers back to them to help focus their attention and feel the presence of another. The brief conversation may go something like this:

What do you notice inside your body?
It hurts.
It hurts inside.
Yes.
Can you point to, or tell me, where?
My head.
Can you describe the hurt for me?
It feels like it's going to explode.
Like it's going to explode.
Yes.
Does it feel hot in there, or tight? What is that explosion feeling like?
It's tight. It hurts. It's pinching down on me.
It's tight and feels like it's pinching down on you.
Yes.
I would like you to focus on those sensations that you just described, that tight, pinching feeling. I'm right here with you. Just watch and see what happens next.

Allow a moment or two of silence so the sensations can move through without the distraction of another question. Look for signs that the sensations are changing, such as a full breath or shift in eye contact or emotion. You will notice that as students continue to focus on sensations within the container of your presence, they will experience a shift or change in the quality of the sensation. They may experience a discharge of the energy and chemicals mobilized during the incident that involves trembling, gentle crying, yawning, heat or facial flushing. Check back with the student.

How does your head feel now?
It doesn't hurt as much.
Just notice now that the hurt has lessened.

Another cycle may follow, during which students feel another uncomfortable sensation and the process would continue until the overall sense of discomfort goes away.

Keep the focus on sensation, discharge, and rest through gentle containment. This is not the time for discussion about the event. Opportunities at another phase of the process will be available to students. They will have the chance later to draw, color, and/or tell stories about what happened.

Normalize the students' physical reactions. Let them know how involuntary crying, trembling, feeling heat, and yawning are all natural, healthy responses after a frightening event. Simply make statements like, "That's it. Just let your body do what it needs to do." Keeping your hand gently on their back can be helpful when offering such reassurance.

The body may want to move in a particular way. This is normal. Students may begin to feel the impulse to run, kick, or hit. These are fight-or-flight behaviors, often thwarted at the time of a crisis due to shock, freeze, extreme fear, or simply the inability to fight or flee. Let the movement happen *only* when it can be kept *very* slow. The brain stem is not sophisticated enough to move through these powerful experiences quickly. The intervention, if it is going to be effective, must occur slowly.

You can slow students down if they begin to give into their impulses too quickly. Just stay calm and use a firm, quiet voice to let them know how important it is that the body may want to move, and that is okay, but it is *absolutely critical* that the movements do not happen quickly. An excellent alternative to having the students slowly engage in the actual movements is to encourage them to imagine themselves, in their mind's eye, giving into the impulse and moving in the way the body wants to move.

Make sure the discharge process is not disrupted. For example, you may notice an urge to stop what is happening. Do not. (The only time to stop is when too much is happening too quickly and the student is becoming overwhelmed.) Notice your own reactions and ground yourself through deep, full breaths and connection to the chair beneath you. The successful completion of the process requires that you trust yourself to observe and provide safe containment, and that you trust the body to complete these natural responses. Do not worry about whether or not you are doing this the "right way." Simply know that things will happen naturally as they are intended.

Watch for signs of completion. Students may be complete after one cycle of noticing an uncomfortable sensation and then experiencing its completion through a gentle discharge involving trembling or heat. Other students may cycle several times between pleasant and unpleasant sensations. One clear way of knowing that they have completed a discharge is orientation back to the room, to you, or to the external world in general.

Make time for students to express their feelings about the event through art, drawing, coloring, or storytelling with an emphasis on highlighting resources, coping, and empowerment. Continue to normalize what they are feeling and expressing. Tell stories of heroism, about other students or adults who experienced a frightening event and then went on to do great things.

If at any point during this process students seem overwhelmed or stuck in unpleasant sensations too long (more than three or four minutes), introduce a resource to them, such as a grounding exercise. You may simply orient them to the room by asking them to find something on the wall that catches their eye, or make a connection with them by having them look into your eyes. Alternatively, you could ask them to imagine their best friend is there with them, giving them support.

Education for Parents and Teachers

Psychoeducation for Parents

Once we have intervened with students, it is important to educate their caregivers about what to expect and how they can be helpful at home. Let parents know about the potential impact a crisis event has on the nervous system. Empower them by giving them a clear sense of the kind of presence they can be for their children that will be most helpful to return the nervous system back to normal. "Building mutual support for the family to surmount this tragedy together" has proven to be very helpful (Walsh 2003, 403).

Parents can be a container for their children at home by providing an overall sense of safety and calm. Reassurance can be provided through simple statements such as, "You are not alone. I am right here with you." Talking too much is not helpful.

Let parents know how important it is that their children do not watch the news or any programs that involve frightening or violent themes.

Tell them about the signs of anxiety and upset that may signal the need for physical proximity and connection with nature, pets, and loved ones. It is precisely these kinds of external resources that will help reinstate calm and balance in the nervous system. When working with the families of students who have experienced a crisis, one of the most important things we can do is identify and fortify key processes for resilience (Walsh 2003).

Parents need to know that offering quiet connection through gentle holding can help facilitate the letting go of anxiety and stress. When holding their children, or offering any kind of physical support, parents may notice their children trembling, shaking, giving off heat or sweating, even yawning excessively. Let them know that these responses should not be interrupted but simply watched and validated through brief statements like, "That's it. That's okay. Just let that happen. I'm right here with you."

In whatever way parents can promote their children's competencies will be an invaluable part of helping them overcome a traumatic event. Getting them involved in activities they are good at, that they derive a sense of pride from, is very useful.

Emphasize to parents that talking about the event may not be helpful. If their children bring it up and seem to really need to talk about it, it is most important for parents to point out their children's resources. As children tell the story, parents can highlight the parts of the story involving who and what helped them get through the event.

Psychoeducation for Teachers

It is important to let teachers know what is helpful and what is harmful in the classroom after a student has experienced a crisis.

Harmful: Having a presence, tone of voice, or body language that is in any way threatening or provocative to the student is harmful. Some students will have had previous traumas and/or few resources before, during, or after the event. As a result, they may become significantly impacted by the crisis and may go in and out of freeze states, even fight-or-flight states, depending on two things: how they responded during the trauma and how well they are currently able to meet the demands of the classroom.

Researchers have found that students who were negatively impacted by trauma have difficulty meeting the demands of their classroom because of the residual effects of the event(s) on the nervous system. Rather than having the ability to simply go with the flow of the classroom and the teacher's directives, they may respond to demands by *not responding*. Their nervous system may no longer have the ebb and flow, fluidity, and flexibility that is essential to making transitions, complying with requests, and persevering in the face of increasing challenges. There is a greater sense of inflexibility about these students, even opposition. This is when teachers are in danger of engaging in threatening stances. Of course, we want the students to comply and do what they need to do. However, becoming harsh, threatening, or provocative in order to exert power over these students is a very bad idea.

Helpful: Having firm boundaries that are reasonable and flexible is helpful. Understanding where students are coming from is the first step. We need to truly appreciate that this is not a compliance issue. This is a capacity issue. Traumatized students do not have the fluid capacity to respond immediately in the moment. Some need ample warning of transitions, such as the daily schedule taped to their desk, as mentioned in chapter 8. Others benefit from the simple intervention of a longer response time when demands are made. This requires extra patience as well as flexibility in the limits and boundaries of the classroom. Flexibility should not lead to abandoning limits and boundaries, however. These are needed for structure and containment. The stability of functioning of students who have been traumatized depends upon the safety and predictability that firm yet flexible limits and boundaries provide.

Harmful: Banning these students to a time-out area or the office over a capacity issue that only *appears* to be a compliance issue is a mistake. We have to know the difference between capacity and compliance. Of course there need to be consequences for any student engaging in problematic behavior, but these students are helped by such consequences when they are held in place with compassion. We do not want to instill in them a deeper sense of hopelessness, shame, or collapse.

Helpful: Use time-out areas as a resource to students where they can go to take a break, a deep breath, and conjure a calming thought or image to bring the nervous system back into balance. Help students undo the damage of their actions or inaction by helping them apologize, correct their previous response with a new more adaptive one, and validate them for that. Remind them that everyone makes mistakes and that what is most important is the repair we do after a mistake to restore peace and a sense of well-being.

Harmful: According to an article written after the nightclub fire in Rhode Island, school psychologists Torem and DePalma indicated that while not speaking of the tragedy would be unnatural, spending too much time in discussion could be counterproductive (Torem and DePalma 2003). They also stated that while scheduled tests should be postponed, the daily schedule should not be veered from too dramatically.

Helpful: Torem and DePalma reported that teachers should be reminded that art, music, and writing activities can be helpful in reducing stress levels, and that simply reassuring students with facts is enough (Torem and DePalma 2003). Also helpful was support given to teachers so they could model appropriately calm and reassuring responses to their students. After-school support groups for teachers were utilized and found to be effective.

Follow-up

Let us briefly review the first three phases of psychophysiological first aid. First, as a crisis response team, we meet and conduct a needs assessment that considers the scope of the event. Once this is complete, we know what we need to do for our second phase: a large or small group intervention, an individual approach, or some combination of two or more of these. Whether we work in a large or small group, or individually, there is a unique emphasis on educating students about their natural physiological responses to threat and how to move through these with ease. At the third phase of psychophysiological first aid, it is important to provide psychoeducation to parents and teachers.

Once the first three phases are complete, we enter the fourth and final stage, follow-up. At this stage, we assess for the potential need for greater assistance, at or outside of school. Some students will need to be seen more than once. A small number may require individual sessions to completely work through the event. An even smaller number may need therapy outside of what can be provided at school. The need for greater assistance, and how intense that help should be, will depend upon the student's previous history of trauma, his or her pre-event level of functioning, and/or his or her lack of available resources before, during, or after the event.

Follow-up sessions involve strengthening students to help them experience a greater sense of balance in their nervous system through the development and experiencing of resources (see chapters 6 and 7 for resource activities). When appropriate, the steps taken during individual psychophysiological first aid also apply. Most helpful are exercises that serve both to resolve the impact of trauma through discharge and to ground students in the here and now by connecting them to both inner and outer resources.

Follow-up should involve consultations with teachers, administrators, and parents, as well as referrals for therapy as needed.

CASE STUDY OF CRISIS INTERVENTION/ PSYCHOPHYSIOLOGICAL FIRST AID

In chapter 2 we heard about Jesus, the ten-year-old boy who was molested on his school campus by a group of his peers. Despite the interventions that Jesus received after the event and prior to coming to the school I served, Jesus continued to have problems on campus. He was unable to play on the playground at recess and lunch. Rather, he went to the office and wept during those periods, asking to see the counselor. This occurred on a daily basis for several weeks.

Psychophysiological first aid would ideally occur immediately following the crisis event to prevent the traumatization that Jesus was experiencing. Weeks later, however, it was not too late to apply the same model to resolve Jesus' traumatic reactions. After two individual sessions and one session of psychoeducation with Jesus' parents, Jesus returned to the playground and enjoyed being a student at our school. The specifics of what Jesus and I did together will be reviewed now as an example of what can be done at the *follow-up* phase of psychophysiological first aid when some students simply need more.

I met Jesus at his school at the request of the school counselor. The counselor had already been meeting with Jesus daily during the times he was in the office crying. The counselor introduced us and let Jesus know that it was he who had asked me to meet with him a few times. Jesus was crying but nodded that he would meet with me. When the counselor left, as Jesus continued to cry, I comforted him by placing my hand on his upper midback. I quietly waited and let him know that I was here to be with him and to help him and that everything was going to be okay. Jesus continued to cry. I decided to do some immediate grounding and invited him to the floor.

We sat right down on the carpet and placed our hands on the ground at our sides. We sat a comfortable distance apart. I gave him a warm blanket that the counselor had in his office. As he cried, I asked Jesus to feel the warm blanket resting on his lap and to get as comfortable as he could as he rubbed his hands over the carpet.

"Can you feel the ground beneath you, Jesus? Do you feel how strong and solid it is and how you are connected to it?"

"Yes," he told me as he continued to rub the floor. I encouraged him to take a moment and feel the parts of his body connected with the floor. I asked him to notice how his body was being supported by the floor, and to notice how his back was being supported by the wall he was leaning into. We took a moment and before long he took a deep breath. His cry became more subdued.

I then told Jesus we were going to do an exercise that might seem a little funny. I told him he would need to squeeze his muscles, hold them a few seconds, and then let them go one at a time. I had him start with his toes and move all the way up his body. He squeezed, held, and released many of his muscle groups. By the time we were done, Jesus was remarkably calmer. I gave him words of encouragement, letting him know what a great job he did with the exercise. We rested a moment.

It was time for a different activity. I asked Jesus to close his eyes if he could, letting him know that he could open his eyes when he needed to. I told him I was going to take him on a fantasy trip just by telling him a story, and asked him if that would be okay. Yes, he told me. Jesus closed his eyes and listened quietly as I led him through a visualization exercise. The specific visualization I chose was from Violet Oaklander's book *Windows to Our Children*. I modified it to help Jesus imagine a safe place. Once I took him gently through the exercise and gave him plenty of time to enjoy being there in his imagination, I let him know that when he was ready he could get up and sit at the table and draw what he saw.

Jesus got up from the floor and sat at the table and saw the page I had left for him there. It was from one of Marge Heegaard's books for children (Heegaard 1993). For the most part, it was a blank sheet of paper, yet at the top of the page were the words, "It is important to have a place that feels very safe. This can be a real place . . . or a pretend place to think about." Jesus read the page then drew a beautiful picture of a grassy meadow that had three red flowers in it and one large solid tree. Jesus drew the sun at the top of the page.

I encouraged Jesus to take a few moments to really look at his safe place, imagining himself there. I let him know what a beautiful job he had done and reminded him that if he ever needed to he could close his eyes and imagine himself in his safe place.

The last activity we did in this first session, which lasted approximately forty-five minutes, was a mostly blank sheet that had the words "I know how I like to be comforted" written on the top, also from one of Heegaard's books. The sheet also read "(draw this . . . and then close your eyes and imagine it)." At the bottom of the page it was written, "I can use words to let others know what I need."

On this sheet, Jesus drew two small pictures. One picture was of him shooting a basketball right into the hoop. The other was of him lying down on the floor playing a video game. The character he drew on the screen of the video game was a strong, muscular man flexing his arm muscles.

The counselor later reported that he noticed a decrease in how upset Jesus would get when he was in the office. However, he still did not want to go out to the playground. We had more work to do. Together, Jesus and I went back to the floor for more grounding. (Sitting on the ground is not necessary for the exercise. It can be done while standing or sitting on a chair. It is about feeling connected to the ground by calling attention to that connection and support.)

Again, I had Jesus feel the ground beneath his hands, buttocks, and legs.

This time, I brought his attention to his breath. I taught him how to take deep breaths that would help center him when he was upset. I modeled a soothing breath, showing Jesus how to do it for himself. Keeping at least one hand on the belly, I explained the importance of taking a deep breath in through the nose and filling up the belly with air like a balloon. Many people shaken by a crisis begin breathing less efficiently, with shorter breaths that permit air to reach down into the body only as far as the midtorso area, filling the lungs but not the belly. When we breathe deeply into the belly through the nose, we engage the parasympathetic nervous system for soothing and relaxation.

Jesus did as I did. He kept one hand on his belly, breathed deeply in through his nose, and filled his belly up like a balloon. It took a couple of tries before he got the hang of it. Once his belly was full, he slowly exhaled through the mouth. We repeated these deep breaths five times. Jesus was much calmer after just a few moments of this exercise.

I revisited with Jesus the coloring worksheets he had done a week earlier. I did this to remind him of his safe place and how he likes to be comforted. I had him take a moment with his safe place to imagine himself there and then asked him what he noticed in his body. This prepared him for the next coloring exercise.

I gave Jesus a worksheet that had a silhouette of a body on it. At the top of the page was the question, "Where are you feeling your feelings today?" There was a grid on the page that matched sensations with colors. I asked Jesus to color in the silhouette where he felt each of the sensations listed according to the grid. With the color blue, which signified "flowing," Jesus lightly colored in the silhouette from the waist down. With the color green, which signified "relaxed," Jesus lightly colored in the silhouette from the waist up. When he was finished, we talked about his picture and I asked him to notice if he could sense those sensations in his body in that moment. He confirmed that that was what he was feeling—relaxed in his upper body and flowing in his lower body. We rested for a moment, taking time to allow for those sensations to be fully experienced.

There was one last worksheet to do. On the top of the mostly blank page it said, "Some people believe they have a higher power, God, or guardian angel to watch over them. Do you?" Jesus took a moment and then drew and colored a picture of his sister in their home with an angel flying over her head. He also drew inside the home a shrine that had another angel flying over it. This is when Jesus began to weep. His cry was different this time. It was quiet and gentle and without hysteria. It was then that I put my hand on his back and said, "It's not your fault, Jesus. Those boys were wrong to do that to you. You did not deserve to have that happen. No one deserves that. It's not your fault." Jesus cried more deeply as he leaned into me with his arms wrapping around my back. I held him for several moments as I reassured him of what a good boy he was and how it was not his fault. He stopped crying and looked at me. I said, "You're going to be okay, Jesus. I know that. I'm meeting with your parents today and we're going to make sure we do everything we can so that you're okay."

At the end of the school day, Jesus' parents came to pick Jesus up. They came together to the office along with Jesus' sisters. Jesus was smiling proudly as he introduced me to his whole family. I met with the parents alone for approximately forty-five minutes. With the help of a translator, I explained to them what I believed was going on inside Jesus' body because of what happened to him. I explained that when terrifying events occur, they happen to the whole person—not just the mind but the body as well. I let them know that Jesus was jumpy inside because he was still scared. He was worried for his sister, which they knew, because of how threatened and violated he was by those boys. He imagined that something terrible could also happen to her. He had become obsessed with taking care of her, to the point of running out of his classroom early every day to pick her up at her classroom before the last bell rang.

I let Jesus' parents know that it was important for them to remain as calm around Jesus as possible. It would be important for them to take care of themselves with the help of their friends and family. That way they would be better equipped to take care of Jesus when he needed them. I asked them to begin to notice how they felt inside when Jesus got upset. If they noticed that they too were getting upset, I encouraged them to take deep breaths to calm themselves. I told them that children pick up on how their parents are feeling and become more anxious as they sense their parents becoming uncomfortable or nervous. It would be soothing to Jesus to be in the arms of his parents when they were calm and centered, breathing deeply and able to be a safe, comfortable place to fall. They said they could do that.

Jesus' parents said they would give him plenty of physical affection as they made reassuring comments about how they would always be there for him to take care of him and his sisters. I let them know that Jesus might shake or tremble in their arms or at other times, or that he might get hot and sweaty. This was a good thing, I told them, and asked them not to stop it. I asked them to let Jesus know that that was his body's way of shaking everything off so he could feel better.

I asked Jesus' parents to turn off the television, especially the news, movies, and shows with frightening and violent content. The calmer they could keep the environment, the calmer Jesus would be. The two most important things to children who have been traumatized are, first, to provide them with as great a sense of safety as possible, and second, to create as many opportunities for competency as possible. I let Jesus' parents know that Jesus needed to be reassured that their roles were to protect him and his sisters, and to keep Jesus involved in activities that would be an outlet for him and a source of pride.

I checked in with the counselor a week later to learn that Jesus had returned to playing out on the playground every recess and lunch. Months later, the counselor reported that Jesus had not been to the office crying since I had seen him last.

UNIQUE TO PSYCHOPHYSIOLOGICAL FIRST AID

This Is a New Language

The brain stem has its own language. Many of us have never thought much about sensations before. We did not know how important they were to intervening with students who had experienced crises. Just because the language of sensations is so different to us, however, does not mean that it is difficult. All we need to do is shift our focus from thoughts and feelings to the deeper core, to what is more basic and primitive. With practice, it gets easier and more comfortable.

The Work Is Subtle

When we are working with sensations, we are engaging the brain stem, the part of the brain most activated by trauma. When we do this, students and crisis counselors alike will notice subtle changes and responses that often fool us into thinking that not much is happening. We are wrong to assume that. Subtle changes and responses happening inside the body are profoundly altering the nervous system and brain to bring the student back into regulated balance. This happens through the discharge of all the mobilized chemistry and energy from the event, releasing what was blocked from either the freeze response, or the inability to fight or flee.

Simply Watch and Do Not Interpret

The lure to talk while this quiet work is happening can be great. We must remember that talking, interpreting, and telling the story or any story while the body is making these subtle changes can completely interrupt the process. When we talk, we shift the students' perceptions away from the reptilian core, the site of the fight/flight response involved in crises, to the more evolved portions of the brain. This breaks the connection we have made through sensation with the part of us that is most important for healing after a crisis.

The Work Is Slow

Even though much can happen, and does, within minutes, the moments may seem long to those of us who have never spoken this language before. There is a natural rhythm inside of us that moves at a much slower pace than to which we are accustomed. That rhythm is beyond our control. We cannot, and we should we not try, to speed things up. We simply must let the students' inner process control the pace. The quiet healing cycles we will observe will involve moving back and forth from a tight, constricted, uncomfortable place, to an open, softer, more relaxed place. This happens naturally without the need for intervention beyond providing a safe container. Something in the students that feels like a rock, for example, may suddenly seem to melt into a warm liquid. This is one cycle. We cannot interpret this cycle; we cannot hurry it, manipulate it, or change it. All we can do is provide containment for cycles to occur, then watch them happen and validate. When we provide time and space, we allow the body to complete its healing mission.

The Necessary Element of Trust

The single most important thing we can provide throughout psychophysiological first aid is our steadfast belief that things will turn out okay. We have nature on our side. We must provide a patient, steady container in order to surround students with a feeling of confidence. All we have to do is wait for nature to take its course. If we are providing a safe place for this to happen, it will. What may most interfere with our capacity to provide what is needed is our own unresolved trauma. Our own previous traumas can be triggered by the crisis events we are called to intervene with. It is our responsibility to seek help for ourselves first.

TRAUMA VERSUS GRIEF

It is important to distinguish between experiences and reactions of trauma and those of grief. They are distinctly different. The general public, as well as many professionals, understand loss and know about grief reactions, but trauma reactions, especially in children, are largely unknown to the public as well as professionals.

1. Grief reactions can occur without trauma reactions. Trauma, on the other hand, also involves grief.
2. The generalized reaction of grief is sadness, whereas with trauma, it is terror.
3. When grieving, most students can talk about what happened. After a traumatic event, many students do not want to talk about what happened.
4. In grief, pain is related to loss. In trauma, pain is related to terror, powerlessness, and fear for safety.
5. In grief, a student's anger is generally not destructive whereas in trauma, a student's anger can lead to physical assault.
6. Grief generally does not attack or disfigure our identity, as evidenced by the drawings of students who are grieving the loss of a loved one. Pictures drawn by traumatized students, however, often show how traumatic events can attack, distort, and disfigure our identity.
7. In grief, guilt involves thoughts and feelings of "I wish I would have" or "I wish I would not have." Trauma guilt is different. It involves thoughts and feelings of "It was my fault. I could have prevented it."
8. The dreams of students who are grieving tend to be about the person who died, whereas the dreams of traumatized students involve themselves dying or being hurt.

CASE STUDY OF A CRISIS EVENT INVOLVING GRIEF

I arrived at work one morning to learn that one of our students had been killed by a drunk driver at 4:45 p.m. the previous evening. The school's crisis response team immediately assembled. It included the counselor, the nurse, the school psychologist, and the mental health specialist. (Although I am also a school psychologist, my role at that particular school was largely as a mental health specialist.) The four of us gathered and supported one another through our own initial reactions to the news. We stayed close to one another to provide physical and emotional support as we simply let our tears come and go. With that containment and support we were able to calmly gather the facts of the event and determine how we were going to respond.

We learned that the nine-year-old third grader, David, was walking across a busy intersection with his teenaged sister. She was holding his hand as they stood on a center median waiting for the cars to stop for them. One car did. David, holding on to his sister's hand, walked ahead of her. Although one car had stopped for them, a second car did not. The impact of that second car jarred David out of his sister's hand and killed him. He was pronounced dead upon arrival to the hospital.

While the surviving sister's reactions were most certainly going to be traumatic, the students at our school were most likely going to experience reactions of grief. We needed to be prepared for that specifically. As a team, we spent valuable time, at least forty-five minutes, supporting each other, getting grounded in our own bodies, and preparing for what we needed to do. That time was crucial to how smoothly everything went from that point forward.

Before we intervened with the large group, David's classroom, we developed a plan of the steps we were going to take and made a photocopy for each member of the team. We made sure that as new members arrived from other schools we gave them the plan and filled them in on the facts. We had clearly defined our roles and had decided who was going to do what. We made sure that each of us felt comfortable with our role. The last thing we did was stand in a circle and hold hands. We knew we had very important jobs to do and reminded ourselves that we had each other for guidance and support.

In the classroom, the nurse and the counselor stood at the front of the class as the rest of us spread out and circled the student body providing as much physical containment as possible. The counselor asked the students if they had heard any rumors about David. They said that they had not. The counselor explained to the students that David had been hit by a car and died. The students gasped as looks of shock spread across their face. They had no idea that this had happened the evening before.

Very quickly we identified four students, all close friends of David, who needed to be seen in a small group. Their tears bordered on hysteria and we knew they needed more support than could be provided within a large group setting. Two school psychologists took the four students with them to the counselor's office where they were comforted during a period of crying and support. The school psychologists asked the students to think about whom they could go to and what they could do to get the help they needed. Together they came up with a plan of how they could get through this difficult time.

In the large group, the students moved through the shock and began to weep. The adults walked around the room slowly and calmly stopped at students' desks to offer them tissues and physical support. We did not try to stop them from crying. We let them know it was a good thing, and that they might feel not only emotions like crying and anger but also sensations like trembling, shaking, sweating, heat, or cold. We normalized all feelings and sensations and encouraged the students not to stop them but to watch them until they changed on their own. A handful of students were not crying so we normalized that also. We let students know that everyone has a different way of experiencing grief and expressing feelings.

I saw from the corner of my eye one student, who was sitting by himself, making a fist. Again, I normalized the feeling of anger to the whole class. I told the boy that I saw his fist and asked him if he was angry. Without hesitation, he said yes. I told him I understood his reaction and that it made a lot of sense to me why he would feel that way. When I went to him and got down on my knees to be face to face with him, I put my hands on his knees. I could see that he was very mad. I asked him what he remembered about David and as he burst into tears he said, "He played with me every day." I consoled him and simply let his tears come, providing support with my calm presence.

After a moment, I asked the boy if there was anyone else he played with at school. He said a name. I asked him to point to that person in the room. He did. That boy was also sitting alone. I suggested to the boy that he sit together with his friend because they needed each other now. He followed me to the boy's desk and they sat together the rest of the day. As I reminded the students of how we all needed to be there for each other, and I reinforced students for being kind to one another, the two boys got closer and closer and eventually sat arm and arm, sharing markers, and offering each other help.

The crisis response team emphasized to the students that we were all working together with the rest of the school and their parents to ensure their safety. We told them that a letter was going home to their parents letting them know what happened and what they could do to help. We asked the students about the rules of crossing the street and reminded them about when not to cross the street. We let them know that the nurse was going to be doing a special presentation on safety when crossing the street the following week.

We began to encourage the use of the students' resources. We asked them to tell us about the things they could do as a class to help each other get through this sad time. They came up with wonderful ideas as we reinforced them for helping each other and being kind to one another. I also let the students know that sometimes, when we are sad or angry, we take our feelings out on other people. I asked them to notice when they were taking their anger out on their classmates. We came up with examples of how and when this could happen. We discussed what they could do instead. The students talked about asking for help from their teacher when they were sad. They talked about noticing other classmates when they are sad and going to them so they would not feel alone. They also suggested giving each other hugs and sharing crayons and markers with one another.

To continue supporting the students in their development of resources, we introduced to them creative activities. This happened after approximately forty-five to sixty minutes of moving through the shock and grief of the event.

The students began drawing pictures and writing letters to David to tell him how much they loved and missed him. As the students completed their pictures, I asked if anyone wanted to share their activity with the class. One girl jumped up and stood at the front of the class. She shared her picture of a heart that said, "We miss you, David. We're going to stick together like super glue." That became our theme for the rest of the day.

The resources came from the students. They thought of the things that would strengthen them and the adults in the room simply reinforced them for their ideas. The students talked about David being in heaven now where he was happy. One student said David would always live in their hearts. Another student wrote on his picture that they could still see each other and would be friends forever. The students did a beautiful job of creating, sharing, and supporting one another.

One boy sat alone and could not stop crying. His name was Juan and he was David's best friend. After coming back from the small group, Juan continued to have great difficulty. When I rested my hand on his upper back for support, he was hot and wet from perspiration. Some students were trying to get him to eat his lunch. The students had brought their lunches back to the class to continue the crisis counseling. After Juan refused, I explained to the students that he was too upset to eat. I pushed the food tray away from him and told him he did not need to worry about eating right now.

Juan immediately pulled out a sheet of paper and began writing David a letter. When he was done, I read it to him. Then he finished a picture of he and David playing basketball together that he had started earlier. The longer Juan worked on these tasks, the calmer he became. Once the two tasks were complete, he was ready to share. He told the class that he had a poem he wanted to read for David.

Juan stood at the front of the class and read a poem about changing the game of tug-of-war to hug-of-war so we could all live in a world of hugs and kisses instead of "tugs and hisses." When he sat back at his desk I asked the class if Juan was going to have to go through this alone. They exclaimed, "No!" I asked the class if we were going to go through this together. They exclaimed, "Yes!" We circled the few people that were still teary and gave group hugs reminding them that they were not alone and we would all do what it took to get through this time together.

The teacher made announcements to her class about rituals and memorials to come. She let the class know that their pictures and letters were going to be made into a book that would be kept in the library where they could go look at it anytime they wanted. She talked to them about keeping David's desk in the classroom and decorating it with notes, pictures, and his favorite colors. She told the students they would be working on cards to give to

David's family and that they were going to plant a tree in David's honor. She also mentioned following through on the students' idea of tying a note written to David by the whole class to a helium balloon and letting it float up into the sky to find David in heaven.

Once the teacher was done making announcements, she moved the students into their workshop, which was part of the original schedule of the day but was not something too academic or demanding. All the students were able to make the transition smoothly. The entire process was complete within four hours.

The crisis team agreed to keep an eye on all the students and to communicate each day with the teacher about the needs and how to respond best. We set up a teacher support group to take place at the end of that day with all of David's teachers and teacher aides throughout his years at our school. Individual support was given to students and teachers as needed.

Weeks and months later, the teacher of the class let me know how helpful the process had been to both her and her students. They continued to grieve and remember David through ritual and team building in the classroom.

12

Final Words: Implications for the Future of Education

We now know how far-reaching trauma is. Stressful pregnancies, complicated births, seemingly benign events such as medical procedures, illnesses and fevers, even minor accidents such as falls, can cause long-lasting difficulty and pain. We now understand how trauma impacts the development of the brain, affecting behavioral functioning, memory, and other processes necessary for learning. We have greater knowledge of what traumatized students look like in the classroom. Some are numb with flat affect, avoidant and fearful. Others are hyper, inattentive, and prone to helplessness or giving up. Traumatized students can fluctuate, sometimes rapidly, from an inability to sit still and be calm to shutting down and withdrawing. In our classrooms, we have seen how many times during the course of one day they can move between states of overarousal and underarousal.

RECONSIDERATION WITHIN GENERAL EDUCATION

The teachers I have worked with have been excellent in sensing when something is wrong with a student. They may not know the name for what is wrong, or where the problem is coming from, but they sense when students are struggling and need help. Teachers within general education need to continue to speak up for these students as early as possible. School counselors and psychologists need to help teachers intervene earlier with these students and their families. We need to educate parents about self-regulation, what it is, why it is so important to learning and behavior, and how it can be restored through a home-school team approach that creates safety, opportunities for mastery, and the building of resources.

We now know to ask parents about falls, accidents, injuries, illnesses, or hospitalizations. Dysregulation may also be due to abuse that the parent may or may not know about, making identification of the source of the trouble more difficult to ascertain. Nonetheless, we must educate parents about the significance of such events and how to offset their impact on the nervous system through relationship and other resources. It is through loving, calm, and consistent relationships that we help balance the nervous system of our students. Trauma tips the scale of the nervous system in one direction, creating dysregulation. By providing safety and reassurance while building resources within the context of a loving relationship, we tip the unbalanced scale back into balance, creating greater flexibility in the regulation between positive and negative states.

Traumatized students will benefit greatly from school personnel knowing both psychophysiological first aid and SRT. Just as we provide other forms of therapy to students—occupational, speech, physical, or cognitive-behavioral—so too can we be trained to provide both first aid and SRT to students who are unregulated. If we do not start identifying and intervening with these students appropriately and effectively, we will only have them to deal with later when the behaviors are more severe, the neural connections more engrained, and thus, the problem more resistant to intervention. It is time to realize that intervening with students later and with an approach that ignores the brain and physiology of the problem fails our students, our schools, and our communities.

SRT is ideal for counselors, school psychologists, social workers, and school-based mental health providers who can see only a limited number of students for a limited amount of time. When we work at the level of physiology incorporating the body into what we are doing, the work is effective faster than when we talk at the cognitive brain where the problem does not primarily lie. When we work with sensation and complete the incomplete behavior, we discharge the stuck energy of trauma, and create space and flexibility within the nervous system where there was little or none before. We begin to see positive change quickly with such an approach. If we concentrated on selecting a handful of our youngest unregulated students each year and provided six sessions of SRT involving their caregivers, we could be engaging in some of the most important preventative work we ever do. From the compilation of research provided by Karr-Morse and Wiley (1997) in *Ghosts from the Nursery: Tracing the Roots of Violence*, we know this is how we can do something to prevent future violence.

School-based practitioners do not have to work alone. Psychologists, counselors, social workers, and psychotherapists can work together to provide SRT. Each one of these professionals would benefit from learning as much as possible about trauma's effect on students and what can be done within the school setting to offset that impact. No school professional should be excluded from learning about the relationship of trauma to the brain and school functioning. Cross-training involving as many school professionals as possible, including OTs who know so much about the importance of self-regulation, is vitally important to the future of our students.

General education normally begins in kindergarten. Therefore, our youngest students are in kindergarten and first grade where our efforts can best be focused on prevention of the exacerbation of the problem in the future. We can start by speaking with teachers who identify unregulated students who are in need of early intervention. Of course, we want to keep in mind the difference between normal kindergarten adjustment and more physiologically imbedded unregulated behaviors. In my experience, many teachers are excellent at recognizing the difference. They know the students who are not, over time, settling in and making the adjustment.

I have had impressive experiences with kindergarten and first-grade teachers who have appropriately identified students who are clearly having difficulty outside the normal range. School support personnel, such as social workers, psychologists, and other mental health providers, need to pay attention at these early stages and have the support of administrators to do so. Observations of, and early intervention plans for, our youngest unregulated students are necessary if we genuinely intend to prevent school and community violence.

Reconsideration of an Intervention Plan

Meet with the caregiver(s) of the student and gather information regarding early development. Should the family identify any early accidents, injuries, illnesses, or hospitalizations that were frightening, this would be the time to educate them about how the nervous system works, and how it becomes sensitized by terrifying events. Caregivers need to know what they can do at home to help create calm and balance for the student.

Take a resource inventory with the caregiver(s) to identify what students have in their lives to offset their strife. Identify what resources they are missing that would be helpful to make available to them. Safety, as well as opportunities to show their strengths and competencies, is very important to offset the impact of trauma.

Caregivers also need to know how their own nervous system functioning affects their children's. The calmer and more balanced they are in their lives, the calmer and more balanced their children will be. They need to take care of themselves first in order to be there for their children in a healthy way.

Caregivers are the most important people in students' lives and have the most power and influence over them. We can help them understand this, that they are the ones who can shift the students' experiences from more to less frightening and from less to more safe and predictable.

Meet with the teacher and provide similar psychoeducation as was provided to the family. Ideas and activities for building safety and competence can be shared, as well as encouragement and support. It is important for teachers to know that, at the school, they have the most direct impact on, and have the most influence over, their students. They are in a powerful position. They can use that power and influence to tip the scales in one direction or the other, toward greater safety and a sense of mastery and competence, or toward greater self-doubt and fear. Although there is a need to rely on other colleagues for help and support, being in the unique position of having students six hours a day, five days a week, cannot be overemphasized. What teachers do or do not do has a demonstrative effect on the traumatized student.

Meet with students and take a resource inventory. Make a note of what and whom they identify as resources in their life. What resources are missing that could be added at school to help students feel safer, more competent and supported. Communicate these needs to the students' caregivers and teachers.

Observe again to determine whether or not the above steps made enough of a difference to the students. If students continue to demonstrate a lack of self-regulated behavior and/or affect, determine the best person to implement SRT, the school psychologist, social worker, or school-based mental health provider, depending upon the resources of the school. Provide two to six sessions. Observe again. Consult with teachers regarding noted changes or improvement and continue SRT as needed.

Now that we know how the brain develops, we understand that the earlier we intervene, the better. The more comprehensive and holistic our intervention approach, the better. We do not have to wait to formally identify these students as requiring special education. We can prevent the need for special education identification and service when we are more precise in our assessments of the problem as well as the need at the earliest of stages. We are more precise when we know what to look for, when we know what to ask about, and when we have the appropriate tools to respond.

RECONSIDERATION WITHIN SPECIAL EDUCATION

With our new knowledge of trauma and its effect on the developing brain, let us reconsider our special education assessments, designations, and services.

Assessments

We have learned the importance of taking detailed developmental histories when we assess our students for special education. Whether or not trauma is part of the student's past is vital information for the development of interventions. We need to ask specific questions, such as whether or not students have experienced falls, accidents, injuries, illnesses, or medical procedures, just as we need to know about exposure to violence, natural disaster, death, or abuse.

Resources in students' lives need to be assessed. We want to know what resources the students have to draw upon in their present lives, as well as what resources were in place before, during, and after the traumatic event(s). We want to determine whether or not there are valuable resources that are missing in the lives of our students that we could help them build and access regularly.

Designations

Autism

From our experiences with autism it would be valuable for us to learn that the earlier we intervene, the better. The more we focus our resources on rehabilitating problematic social-emotional behaviors, the better. We have improved upon early identification and intervention with students with autism, speech deficits, physical disabilities, and sensory-motor problems, but we have not yet made that same effort with students with behavioral problems.

Some students with severe behaviors are identified early with ED and placed in classrooms for young ED students, but this is done rarely because of how hesitant school psychologists and others are to give young students such a grave label. We used to avoid or postpone the label of autism as well, and still do sometimes, but have now learned the benefit of assessing earlier, identifying earlier, and providing much-needed services as soon as possible.

When students are very young, labels may be given but they can also be taken away. Many students identified with speech, physical, or occupational therapy needs receive services for one or two years and then do not need the services anymore. "Exit" IEPs are held often to recognize the success of interventions provided and to remove special education labels from students when they are no longer needed. This can also happen for students identified with behavioral, self-regulatory problems.

Other inconsistencies in practice exist depending upon whether the designation is autism or ED. Once ED students are identified through special education, they are not provided with the same designated instructional services

(DIS) as students with autism. Behavior specialists are one example. Educators are hearing more about behavior specialists working with students with autism while our ED students, who have many of the same behaviors, go without services. Rather, ED students are placed in self-contained classrooms that consist of more students with severe behaviors, with little, if any, adjunct services. What we are failing to recognize is that the same dysregulation that underlies the challenges of students with autism underlies students with and without other special education designations, including ED.

Students with autism are not only provided with behavior specialists when needed, but also receive sensory integration intervention from OTs that sometimes involves the Alert Program for Self-Regulation. Again, we readily recognize the needs of students with autism and fail to recognize the needs of some of our other most troubled students. The discrepancies and inconsistencies in services depending upon the designation of students are appalling, especially considering that the same fundamental inability to self-regulate underlies many of these designated conditions. Without going into the social-political context within which these decisions are made, it is time educators take a long hard look at how we are contributing to the perpetuation of the cycle of violence in specific populations of students. Thinking that these cycles of violence are not impacting all of us as a society is a level of denial that we can no longer afford to tolerate.

Developmental Delays (Ages Three to Nine)

This has been a helpful addition to the list of special education designating categories. It is useful because it recognizes that there is a problem that requires remedial services through special education immediately, whether or not a more specific designation can be determined. In other words, we know that there is something wrong, that skills are delayed, but we cannot yet determine whether or not the problem is autism or mental retardation, for example.

The designation of developmental delays is considered for students aged three to nine who demonstrate delayed development in specific areas including communication, academic/cognitive, gross and/or fine motor, and adaptive/self-help skills. The list of skills to be assessed in this category also formally includes social-emotional development. However, students whose disabilities are primarily in the emotional and behavioral domains are often overlooked in eligibility-driven assessments, possibly due to the unavailability of measures used to assess for such problems (Evangelista and McLellan 2004). According to some researchers, the assessment of social and emotional functions is more difficult to quantify using a standard of delay and thus is de-emphasized in assessments for developmental delays, perhaps even ignored (DelCarmen-Wiggins and Carter 2001).

Ignoring the social-emotional and behavioral needs of our youngest students is a costly mistake. This is how we pave the way for future violence to occur. Whatever our excuses are for not identifying and intervening with these students as soon as possible will pale in comparison to the violence some of them will commit at later stages of their development. How much longer can we ignore the research that makes this link clear? How many more school shootings need to happen before we pay attention and do more than offer lip service to prevention of violence? Identifying delays in self-regulation and intervening as early as possible will do much not only to prevent future violence, but also to prepare students for school success. As we now know, the ability to self-regulate is the very foundation from which numerous other skills, academic and adaptive included, develop normally or not.

Specific Learning Disability (SLD)

When assessing for SLD, as with ADHD, it is important to consider the source of the symptoms in question. If students' memory deficits or inability to focus attention, for example, are related to a traumatic event or series of events, students may not have an actual SLD. Their learning challenges may have more to do with unresolved trauma than an intrinsic lifelong condition of SLD.

Although once thought that the challenges of posttraumatic symptoms could only be *managed* throughout life, somatic approaches to healing trauma based on the last decade of brain research tell a different story. Post-trauma conditions, whether they involve learning, behavior, or affect, can be healed. Many anecdotal cases are now being documented and published in various books in the field that indicate that people who were once illiterate are learning to read after receiving somatic treatment much like SRT. When the traumatized state is resolved, students gain back their abilities to attend, retain information, and meet the expectations of traditional classrooms.

This does not mean that students who are struggling academically who have been traumatized should not receive special education assessments and designations for services. It does mean, however, that we need to be more accurate and precise in our assessments and in the use of our designations. SLD is a lifelong condition, many times passed on from one generation to the next due to genetics, much like ADHD. Trauma-induced signs and symptoms of what only *appears* to be SLD or ADHD, on the other hand, can be healed. They need not be considered chronic conditions that require a lifelong label. We know that approximately 50 percent of the cases of ADHD are environmentally caused by pre- and perinatal stress and trauma, and that a percentage of these cases involve what looks like SLD (Karr-Morse and Wiley 1997). Brain research is now informing us that these trauma-induced conditions can change over time, given the appropriate intervention.

Let us consider an assessment of a student struggling with learning in the classroom. We find that the student has a history of trauma and may have been traumatized by one or more events. We have a different student in this case than one who is struggling with learning whose biological mother and/ or father also struggled and there is no history of traumatization indicated. In the first case, when we designate SLD and provide resource support through special education (RSP: small group instruction with a special education teacher), for example, without SRT to address the fundamental underlying issue of a lack of self-regulation due to trauma, we do not intervene with the actual source of the problem. SLD would be an incomprehensive designation and RSP would be an inappropriate, ineffective intervention. Using special education designations and services in this way may be part of the reason why some students continue to fall further behind despite intervention.

Emotional Disturbance (ED)

This has become a catch-all category for those students who, at the earliest stages of their education, baffle educators as to what to do to make a marked difference. Many of these troubled students do not get to our preschool assessment centers. The ones who do are those we often fail to formally identify and provide with appropriate intervention at that early time in their development. Rather than formally recognize a developmental delay in social-emotional functioning, for example, we hope they will outgrow their behaviors. Instead, they often get worse. These students later show up to our kindergarten and first-grade classrooms unable to self-regulate both their behavior and affect and begin a long history of negative experiences with school that involves suspensions, disciplinary transfers, and referrals for immediate action, all of which make the problems worse rather than better.

Instead of being accurately identified as lacking a key ability needed for school success and receiving interventions to develop that ability, our most troubled students are removed from both classes and schools, housed in various alternative settings for "naughty" students, and provided with anger-management training. When our interventions do not work the first time, we give them a second time. When they do not work the second time, we give them a third time. We continue to do what does not work, until finally, we label the students ED. Not only have our ineffective and inappropriate interventions not worked, but they also contributed to the students' condition getting worse.

Traumatized students can be harmed by anger management training because of its potential to further engrain a state of shame. They may develop insight with the approach—but with little or no physiological capacity to support the better choices they want to make, traumatized students are left feeling more hopeless.

Traumatized students are also harmed by disciplinary transfers that force them to adjust to new environments and situations, no matter what we tell ourselves about giving them a "fresh start." This is a lie, and we have to stop telling it. Our rationalizations include a belief that we reinforce the behavior when we keep students in our schools after they have "crossed the line." We ask ourselves, "What kind of a message would it be to send to other students in the school?" These justifications perpetuate the problems of our most troubled students and contribute to the violence we say we want to stop. What could be more violent than discarding a child? We discard children every time we give them a "fresh start."

We need to start taking ownership in the problem of the perpetuation of violence in our schools and communities. It begins with understanding our students better. We need to precisely identify where the problems are coming from, what the fundamental underlying problem is, and provide early intervention for that. If we really want to see the number of our ED students decline, we will start earlier in both our identification and intervention. We will also more directly match our interventions to accurately defined problems.

ED designations would be used much less if we identified the source of the students' problems and then selected a designation to reflect the source. Such an approach specifically informs intervention. Two designations that take the source of the problem into primary consideration are traumatic brain injury (TBI) and other health impairment (OHI).

Traumatic Brain Injury (TBI)

This is the only category that exists that recognizes the impact of trauma on the brain and later functioning across areas. With this category we can precisely acknowledge what went wrong, how it is that students have come to have such difficulty, and then tailor our interventions accordingly.

There are more students suffering with TBI than we realize. As educators, school psychologists, and special education teachers particularly, we need to know more about what TBI is, how to diagnose it, and how to help most effectively.

I have had numerous cases of students suffering terribly for years with little support, some of whom fell from their second-story balconies, others who were hit by cars, all at critical ages between one and three, when a large amount of brain development is taking place. A number of these students had visible scars on their head and still went unnoticed.

They go unnoticed partly because parents do not speak up. Parents are often told by medical doctors in emergency rooms that everything is fine. Doctors do not observe the behavioral sequelae of such life-altering accidents. Educators do. Whatever tests medical doctors run in emergency rooms do not reveal the brain damage that is done by such falls, and certainly not the damage that is done to these students' self-regulatory capacity.

It is up to nurses, psychologists, social workers, and mental health providers who work in schools to start educating themselves about the damage such accidents can cause and to start bringing that knowledge to schools and students who need us to tell their story and get them help. We know now that serious damage can be done to the brain and autonomic nervous system with falls, accidents, medical procedures, and other traumas. It is up to us to acknowledge this fact and do something about it.

Other Health Impairment (OHI)

It is vital that we consider using the designating category of OHI to recognize the damage caused to the health of our students when traumatized. Once traumatized, the brain and nervous system functioning of our students is changed, making many everyday academic and behavioral challenges much more difficult. Rather than having healthy self-regulation that helps them manage upsets and tolerate stress, traumatized students are unregulated. They are more easily upset, to a greater degree, and for a longer period of time than their peers who have not been traumatized. Many have greater trouble focusing their attention, retaining information, and sustaining their effort with a challenging task. Their nervous system can become so inflexible, so exquisitely sensitive, that any slight change becomes too difficult to tolerate. In fact, most things that used to be only slightly annoying, for example, become the "end of the world." Rigidity, inflexibility, and sensitivity of the nervous system can make mountains out of molehills. Education, and all that it requires, is Mount Everest to these students.

We can help. We can educate ourselves so that we understand what our students are going through and what they need in order to be successful. If after our efforts within general education they continue to need help, we can recognize their health impairment. We can acknowledge how their traumatic experience(s) changed them by providing them with an IEP through the designation of OHI.

The ED category need not be a catch-all category for these students. When we identify them early enough they need never become ED. They are not "disturbed" students. They have been traumatized. Their responses to their experiences are natural; they are simply incomplete and unresolved causing the difficulties we see. Traumatized students need specific interventions that are tailored to their unique needs, such as SRT. When we respond in a timely fashion, we prevent the unnecessary labeling and subsequent experiences of the ED student.

The more appropriate designation for traumatized students when one is needed is OHI (unless TBI or a developmental delay in social-emotional functioning is warranted). By identifying the source of their challenges and understanding the health impairment that it causes, we are more precise in our conceptualizations of the students we serve. When we are precise, we do for students and their families what medical doctors were unable to do, recognize the damage caused by trauma. We finally understand the child, and when we do, the relief and gratitude of the families is tremendous. They always knew something about their child was changed by "the thing" that happened. The doctors did not see it, but they did. Some went to multiple therapists and other mental health professionals to get help, but no one ever seemed to understand what it was, until someone talked to them about trauma and its effect on the nervous system.

We are in a powerful position as educators to make a huge difference to the life of a child. Let us not hesitate in using every resource we have, including our designating categories where appropriate, to move one traumatized student at a time toward greater educational success.

Services

Currently, the services provided through special education that are relevant to this discussion include resource support for academics, self-contained classrooms (e.g., for ED students), and designated instructional services (DIS), such as occupational therapy (OT), behavior specialist support, and counseling.

There is no question that when it comes to students with learning and behavior problems who require IEPs, educators are doing their best to provide the services students need. Many students with IEPs designated as SLD, ED, OHI (often for ADHD), and TBI receive resource support for academics, placements in self-contained classrooms for smaller student to teacher ratios, and DIS psychological services in the form of anger management or counseling. What many students who need it do not receive, however, is support from an OT or behavior specialist. OTs specifically address problems with self-regulation and behavior specialists specifically address challenging behaviors. The students discussed in this book have great difficulty with both, yet OT and behavior specialist services are rarely even considered for them.

Both OT and behavior specialist services have largely been reserved for students with autism. For some reason, students with autism seem to be more readily recognized as having self-regulatory problems and dangerous behaviors. Their difficulties are understood as involving an inability to regulate that requires formal remedial services. While over the years I have heard OTs mention the need to work with ED students, I have never seen this happen. I have heard, rather, that the behavior problems of ED students are too severe to benefit from the interventions of OTs. However, when we consider that the behaviors of students with autism can be just as severe, if not more severe, it seems we have created yet another rationalization.

Already discussed was the fact that psychological services in the form of counseling, especially when it involves a focus on anger and how to manage it cognitively, is largely ineffective with traumatized students. It is not that anger management is not effective with some students some of the time. It is that we try to apply the same methodology to every student.

Anger management is not a one-size-fits-all approach. We need to assess and intervene with accuracy and precision. We must know who our students are before we decide what intervention is most appropriate. Taking histories of our students to understand where their anger is coming from would better help us know whether or not to provide anger management or SRT. We have to study their behaviors to recognize the difference between the student with an anger problem, the student who has been traumatized, and the student who struggles with both.

Whether it is through the OT department or psychological services or it becomes its own adjunct service, SRT would be well considered as a crucial addition to students' programs when they are suffering in the aftermath of trauma. The future of our students will depend upon how educators respond to recent brain research implicating trauma as the culprit in a host of problems with self-regulation impairment at their root. This research must inform our assessments, our designations, and the services we provide.

Support personnel need to come together to educate themselves about this research, and to consider the use of psychophysiological first aid and SRT as responses to this new evidence. Interventions that engage the physiology of our students have the potential to resolve their traumatic conditions. As educators we can demand training and support to provide these approaches in a timely fashion to those in need. When we restore self-regulation in our students, we give them their lives back. Only then will they have what it takes to meet the demands of their world. Only then will no student be left behind.

THE IMPORTANCE OF EARLY INTERVENTION: BIRTH TO AGE FIVE

Education has progressively done a better job at recognizing the importance of identifying and intervening with problems early. Most school districts have preschool assessment centers, usually for children aged three to five. Many young students receive special education services before entering kindergarten, at which time they often no longer require them. This is the case when we are accurate and precise in both our diagnoses and designations and when we specifically match our interventions to the need.

Brain research from the last decade is indicating the need to intervene earlier than ages three to five. Early childhood services are expanding to include children aged "zero to three." In fact, the National Center for Clinical Infant Programs has developed the Diagnostic and Classification of Mental Health and Developmental Disorders of Infancy and Early Childhood (DC: 0–3) to meet the needs of our youngest children. This is an alternative diagnostic framework to the DSM-IV-TR. It offers more developmentally appropriate diagnoses and a structured format to consider the impact of family and contextual factors on children's behaviors (Evangelista and McLellan 2004).

While educators have always seemed to understand the importance of intervening early with cognitive problems, motor delays, and speech and language issues, this has not been the case with students with behavioral and/or social-emotional problems. We have largely neglected to intervene appropriately with social-emotional difficulties at these early stages of development despite the fact that infant and toddler conduct problems are related to behavioral challenges in early school years (Lavigne, Arend, Rosenbaum, Binns, Christoffel, and Gibbons 1998), in middle childhood and adolescence (Olson, Bates, Sandy, and Lanthier 2000), and in adulthood (Caspi, Moffitt, Newman, and Silva 1996).

Most brain development occurs between the ages of zero to three. What we do during this time contributes to either healthy self-regulation or autonomic dysregulation. Considering the importance of parenting approaches and parent-child interactions to brain growth and the development of self-regulation, we must intervene with parents as early as possible. Contextual factors, such as parenting and the presence or absence of trauma, are pivotal to understanding derailment of healthy adaptive functioning in young children. This is why the DC: 0–3 is so important. Rather than having a primary focus on the "identified patient" as the DSM-IV-TR does, the DC: 0–3 incorporates the context as a primary component of the clinical picture (Jensen and Hoagwood 1997).

The DC: 0–3 may be of great importance to us as educators as we begin to recognize the need to focus more on early intervention. As our knowledge base has expanded with current research, diagnoses have changed to include in the DC: 0–3 regulatory disorders. No parallel DSM-IV-TR category exists at the present time. The DC: 0–3 recognizes that autonomic dysregulation in young children exists, it needs to be recognized, and it requires early intervention.

IMPLICATIONS FOR FUTURE RESEARCH

There are no empirical studies examining the efficacy of psychophysiological first aid and SRT as outlined in this book. Developing and implementing these approaches in schools and assessing their effectiveness in the form of a pilot study is proposed. Considering the growing number of anecdotal cases and preliminary evidence demonstrating the efficacy of similar forms of self-regulation therapy (Zettl 1998), as well as other somatic approaches, such a study seems warranted to the future of our traumatized students.

An empirical examination of the vast differences in students diagnosed with ADHD is also needed. If we can determine the source of the behaviors evidenced by the students, whether genetically or environmentally invoked, we may do a better job of predicting which intervention approach would be most efficacious. For instance, if we determine that the student with an ADHD-looking profile most likely acquired the symptoms genetically, treatment with psychostimulant medication, effective with up to 75 percent of accurately diagnosed cases, may be the most effective approach. However, the ADHD-looking students who demonstrate not only resistance to, but also exacerbation of symptoms with, these particular medications may be the students who acquired their conditions from a history of pre- and perinatal stress and trauma.

Does the source of the problem make an empirical difference in terms of what treatments work best? As may be clear from the arguments I have made in this book, I believe the answer is yes. For instance, both biofeedback and neurofeedback intervention programs targeted for behaviors exhibited by ADHD students commence with a neurological assessment to determine whether or not abnormalities in the prefrontal lobe of the brain exist. It is only when such abnormalities exist that these approaches are found to be an appropriate intervention (Ferrari 2004). Many professionals in the field today believe that unless these particular abnormalities are found in that specific region of the brain, students are not ADHD (Lawlis 2005).

I believe that, in the pursuit of an empirical answer through scientific research, we will find a difference in responses to various treatments between students whose ADHD-looking behaviors have different sources. Perhaps the students' whose symptoms were genetically passed down, for example, also inherited the specific abnormalities in the prefrontal cortex required for biofeedback and neurofeedback approaches and would therefore respond well to these approaches. Alternatively, the students whose ADHD-*looking* behaviors developed as a result of pre- or perinatal stress or trauma may not have abnormalities in that particular region of the brain and, therefore, would not benefit from such interventions. Their behaviors, better understood as traumatic stress responses, may be related to abnormalities in a different region of the brain, a possibility that recent research is beginning to confirm.

The observations we are making in our schools today need to be empirically validated. Posttraumatic stress responses when misunderstood as ADHD behaviors may, in fact, be exacerbated by psychostimulant and antidepressant medication, as well as by some cognitive approaches including anger management. Traumatized students may better respond to interventions that restore autonomic regulation between the sympathetic and parasympathetic nervous system. Sensory based/somatic approaches to healing trauma are now receiving a great deal of attention from the country's leading researchers in the field. This is because they are showing such promise in their power to return the imbalanced, unregulated nervous system back to a healthy state of tolerance and well-being, a state that is vitally important to the learning and behavior of our students.

There is no reason for educators to continue using approaches that are contraindicated and ineffective. The psychophysiological first aid and SRT models proposed in this book were designed specifically for educators to have access to practice that is congruent with current and mounting empirical evidence. Equipped with comprehensive knowledge and excellent training, they too can do their part not only in preventing violence but also in fostering the success of every student.

Appendix A: IDEA Categories

The following eight disabilities will be defined for the purposes of a thorough overview of each of the designating categories of special education included in IDEA (see chapter 1 for the other categories): deaf-blindness, deafness, hearing impairment, mental retardation, multiple disabilities, orthopedic impairment, speech or language impairment, visual impairment including blindness.

Deaf-Blindness: Deaf-blindness means concomitant hearing and visual impairments, the combination of which causes such severe communication and other developmental and educational needs that they cannot be accommodated in special education programs solely for children with deafness or children with blindness.

Deafness: Deafness involves a hearing impairment that is so severe that the child is impaired in processing linguistic information through hearing with or without amplification that adversely affects a child's educational performance.

Hearing Impairment: This category includes students with impairment in hearing, whether permanent or fluctuating, that adversely affects their educational performance but that is not included under the definition of deafness in this section.

Mental Retardation: Mental retardation is significantly subaverage general intellectual functioning, existing concurrently with deficits in adaptive behavior and manifested during the developmental period, that adversely affects a child's educational performance. Practically, this category is reserved for students who demonstrate significantly delayed cognitive development, at least two standard deviations below the mean, as well as deficits in adaptive behavior. Adaptive behavior includes self-help skills, such as dressing, toileting, and feeding. Students may be mildly, moderately, or severely delayed and receive services accordingly.

Multiple Disabilities: Multiple disabilities refers to concomitant impairments (such as mental retardation-blindness, mental retardation-orthopedic impairment, etc.), the combination of which causes such severe educational needs that they cannot be accommodated in special education programs solely for one of the impairments. The term does not include deaf-blindness.

Orthopedic Impairment: Orthopedic impairment refers to severe orthopedic impairment that adversely affects a child's educational performance. The term includes impairments caused by congenital anomaly (e.g., clubfoot, absence of some member, etc.), impairments caused by disease (e.g., poliomyelitis, bone tuberculosis, etc.), and impairments from other causes (e.g., cerebral palsy, amputations, and fractures or burns that cause contractures).

Speech or Language Impairment: Speech or language impairment includes communication disorders, such as stuttering, impaired articulation, language impairment, or voice impairment that adversely affects a child's educational performance.

In most cases, one or more of the following criteria must be met in order for this designating category to be used as the appropriate identification of a student: (1) articulation disorder (when the disability is more than an abnormal swallowing pattern); (2) abnormal voice (characterized by persistent, defective voice quality, pitch, or loudness); (3) fluency disorder (when the flow of verbal expression including rate and rhythm adversely affects communication between the student and listener); (4) language disorder (when the student scores at least one-and-a-half standard deviations below the mean or below the seventh percentile for his or her age or developmental level on two or more standardized tests in morphology, syntax, semantics, or pragmatics—or when the student displays inappropriate or inadequate usage of expressive or receptive language as measured by a representative spontaneous or elicited language sample of a minimum of fifty utterances).

Visual Impairment Including Blindness: This term refers to students with impairments in vision that, even with correction, adversely affect their educational performance. The category includes both partial sight and blindness.

Appendix B: Resources

Books:

Please see the references section in this book.

Audio:

Levine, P. A. *It won't hurt forever: Guiding your child through trauma.* Produced by Sounds True, 2001.

Websites:

www.traumahealing.com (Dr. Peter Levine's Foundation for Human Enrichment)

www.HealingResources.info (in partnership with the Santa Barbara Graduate Institute and Neurons to Neighborhoods conferences)

www.cftre.com (The Canadian Foundation for Trauma Research and Education)

References

Arendt, M., and A. Elklit. 2001. Effectiveness of psychological debriefing. *Acta Psychiatrica Scandinavica* 104, no. 6: 423–438.

Baker, L. 2002. *Protecting your children from sexual offenders.* New York: St. Martin's Press.

ban Breathnach, S. 1995. *Simple abundance: A daybook of comfort and joy.* New York: Warner Books.

Begley, S. 2003. Is trauma debriefing worse than letting victims heal naturally? *Wall Street Journal* (Eastern Edition), September 12.

Bisson, J. I., P. L. Jenkins, J. Alexander, and C. Bannister. 1997. Randomized control trial of psychological debriefing for victims of acute burn trauma. *British Journal of Psychiatry* 171:78–81.

Boscarino, J. A., S. Galea, J. Ahern, H. Resnick, and D. Vlahov. 2002. Utilization of mental health services following the September 11th terrorist attacks in Manhattan, New York City. *International Journal of Emergency Mental Health* 4:143–55.

Bremmer, J. D., J. H. Krystal, D. S. Charnez, and S. M. Southwick. 1996. Neural mechanisms in dissociative amnesia for childhood abuse: Relevance to the current controversy surrounding false memory syndrome. *American Journal of Psychiatry* 153:71–80.

Brennan, P. A., and S. A. Mednick. 1997. Perinatal and medical histories of antisocial individuals. In *Handbook of antisocial behavior*, edited by D. Stoff, J. Breiling, and D. Maser, 269–79. Toronto: John Wiley & Sons.

Brock, S. E. 2002. *Overview of crisis response in our schools & advanced training in school crisis intervention.* A two-day training for school psychologists. Long Beach, California: Long Beach Unified School District, November.

Brock, S. E., and S. R. Jimerson. 2002. *Characteristics and consequences of crisis events: A primer for the school psychologist.* Sacramento: California Association of School Psychologists.

California Special Education Programs: A Composite of Laws, 24th ed. 2002. Sacramento: California Department of Education.

Campfield, K. M., and A. M. Hill. 2001. Effect of timing of critical incident stress debriefing (CISD) on posttraumatic symptoms. *Journal of Traumatic Stress* 14:327–40.

Caspi, A., T. E. Moffitt, D. L. Newman, and P. A. Silva. 1996. Behavioral observations at three years predict adult psychiatric disorders: Longitudinal evidence from a birth cohort. *Archives of General Psychiatry* 53:1033–39.

Chamberlain, D. 1995. What babies are teaching us about violence. *Pre- and Perinatal Psychology Journal* 10:51–74.

Chemtob, C. M., S. Thomas, W. Law, and D. Cremniter. 1997. Postdisaster psychosocial intervention: A field study of the impact of debriefing on psychological distress. *American Journal of Psychiatry* 154:415–17.

Christner, R. W. 2003. Early intervention for trauma: Current status and future directions. *Communique* 32, no. 4 (December).

Clay, R. A. 1998. School psychologists work with families and communities to improve mental health services. *APA Monitor* 19 (January).

Dacey, J. S., and L. B. Fiore. 2002. *Your anxious child: How parents and teachers can relieve anxiety in children.* San Francisco: Jossey-Bass.

Damasio, A. 2003. *Looking for Spinoza: Joy, sorrow, and the feeling brain.* Orlando, Fla.: Harcourt.

Deahl, M. P., A. B. Gillham, J. Thomas, M. M. Searle, and M. Srinivasan. 1994. Psychological sequelae following the Gulf War. *British Journal of Psychiatry* 165:60–65.

Deahl, M. P., M. Srinivsan, N. Jones, J. Thomas, D. Neblett, and A. Jolly. 2000. Preventing psychological trauma in soldiers: The role of operational stress training and psychological debriefing. *British Journal of Medical Psychology* 73:77–85.

DeAngelis, T. 2003. When anger's a plus. *Monitor on Psychology* 34, no. 3 (March).

DeBellis, M. D., A. S. Baum, B. Birmaher, M. S. Keshavan, C. H. Eccard, A. M. Boring, F. J. Jenkins, and N. D. Ryan. 1999. Developmental traumatology (Part I): Biological stress systems. *Biological Psychiatry* 45:1259–70.

DeBellis, M. D., M. S. Keshavan, D. B. Clark, B. J. Casey, J. N. Giedd, A. M. Boring, K. Frustaci, and N. D. Ryan. 1999. Developmental traumatology (Part II): Brain development. *Biological Psychiatry* 45:1271–84.

DelCarmen-Wiggins, R., and A. S. Carter. 2001. Assessment of infant and toddler mental health: Advances and challenges. *Journal of the American Academy of Child and Adolescent Psychiatry* 40:8–10.

Diagnostic and Statistical Manual of Mental Disorders: Fourth Edition: Text Revision. 2000. Washington, D.C.: American Psychiatric Association.

Elliott, F. A. 1992. Violence: The neurological contribution: An overview. *Archives of Neurology* 49:595–603.

Evangelista, N., and M. J. McLellan. 2004. The zero to three diagnostic system: A framework for considering emotional and behavioral problems in young children. *School Psychology Review* 33:159–73.

Ferrari, S. A. 2004. *Alta neuro-imaging neurofeedback.* Personal communication, Brea, California (March).

Fonagy, P., and M. Target. 2002. Early intervention and the development of self-regulation. *Psychoanalytic Inquiry* 22, no. 3: 307–35.

Gabriel, M. A. 1992. Anniversary reactions: Trauma revisited. *Clinical Social Work Journal* 20:179–92.

Gendlin, E. T. 1981. *Focusing.* New York: Bantam Books.

Gideonse, T. 1998. Music is good medicine. *Newsweek* (September 21).

Gillis, S. 2003. Autogenics visualization. At http://www.trigenics.net/journals/Steve Gillis-AutogenicVisualization.htm.

Gist, R., and G. J. Devilly. 2002. Post-trauma debriefing: The road too frequently traveled. *Lancet,* no. 360: 741–42.

Gist, R., B. Lubin, and B. G. Redburn. 1998. Psychosocial, ecological, and community perspectives on disaster response. *Journal of Personal and Interpersonal Loss* 3:25–51.

Golden, C. J., M. L. Jackson, A. Peterson-Rohne, and S. T. Gontkovsky. 1996. Neuropsychological correlates of violence and aggression: A review of the clinical literature. *Aggression and Violent Behavior* 1:3–25.

Groopman, J. 2004. The grief industry. *New Yorker* (January 26).

Hass, M. 2002. *Solution focused brief counseling.* A professional talk for school psychologists, Long Beach, California: Long Beach Unified School District, August.

Heegaard, M. 1993. *When something terrible happens: Children can learn to cope with grief.* Minneapolis, Minn.: Woodland Press.

Hendricks, G., and R. Wills. 1975. *The centering book: Awareness activities for children, parents, and teachers.* New York: Prentice-Hall.

Herman, J. L. 1992. *Trauma and recovery.* New York: Basic Books.

Janet, P. 1889. *L'Automatisme psychologique.* Paris: Alcan.

———. 1909. *Les neuroses.* Paris: Flammarion.

Jensen, P. S., and K. Hoagwood. 1997. The book of names: DSM-IV in context. *Development and Psychopathology* 9:231–49.

Johnson, S. 2003. The brain and emotions: Fear. *Discover Magazine* (March).

Kandel, E. 1998. A new intellectual framework for psychiatry. *American Journal of Psychiatry* 155:457–69.

Kandel, E., and S. Mednick. 1993. Perinatal complications predict violent offending. *Criminology* 29:519–29.

Karr-Morse, R., and M. S. Wiley. 1997. *Ghosts from the nursery: Tracing the roots of violence.* New York: Atlantic Monthly Press.

Knapp, P. H. 1967. Purging and curbing: An inquiry into disgust, satiety, and shame. *Journal of Nervous and Mental Disease* 144:514–44.

Larson, J. 2005. *Think first: Addressing aggressive behavior in secondary schools.* New York: Guilford Press.

Larsson, G., P. Michel, and T. Lundin. 2000. Systematic assessment of mental health following various types of posttrauma support. *Military Psychology* 12:21–35.

Lavigne, J. V., R. Arend, D. Rosenbaum, H. J. Binns, K. K. Christoffel, and R. D. Gibbons. 1998. Psychiatric disorders with onset in the preschool years: II. Correlates and predictors of stable case status. *Journal of the American Academy of Child and Adolescent Psychiatry* 37:1255–61.

Lawlis, F. 2005. *The ADD answer: How to help your child now.* New York: Plume.

LeDoux, J. 1993. Emotional memory systems in the brain. *Behavioral Brain Research* 58:69–79.

———. 1996. *The emotional brain.* New York: Simon & Schuster.

———. 2002. *Synaptic self.* New York: Viking Press.

Leeds, M. 2003. *The many faces of anger.* FACES: A national conference, mastering counseling skills with the masters, San Diego, October.

Levine, P. A. 1997. *Waking the tiger: Healing trauma.* Berkeley, Calif.: North Atlantic Books.

————. 2003. *Tools for times of terror and turbulence: A body-based approach to trauma treatment.* A professional talk at the University of San Diego, February.

Levy, D. 1945. Psychic trauma of operations in children. *American Journal of the Diseases of Childhood* 69:7–25.

Lindamood, P., N. Bell, and P. Lindamood. 1997. Sensory-cognitive factors in the controversy over reading instruction. *Journal of Developmental and Learning Disorders* 1:143–82.

Litz, B. T., M. J. Gray, R. A. Bryant, and A. B. Adler. 2002. Early intervention for trauma: Current status and future directions. *Clinical Psychology and Scientific Practice* 9:112–34.

Maine, M., and E. Hesse. 1990. Parents' unresolved traumatic experiences are related to infant disorganized status: Is frightened and/or frightening parental behavior the linking mechanism? In *Attachment in the preschool years,* edited by M. Greenberg, D. Cicchetti, and M. Cummings, 161–82. Chicago: University of Chicago Press.

May, R. 1978. *The art of counseling.* Nashville, Tenn.: Abingdon.

Mayou, R. A., A. Ehlers, and M. Hobbs. 2000. Psychological debriefing for road traffic accident victims: Three-year follow-up of a randomized controlled trial. *British Journal of Psychiatry* 176:589–93.

Menvielle, E. J. 1998. Mellon Project Mental Health Sub-Studies at www.cnmc.org (Children's National Medical Center).

Mercer, C. D., and M. E. Snell. 1977. *Learning theory in mental retardation: Implications for teaching.* Columbus, Ohio: Charles E. Merrill.

Mitchell, J. T., and G. S. Everly. 1996. *Critical incident stress debriefing: An operations manual for the prevention of traumatic stress among emergency services and disaster workers.* 2nd ed., Rev. Ellicott City, Md.: Chevron.

Murphy, J. 1997. Turn brief interviews into problem-solving opportunities. *Today's School Psychologist* 1, no. 1 (August).

Nader, K., and P. Muni. 2002. Individual crisis intervention. In *Best practices in school crisis prevention and intervention,* edited by S. E. Brock, P. J. Lazarus, and S. R. Jimerson, 405–28. Bethesda, Md.: National Association of School Psychologists.

Oaklander, V. 1988. *Windows to our children.* New York: Gestalt Journal Press.

Ogden, P. 2003. *Integrating cognitive and somatic approaches in trauma treatment.* Presented at Neurons to Neighborhoods: The Neurobiology of Emotional Trauma: Innovative Methods for Healing Children and Adults, Los Angeles, California, May.

Olson, S. L., J. E. Bates, J. M. Sandy, and R. Lanthier. 2000. Early developmental precursors of externalizing behavior in middle childhood and adolescence. *Journal of Abnormal Child Psychology* 28:119–33.

O'Neill, C. 1993. *Relax.* Toronto: Child's Play (International).

Pfferbaum, B., S. J. Nixon, R. D. Tivis, D. E. Doughty, R. S. Pynoos, R. H. Gurwithch, and E. W. Foy. 2001. Television exposure in children after a terrorist incident. *Psychiatry* 64:202–11.

Perry, B. D. 1997. Incubated in terror: Neurodevelopmental factors in the cycle of violence. In *Children in a violent society,* edited by J. D. Osofsky, 124–49. New York: Guilford.

———. 2003. *Nature and nurture of brain development: How early experience shapes child and culture.* Presented at From Neurons to Neighborhoods: The Neurobiology of Emotional Trauma: Innovative Methods for Healing Children and Adults, Los Angeles, May.

Perry, B. D., R. A. Pollard, T. L. Blakley, W. L. Baker, and D. Vigilante. 1995. Childhood trauma, the neurobiology of adaptation, and "use-dependent" development of the brain: How "states" become "traits." *Infant Mental Health* 16:271–91.

Reed, N. L. 2000. Assessment and accommodation of students with learning disabilities. Presentation to the Academic Affairs Council, Atlanta Metropolitan College, Atlanta, Georgia, April.

Reynolds, C. R., and R. W. Kamphaus. 1992. *Behavior assessment system for children.* Circle Pines, Minn.: American Guidance Service.

Richards, D. 2001. A field study of critical incident stress debriefing versus critical incident stress management. *Journal of Mental Health* 10:351–62.

Rothschild, B. 1996. Applying the brakes: Theory and tools for understanding, slowing down and reducing autonomic nervous system activation in traumatized clients—both in therapy and in their daily lives. Paper presented at the 10th Scandinavian Conference for Psychotherapists working with Traumatized Refugees, Finland, May.

Rothschild, B. 2000. *The body remembers: The psychophysiology of trauma and trauma treatment.* New York: W. W. Norton.

Saltzman, B. 2003. *Early intervention: Psychological first aid: A developmental approach.* A professional talk for school psychologists. Long Beach, California: Long Beach Unified School District, August.

Sattler, J. M. 1992. *Assessment of children.* San Diego, Calif.: Jerome M. Sattler.

Scaer, R. C. 2001. *The body bears the burden: Trauma, dissociation, and disease.* New York: Haworth Medical Press.

Schore, A. N. 1994. *Affect regulation and the origin of the self.* Hillsdale, N.J.: Lawrence Erlbaum.

———. 1998. Early shame experience and the development of the infant brain. In *Shame, interpersonal behavior, psychopathology, and culture,* edited by P. Gilbert and B. Andrews, 57–77. London: Oxford University Press.

———. 2001a. The effects of early relational trauma on right-brain development, affect, regulation, and infant mental health. *Infant Mental Health* 22:7–66.

———. 2001b. The effects of early relational trauma on right-brain development, affect, regulation, and infant mental health. *Infant Mental Health* 22:201–69.

———. 2003. *Affect regulation and repair of the self.* R. Cassidy Seminars. Santa Rosa, Calif.: R. Cassidy Seminars.

Shalev, A. Y., T. Peri, Y. Rogel-Fuchs, R. J. Ursano, and D. Marlowe. 1998. Historical group debriefing after combat exposure. *Military Medicine* 163:494–98.

Siegel, D. 2003. *Attachment and self-understanding: Parenting with the brain in mind.* FACES: A national conference, mastering counseling with the masters, San Diego, October.

Silver, L. B. 1984. *Misunderstood student: Understanding and coping with your child's learning disabilities.* New York: McGraw-Hill.

Silverman, W. K., and A. M. LaGreca. 2002. Children experiencing disasters: Definitions, reactions, and predictors of outcomes. In *Helping children cope with disasters and ter-*

rorism, edited by A. M. LaGreca, W. K. Silverman, E. M. Vernberg, and M. C. Roberts, 11–33. Washington, D.C.: American Psychological Association.

Starknum, M. N., S. S. Gebarski, S. Berent, and D. E. Schterngart. 1992. Hippocampal formation volume, memory of dysfunction, and cortisol levels in patients with Cushing's Syndrome. *Biology Psychiatry* 32:756–65.

Steele, W., and M. Raider. 2001. *Structured sensory interventions for children, adolescents, and parents.* New York: Edwin Mellen Press.

Stern, D. N. 1985. *The interpersonal world of the infant: A view from psychoanalysis and developmental psychology.* New York: Basic Books.

Stewart, J. 1998. *Understanding and programming for the severely acting-out and aggressive child in the public school setting.* Gorham, Me.: Hastings Clinical Associates.

Stroufe, A. 1996. *Emotional development: The organization of emotional life in the early years.* New York: Cambridge University Press.

Tavris, C. 1989. *Anger: The misunderstood emotion.* New York: Simon & Schuster.

Teicher, M. 2000. The neurobiology of child abuse. *Scientific American*, 68–75.

Terr, L. 1990. *Too scared to cry: How trauma affects children and ultimately us all.* New York: Basic Books.

Torem, C., and J. DePalma. 2003. Crisis intervention: Community disaster. *Communique* 31, no. 7 (May).

Utley, G. 2001. *Gray matters: Trauma and the brain.* Washington, D.C.: Dana Alliance for Brain Initiatives.

van der Kolk, B. A. 1993. Biological considerations about emotions, trauma, memory, and the brain. In *Human feelings: Explorations in affect development and meaning*, edited by S. Ablon, D. Brown, S. Khnatsian, and J. Mack, 221–40. Hillsdale, N.J.: Analytic Press.

———. 2001. The assessment and treatment of complex PTSD. In *Traumatic stress*, edited by R. Yehuda, 1–29. American Psychiatric Press, Inc. (at www.traumacenter .org/van_der_kolk_Complex_PTSD.pdf).

———. 2002. *The effects of trauma on the self: The aftermath of terror.* FACES: A national conference, mastering counseling with the masters, San Diego, November.

van der Kolk, B. A., A. C. McFarlane, and L. Weisaeth. 1996. *Traumatic stress: The effects of overwhelming experience on mind, body, and society.* New York: Guilford Press.

van Emmerik, A. A., J. H. Kamphuis, A. M. Hulsbosch, and P. M. Emmelkamp. 2002. Single session debriefing after psychological trauma: A meta-analysis. *Lancet*, no. 360: 766–71.

Vogel, J. M., and E. M. Vernberg. 1993. Psychological responses of children to natural and human-made disasters: I. Children's psychological responses to disasters. *Journal of Clinical Child Psychology* 22:464–84.

Walsh, F. 2003. Family resilience: Strengths forged through adversity. In *Normal family processes: Growing diversity and complexity*, 3rd ed., edited by F. Walsh, 399–423. New York: Guilford Press.

Weiss, R. 1994. *Music therapy: Doctors explore the healing potential of rhythm and song.* Silver Spring, Md.: American Music Therapy Association.

Wenar, C. 1990. *Developmental psychopathology: From infancy through adolescence*, 2nd ed. New York: McGraw-Hill.

Wilbarger, P., and J. L. Wilbarger. 1991. *Sensory defensiveness in children aged 2–12: An intervention guide for parents and other caretakers.* Denver, Colo.: Avanti Educational Programs.

Williams, M. S., and S. Shellenberger. 1996. *How does your engine run? The Alert program for self-regulation.* Albuquerque, N. Mex.: Therapy Works.

Winston, F. K., N. Kassam-Adams, F. Garcia-Espana, R. Ittenbach, and A. Cnaan. 2003. Screening for risk of persistent post-traumatic stress in injured children and their parents. *Journal of the American Medical Association,* no. 290: 643–49.

Wissel, H. 1994. Shooting: A state of mind. *Scholastic Coach* (January).

Yang, B., and G. A. Clum. 2000. Childhood stress leads to later suicidality via its effects on cognitive functioning. *Suicide and Life Threatening Behavior* 30:83–189.

Zettl, L. 1998. Knights in shining armor: A phenomenological exploration of the experience of trauma in emergency service personnel and the impact of psycho-physiological deactivation. *Canadian Foundation for Trauma Research and Education,* from http://cftre.com/research.php.

About the Author

Regalena ("Reggie") Melrose is a licensed clinical and credentialed school psychologist. She earned a bachelor of arts degree in psychology, a master of arts degree in developmental psychology, and a PhD with a double major in both clinical child and school psychology from McGill University in Montreal, Canada.

Dr. Melrose worked as an intern in Eastern Canada and Southern California before commencing her work with the Long Beach Unified School District, recently distinguished as the best urban public school district in the country. There she performed various roles, as a school psychologist, districtwide coordinator of the school-based mental health program in partnership with the county department of mental health, lead psychologist for elementary schools, and member of the task force for students with emotional disturbance. She most enjoyed sharing with her colleagues new and relevant research findings, current best practices, and examples of her own experiences with students through presentations and in-services.

After thirteen years in the field, Dr. Melrose recently began working from home so she can help raise, together with her beloved husband, their beautiful son, Jules.